Jaap van Ginneken was born in the Netherlands in 1943.
He studied social psychology and consequently taught at
the Baschwitz Institute for Mass Psychology in the
Political Science Department of Amsterdam University
and at the South-East Asia Branch of the Centre of
Anthropology and Sociology. A journalist, he writes
mainly on socialism in developing countries and has
visited China, North Vietnam and North Korea several
times. He is at present living in Paris, completing a thesis
on the social origins and ideological uses of Western
theories about political mass movements.

Jaap van Ginneken

The Rise and Fall of Lin Piao

Translated by Danielle Adkinson

Penguin Books

Penguin Books Ltd,
Harmondsworth, Middlesex, England
Penguin Books,
625 Madison Avenue, New York, New York 10022, U.S.A.
Penguin Books Australia Ltd,
Ringwood, Victoria, Australia
Penguin Books Canada Ltd,
41 Steelcase Road West, Markham, Ontario, Canada
Penguin Books (N.Z.) Ltd,
182–190 Wairau Road, Auckland 10, New Zealand

First published as *De linkse stroming in China* by Uitgeverij en
boekhandel, Van Gennep, Amsterdam, 1974
Copyright © Uitgeverij en boekhandel, Van Gennep, Amsterdam, 1972
This translation first published 1976
Translation copyright © Danielle Adkinson, 1976

Made and printed in Great Britain by
Hazell Watson & Viney Ltd,
Aylesbury, Bucks
Set in Linotype Times

Contents

Past experience had taught us that 'Left' errors were liable to crop up after our Party had corrected Right errors, and that Right errors were liable to crop up after it had corrected 'Left' errors.

Lin Piao, *Long Live the Victory of the People's War*, September 1965

Part One
The Crisis: September 1971

1: Confusion in the Media

11 September 1971 was the day on which the greatest crisis (but one) that the Chinese People's Republic had ever experienced came to a head. It was also the last day of my first visit to the country. Outwardly, there were no signs of tension. On the Central Square of the Gate of Heavenly Peace in the capital, tens of thousands of school children with colourful paper flowers were preparing themselves for the procession commemorating the twenty-second anniversary of the People's Republic, two and a half weeks later. Trucks carrying young people from the districts around passed to and fro. Even the military-style student battalions helped to increase the festive atmosphere. Martial music was played over the loud-speakers, punctuated with instructions for the procession rehearsals.

Only when darkness descended did the square become silent. Along one of the sides of the square stands the People's Palace, where all large and important political meetings are held. Suddenly, the quiet was broken from several directions as a number of black limousines swept up to the People's Palace. A foreigner who happened to be passing estimated their number at about fifty. Too many for the transport of a few casual visitors, but exactly enough for an emergency meeting of the Party leadership. Somewhere in Peking, a Japanese delegation waited in vain: they were to have had a meeting with Premier Chou En-lai that day, but the latter had cancelled the meeting at the last moment and postponed it to more than a week afterwards. That in itself was very unusual. But the immediate concern among the highest leadership of the Party was the fear that the central army command would use its military power in the current political struggle.

Chou En-lai had already received indications that this could happen, and these were no doubt brought up by him at the nocturnal session at the People's Palace. Mao Tse-tung was also present. His sudden return from Shanghai was very significant, but the incidents which had accompanied it were even more so. Lin Piao, since the Cultural Revolution Mao's closest comrade-in-arms' and chosen successor, first vice-chairman of the Party and Minister of Defence, was the most notable absentee.

In the past few months, a number of contradictions that had been latent since the Cultural Revolution had suddenly become dramatically apparent. The leadership was divided over issues arising from the danger of war with the Soviet Union and the attempt at normalizing relations with the United States. While Mao fully supported Chou En-lai's position on this issue, Lin Piao very much questioned the line taken. On internal affairs there had also been serious conflicts. The press had made this fairly clear. If one read between the lines, it was evident that a propaganda battle was also being waged. The *Red Flag* had already, in May, broken with the established practice of having a portrait of Mao alone on the front page; the covers of numbers 5, 7/8, and 9 had made great play of showing Mao and Lin together, while the sixth number had been completely devoted to the letter of 7 May 1966, which linked Lin to Mao. The pro-Lin press now repeatedly stated that only Lin could guarantee and safeguard the radical achievements of the Cultural Revolution. Only a very small circle of people in Peking had known what differences had occurred in the top Party leadership over the last year. Even some of the members of the Central Committee had not yet understood what was taking place before their very eyes, let alone the middle and lower cadres. The fact that the conflict had not yet been properly defined in the open was taken as a point in their favour by Lin and his supporters.

A remarkable and perhaps characteristic example of what was happening in the media is provided by the fate of the photographic album of Mao Tse-tung which was to have been published on 1 July, on the fiftieth anniversary of the Party. The date of publication was continually postponed, probably because there was some doubt about the suitability of such a pub-

lication at that time, and also about the prominence which Lin
Piao was to be accorded in it. Suddenly, however, a decision was
made by someone who thought that enough time had been
wasted. When the participants in the nocturnal meeting at the
People's Palace picked up their copies of the *People's Daily* on
12 September, they must have been very astonished to see that
the newspaper had announced the publication of the album,
adding:

> Some photographs in this album in which Chairman Mao and his
> intimate comrade-in-arms Lin appear together convey the feeling
> that comrade Lin Piao has always lifted high the Great Red Flag of
> the Thoughts of Mao Tse-tung, has always firmly put into practice
> and protected the proletarian revolutionary line of Chairman Mao,
> and has always been a shining example to the whole Party, to the
> whole Army, and to the people of the whole country.

The surprise among the people who read this in the People's
Palace must have been twofold: these terms of praise for Lin
would have seemed exaggerated even a year ago, and they had
certainly reached very different conclusions about him now.

Conjectures and conclusions

What, then, were the grounds for the anxiety of the people at the
session at the People's Palace about the activities of Lin Piao?
In the first place, there was Lin's controversial speech of 18 May
1966 on the subject of a military *coup d'état*. 'There are two prerequisites for a *coup d'état*. One is propaganda organs, viz.
newspapers, broadcasting . . . and publications, which are related
to ideological works. Subversive activities . . . need ideological
leadership in order to create confusion in the people's ideology.
The other is military work to control the armed forces.'

The more these opinions were linked to the current situation,
the greater seemed the justification for anxiety.

In 1966 Mao had already pointed out that Lin Piao's speech
was so dogmatic as to reduce the question of deep political differences of opinion to the level of military conflict. If Lin had
held that opinion then in relation to others, why should he not
hold it now in relation to Chou En-lai? And if Lin and his

central army command had, during the Cultural Revolution, justified propaganda offensives and their extension of military controls on the grounds that it was to prevent the 'conservative' regional commanders from gaining power, why should the same tactics not be used in the present instance?

There were indications that the Lin group was busily putting itself in the position of controlling the two fields mentioned earlier as being prerequisites for a *coup d'état*. The propaganda media controlled by his supporters were clearly mobilizing public opinion; and the orientation of the new groups of political activists in the army and their 'cultural congresses' had begun to create suspicion.

Reports from the military intelligence service (which was now under the control of the Ministry of Public Security, and no longer under the Ministry of Defence) reinforced this suspicion. A number of the political activist groups in the army had begun to look more like commando units, and were largely recruited from young cadres who had in the past been active in 'ultra-leftist' Red Guard organizations. They were now undergoing special military training, in addition to ideological instruction.

It is probable that other sources of information indicated that Lin Piao attempted to form a faction around him. It is reported that he and his closest supporters entered into frenzied consultation at the end of August and the beginning of September to see how the trend of events could be reversed.

Clearly, though, these reports did not amount to concrete evidence of 'plotting'. It took more than that for suspicion to become certainty.

Attempts on Mao Tse-tung

This information probably came from General Wang Tung-hsing, Vice-Minister of Public Security, chief of the special security service of the Military Commission of the Central Committee, who was directly responsible for Mao Tse-tung's personal bodyguard. This service was completely separate from the rest of the army and any political bodies. It had complete powers to protect the Chairman on his journeys, which were usually kept secret, and when he was staying in his heavily-guarded residences in Shanghai and Peking.

The information from General Wang dealt with the events surrounding the return of the Chairman to Peking, and this in itself was a sufficient inducement for as many of the Party leaders as were present in the capital to attend the emergency meeting. The reports of these events reaching the outside world were fragmentary and often contradictory, but were unanimous about one thing: between 8 and 10 September, a series of abortive attacks had been made on Mao. Some weeks later, the Hong Kong newspaper, *Ming Pao*, reported that one or more unidentified aircraft had carried out a raid on Mao's residence in Shanghai. The Chairman had escaped unscathed, but a number of his bodyguards had been killed or wounded. This version of events is probably based, however, on a misinterpretation of partial reports.

Much later rumours reported that Mao's return to Peking had not been without incident, and included an account about the train in which Mao travelled being attacked from the air. According to later confessions by those involved, the flights of the aircraft had to coincide with a false alert in the province of Fukien, so that blame could be placed on the régime of Taiwan. Other reports claimed that plans had been made to blow the train up, just north of Nanking, but that the officer responsible had hesitated to do this, and had been reported to the authorities by his wife. It also said that when Mao had arrived in the capital, a courier had announced himself at the Chairman's residence and had insisted on delivering a message personally to him; after his arrest, however, this man confessed that he had intended to make an attempt on the Chairman's life.[1] All evidence pointed to a widespread plot within the centrally-commanded army units, like the air force and logistics department, which controlled the railways. In addition, the high degree of co-ordination of the plans and the exact knowledge of Mao's movements pointed to complicity at the highest level.

Who could have benefited from Mao's disappearance at that moment? Whichever way the question is put, Lin Piao is the most probable answer. Lin would become Party Chairman and commander of all military forces; in addition, the declaration of a state of emergency would make it easy to eliminate any opposition. Even if the Lin Piao faction was not involved in the attempts, the conspiracy was clearly meant to play into his hands. But in any case, the possibility that Lin Piao and his group were involved personally was too great to be ignored.

Where is Lin Piao?

While those present at the meeting were reasoning along the lines indicated above, a strange item of information came to light through Lin's daughter, Tou-tou (born in 1941 from Lin's first marriage; her name means 'little bean', which is said to have been given her because of her father's habit of chewing roasted beans) who told Chou En-lai that her parents were preparing a night flight about which the Party leadership knew nothing.[2] Chou En-lai telephoned Lin's country residence in Peitaiho, on the coast a few hundred kilometres from Peking. He spoke to Lin's wife, Yeh Chun, who told him that Lin had gone to a concert, and that this was all she knew about his movements. Immediately after this conversation, she managed to get Lin to leave the concert. Soon afterwards a convoy of cars left in the direction of the airport. A chauffeur who hesitated to carry out orders is said to have been shot by Lin's son, Lin Li-kuo, and pushed out of a fast-moving car. At the airport, it seemed initially that all traffic had been halted by orders of the Party leadership. Permission for exceptions to this rule could only be given by Chou, Lin and a third member of the leadership together. Lin, however, managed to bluff the control tower by saying that the message must have been misunderstood, and that the signature of one of the leaders named would be sufficient. An aircraft was prepared for flight almost immediately and fuelled. But while the aircraft was trundling towards the runway, the alarm was given – perhaps after the discovery of Lin's badly wounded chauffeur. The aircraft, however, managed to become airborne in the nick of time. Some reports say that the plane (a British Trident, a civil aircraft which had already been requisitioned for Lin's own use) made a landing at an air force base near Huhehot, capital of the province of Inner Mongolia, where Lin Li-kuo was deputy air force commander. Other reports, however, claimed that the machine disappeared without trace from Chinese airspace after a short time.

2 : Weeks of Uncertainty

Actions by the Central Committee

The Central Committee was now sufficiently in possession of the facts to take action. Some information on the events had already fallen into their hands after the incidents at Peitaiho Airport. Shortly after the take-off of Lin Piao's jet, a helicopter carrying three of the plotters also took off. The pilot is reported to have been shot when he refused to carry out orders; whatever happened, the machine was forced to land again. Two of the plotters are said to have committed suicide and, although one still remained alive, the most important documents on board could not be destroyed in time. During the arrests and hearings which followed, the rest of the plot is reported to have been revealed. The remaining members of the Lin Piao faction were taken into custody, including chief-of-staff Huang Yung-sheng, his deputies Wu Fa-hsien and Li Tso-peng of the air force and navy. They were no longer seen in public after 11 September. Chiu Hui-tso, head of the logistics department, was also arrested later.

During the days which followed, twenty more high-ranking officers are reported to have been arrested while trying to cross the frontier into Hong Kong, while a last group was arrested while making another attempt to flee the country. The material evidence found was of course very disquieting, but in the last analysis it was impossible to tell how far the plot had progressed. What was going to happen now?

Where was Lin Piao again?

Early in the morning of 13 September, the Party leadership, together with a couple of top army officers, reviewed the situation which had now arisen. Nobody knew where Lin Piao had gone. There were several possibilities, and all those possibilities represented serious risks. The first possibility was the most probable: that Lin had flown to another province with friendly military and civil administrations, where he could prepare the proclamation of secession or civil war. A second possibility was that he had tried to leave the country. In that case, his most obvious route would be via Mongolia to Irkutsk in the Soviet Union. This would have meant that all Chinese state secrets would have fallen into the hands of the enemy at one fell swoop, at a time when a massive offensive in subversion was imminent. Another possibility, following the same direction of thought, was that Lin's aircraft had been shot down by Mongolian or Soviet anti-aircraft artillery. Such an incident could have been taken to be provocation and used as a pretext to carry out the long-awaited 'Blitzkrieg'. A last possibility, although not one which was immediately considered (unless Chinese fighter pilots had claimed that they had shot Lin's aircraft down) was that it had crashed.[1] A large number of decrees were issued which indicated that the leadership regarded the circumstances as constituting a state of emergency. Although no one outside a very limited group in Peking knew what was happening, and no foreign observer in Hong Kong, Taipei or Tokyo knew anything, it was to become obvious to everyone in the following weeks that a very alarming situation had arisen in Peking.

Indications for outsiders

First of all there were a number of astonishing military facts. Almost the whole central army command seemed to have disappeared from public life. There had been a complete ban in China for several days on all civil and military flights; according to the commander of the American forces in the Pacific area, John McCain, it was at least five full weeks before normal flying activities were resumed. In Japan a Government spokesman announced that radio messages had been clearly picked up which said that all army leave had been cancelled with immediate effect; all military personnel had been recalled to their divisions 'because of an unprecedented incident and in order to prevent chaos'.

Then there were a number of unexpected developments with regard to China's foreign relations. Discussions which a Japanese goodwill mission were supposed to hold with Chou En-lai on 11 September were postponed for five days at only two hours' notice. A diplomatic telegram from Peking to one of the overseas embassies was intercepted; in it mention was made of serious differences of opinion at home in connection with the opening of the dialogue with Nixon. A high-ranking Rumanian military delegation, which was to have visited the Chinese People's Republic, cancelled their journey at the last minute without offering any good reason.

And, finally, there were a number of interesting political measures. There were reports that many important political documents for which Lin Piao had been responsible, or which were related to his position, were being subjected to thorough ideological examination; these included certain reports from the Ninth Congress, a number of texts related to the Second Plenum, which were still being considered, such as the project for a new constitution, and other articles by Lin Piao. The most important and significant measure, however, was that the preparations for the annual mass procession for the Party leadership, to have taken place on 1 October, were cancelled on 20 September.

It was this last decision especially which attracted the attention of all observers at home and abroad who were interested in what was happening in the Forbidden City and the People's Palace in Peking. The official reason given for this decision was that it had been decided to make the celebrations more sober; little can be said about this, since the celebrations for the Fiftieth Anniversary of the Party on 1 July had been strikingly subdued. Richard Harris of *The Times* laconically established that only two people were really necessary on the podium in Tien An-men Square on the national feast day: Mao and Lin. If one of them was not present, the reasons could only be the death of Mao Tse-tung or the purge of Lin Piao.

The celebrations on 1 October

The end of the month came. The streets of Peking were decorated with countless little lamps and lanterns. Although the yearly meeting of an excited crowd of millions of people with the Party leadership had been cancelled, the Twenty-second Anniversary of the People's Republic was celebrated all the same. Instead of having one central procession, however, the festivities were spread all over Peking. Cultural propaganda teams had organized hundreds of presentations in the parks of the city: performances of music, sports events, and folk dancing by groups from the national minorities of the autonomous areas of China. And instead of all the members of the Standing Committee of the Political Bureau appearing together above the entrance gate to the Forbidden City, five separate receptions were held, at which a large section of the Party leadership made public appearances.

On the evening of 30 September a large diplomatic reception was held in the People's Palace for some 700 representatives of foreign nations. There were two hosts: Chi Peng-fei, Deputy Minister for Foreign Affairs (minister Chen I was to die two months later) and Wang Hsin-ting, deputy to the chief-of-staff Huang Yung-sheng, who had most probably been arrested, and three adjutants. All the other hosts present were deputies: Tung Pi-wu (as Vice-President of the Republic), Li Hsien-nien (as Vice-Premier of the Government) and Ngapo Ngawang-jigme (as Vice-Chairman of the People's Congress). No one from the highest echelon of the leadership was present.

On the same day, at another location in Peking, a reception was given for 'comrades of Marxist-Leninist brother parties and organizations from various countries, as well as other foreign friends'. The host at this reception was Keng Piao, director of the International Liaison Branch of the Central Committee. The most notable absentee, probably because of illness, was the fifth member of the Standing Committee, Kang Sheng, who had always involved himself in this kind of reception in the past. The young ideologue, Yao Wen-yuan, however, was present, and now seemed to be on the way to a more powerful position.

There were also a number of members of the Central Committee present.

The largest gathering took place on the following day, on the occasion of a boat-trip which had been specially arranged for the Cambodian head-of-state, Prince Sihanouk and his wife. Many people were surprised to see Chou En-lai himself put in an appearance as host, assisted by Vice-Premier Li Hsien-nien, the Vice-Chairman of the Military Commission, Yeh Chien-ying, and the Vice-Chairman of the People's Congress, Kuo Mo-jo. Pride of place was given to this reception in the propaganda film which was made about the day's festivities. In it, Chou En-lai appears as relaxed, charming and cheerful as ever, and can be seen joking with the guests.

In the evening another reception was held at which Chou En-lai again appeared; this was organized by the Association for Friendship with other Countries and the Government's Culture Group. The hosts for the 700 foreign guests were Wang Kuo-chuan and Wu Te, who represented both organizations. Others present were Chiang Ching, Mao's wife, and the other member of the Shanghai section of the Cultural Revolution Group, Chang Chun-chiao. Finally, there was yet another gathering organized by the relevant Government branch for the representatives of the overseas Chinese in Hong Kong and Macao.

Altogether, there was still a lot of activity for the occasion. But the Political Bureau as such had not made a public appearance, and a large number of its most prominent members were not seen at all. To begin with, almost all the strong military men, both from the central army command and the regions, were absent. Almost all the principal provincial commanders were absent, especially those from Eastern China and the strategic border areas. One question, however, overshadowed all others: why had Chou not appeared at the important reception of 30 September, but at the less important reception of the following day? And why had Mao Tse-tung and Lin Piao not appeared at all? They were now mentioned less frequently than they had been in previous years, and some observers noted that there were fewer portraits of Mao in the city. This also drew attention to the fact that the *People's Daily* of that date carried no photograph of Mao (or Mao and Lin) on the front page (although there was a poem by him on the back). And the traditional joint leading article by the *People's Liberation Daily* and the *Red Flag* failed to appear. Had the front page been changed at the last moment? The number of references to Lin Piao had diminished considerably. In the capital there were very few references to him on the centrally produced banners, but somewhat more in the texts put out by the district committees. In the provinces, the frequency with which Lin's name was mentioned varied considerably. In the central provinces, the name of Lin Piao was hardly in evidence, but in remote and relatively inaccessible areas there was an obvious lack of knowledge about recent events. Radio bulletins in Inner Mongolia, Ninghsia, Chinghai and Yunnan did not even mention the widespread festivities in Peking – obviously believing that all the celebrations had been cancelled. In the provinces of Kansu and Chinghai, in the remote west, radio broadcasts appealed to the population 'to unite closely around the administration of the Party, with Chairman Mao as leader and Vice-Chairman Lin as second in command'. But a radio station in the south-eastern province of Kiangsi, having used the same formula on 30 September, changed it the next day in its appeal to 'unite even more closely round Chairman Mao and the administration of the Party'. It is obvious that the news of what had happened was beginning to reach all parts of the country.

3: The Incident of the Aeroplane

Lin's aircraft seems to have crashed

What had happened between 30 September and 1 October to change the situation (though so little, that the difference only became apparent later)? What was significant were small details like the absence of Chou En-lai from the traditionally most important receptions on 30 September, and his presence at less important receptions on the following day. And this was not only true in Chou's case, it was also true for other important figures like Chiang Ching and Yeh Chien-ying. The situation had indeed changed from one day to the next: on 30 September a fascinating report appeared in Ulan Bator, the capital of the People's Republic of Mongolia (an independent republic, but strongly orientated towards Moscow) in the official daily paper *Unen*. It simply recorded a Government announcement to the effect that, seventeen days ago, a Chinese jet aircraft of British make had crashed near Khentiiaimat, at 111° 15′ East, 47° 42′ North. The aircraft had entered Mongolian air-space during the night at 1.55 a.m., and had crashed after a few hundred miles.

A similar report was issued on the same day in Moscow by the press agency Tass, and published inconspicuously on one of the inside pages of the party paper *Pravda* and the government paper *Izvestia*:

The causes of this catastrophe are not known. The half-burnt corpses of nine people, weapons, documents and equipment, which indicate that the machine belonged to the Chinese air force, have been found on the scene of the accident.

More details were not given. Ulan Bator, in indignant tones, asked Peking for an explanation; relations between the two countries had just become normal again, and the new Chinese ambassador Hsu Wen-yi had only been in Mongolia for two weeks when the incident took place.

A diplomatic incident

The news finally reached Peking on the night of 30 September–1 October, giving rise to both relief and caution. Relief, because if the report was true, then the danger from Lin Piao was over. It was clear that Lin had decided to flee the country, and if he had reached the Soviet Union the consequences would have been incalculable. At the same time, there was still reason to be cautious: there was still no guarantee that Mongolia and the Soviet Union would not judge the incident to be military provocation and consider retaliation. There was also anxiety about the documents which had been found in the aircraft. It was decided in Peking not to make any comment for the time being. On 3 October an official reply was issued which said that the aircraft was a civil and not a military machine, which had gone off course and thus entered Mongolia. A similar explanation was issued in Moscow, which finally reached the West. But the Mongolian authorities were not satisfied with this explanation. They pointed out that the aeroplane had crashed at too great a distance from the nearest Chinese civil airports for it to be plausible that it was off course. On the other hand, the accident had occurred very close to a very important rocket base in Mongolia, it was claimed. A more complete explanation was demanded and the credentials of the new Chinese ambassador in Ulan Bator were temporarily refused acceptance. There was even a possibility that diplomatic relations would be broken completely, and the Mongolians reserved the right to take further steps. The Chinese ambassador contacted the Minister of Foreign Affairs to try to discover how much he knew or suspected. The conversations were extremely harsh, because of mutual distrust: Peking did not know if Lin had had contacts with Moscow and Ulan Bator, and naturally had no wish to comment on this aspect. Ulan Bator did not know whether the aircraft was on a secret military mission, nor did Peking wish to enlighten them on the subject. Successive meetings took place in November, December, January and February. But the credentials of the ambassador were still not accepted.[1]

In the meantime, the time-honoured propaganda battle against Peking was resumed, with attacks on Chinese anti-Sovietism, 'reactionary Maoism', and 'Mao Tse-tung's nationalist superpower ideology'. The same formulae, with different prefixes, were used on the other side to describe the 'plotting' of Mongolia and the Soviet Union. It was only towards the spring of 1972 that a solution seemed to be in sight: Hsu Wen-yi had been allowed to inspect the wreckage of the aircraft, and Ulan Bator had by now also learned from other sources, such as intercepted Chinese Communist Party documents, what Peking's opinion of the whole matter really was. This meant that the incident could be considered closed.

Whatever the outcome, the affair had been elevated into a real diplomatic incident, which now started to take on an existence of its own. There was no pekingologist or kremlinologist, no newspaper or press agency which did not have an opinion about what had really happened. And because Peking had not said anything, and only made a public statement on the affair at the end of July, the conditions for speculation to thrive were ideal. The fact that the report of the plane crash did not come directly or indirectly from Chinese sources made it doubly interesting to foreign observers. Closer consideration of the alternative interpretations, however, showed them to be even more improbable than the reconstruction outlined here.

The Soviet Union and the incident

There was another fact to be taken into consideration: the current version of the affair was largely agreed on by the three principal enemies of the Peking government. Firstly, the information services of the Taiwan régime claimed to have intercepted several Central Committee documents at the end of 1971 and the beginning of 1972 on the mainland, which largely substantiated the version of events given above and remained uncontested on essential points even when the documents were published. Secondly, the information services of the Japanese,

American and British in Tokyo and Hong Kong accepted the official version as being substantially correct; any difference of interpretation related only to secondary points. And, last but not least, it was striking that Moscow, which was more likely than anyone else to have been in possession of evidence which could have shown the Peking version to be incorrect, did not contradict the Chinese. Obviously a number of Soviet publications did try to make political capital out of the incident, but it would not have been difficult for the Russians to come up with decisive evidence on the matter, if their findings had really been in contradiction to those of the Chinese.

Let us go back for a moment to 13 September. The plane crashed in the early hours of the morning. In the tense situation existing on the borders between the Soviet Union and China, it is hardly possible that the presence of the aircraft remained unnoticed for long by the hundreds of thousands of Soviet military advisers in Mongolia. It is probable that a special investigation unit was on the scene of the crash on the day it occurred. It was later stated that certain documents had been found, and there can be no doubt that these contained important indications as to the identity of the passengers and the reason for their flight. There could have been no difficulty in verifying the identity of the most important ones: Lin Piao had spent several years in the Soviet Union during the initial stages of the Second World War for specialist medical treatment. Although the bodies had been half-burnt (which indicates a fire in the wreck) there would certainly be enough traces left to recognize any corpse thought to be that of Lin. There would, for instance, be clinical data on his teeth at some dentist's. In any case, it would hardly take the experts more than a couple of days to form serious suspicions in certain directions. Furthermore, the information services of the Soviet Union must obviously have known that a serious conflict among the Chinese leadership had been developing during the past year. Therefore it was not too difficult to reach a conclusion about the nature of the incident. But both Moscow and Ulan Bator remained silent. No diplomatic or even propaganda offensive followed, and nothing further occurred during subsequent weeks. The reason for this silence was a source of some puzzlement to China observers and interested journalists. It was taken by some to mean that events had in fact been different from the subsequent versions of them. There is, however, no sure indication that this was so. Other observers took it as proof of a degree of uncertainty on both sides regarding the nature of the incident. This seems quite possible, but does not provide us with an explanation.

An article by Gilles Martinet and Yann Govello in *Le Nouvel Observateur* seems to offer the most plausible account.[2] The authors refer to the battle of words which followed the accident. On 22 September, Peking announced to the outside world that the parade to be held on 1 October had been cancelled. No reason was given, though there were hints that there were threats of war from the Soviet Union. Moscow then decided to take the offensive to Peking in a warning against any such suggestion. On 24 September the Russian news agency Tass commented sarcastically on Western speculation on events in China and the Chinese suggestion that war had been threatened. The French article continues: 'One thing is clear: a number of significant domestic events were strongly influencing the situation within the People's Republic of China.' And it goes on to add very significantly: 'But all measures were being taken in Chinese circles to keep what was happening as secret as possible.' The article goes on:

The state of tension cannot last for ever, however. The Russians would certainly feel in a very strong position if they had Lin Piao alive. *But they only have a corpse.* Brezhnev and the other members of the Political Bureau of the C.P.S.U. have now entered the game of chess. But it is not sufficient simply to advance a pawn; the possible reaction of the opponent has also to be judged. If the Soviet authorities announce that Lin Piao was in the plane which crashed on 13 September, then they would certainly make a successful propaganda point. But what would this result in? The Chinese can then claim that Lin Piao's plane was shot down by Soviet fighters and that this constitutes a provocation preparatory to war against China. This would automatically restore the unity of the Chinese Communist Party and, in any case, Lin Piao cannot be restored to life – and he was no friend of the Soviets anyway. There would thus be no advantage to be gained from announcing that Lin Piao was in the plane on 13 September.

This was the reason, then, why it was decided to make vague announcements at a suitable moment, to be followed by further announcements, which would be made after an eventual Chinese reaction. The moment chosen was 30 September, and while it was true that a large part of the Chinese festivities had been cancelled anyway, it was expected that the impact would be considerable. In fact, the effect came nowhere near expectations. It is true that the references to 'half-burnt corpses' and 'documents' (which had – it was implied – not been burnt) were sufficiently vague to make Peking react with prudence; in fact the political crisis in Peking had advanced so far that the announcement had little effect on internal relationships. These, then, were the considerations which led to the cat-and-mouse game which took place around the plane crash, the circumstances of which can now be accepted as having been those described in the standard version of the story.

But even if one accepts that Lin Piao was involved in the plane crash, there is still an overwhelming number of questions to be answered. Why did Lin Piao try to fly to the Soviet Union? Did he really plot against Mao or were others trying to use him? Why did the differences of opinion on external and internal policy in 1971 take such a dramatic turn and what are the roots of these divergencies? To answer these questions we have to go back to the Great Leap Forward, the Great Proletarian Cultural Revolution and the way in which Lin Piao finally reached his number two position.

Part Two
The Roots

The assumption of political power depends on gun-barrels
and ink-wells. We must give them our attention ...

Lin Piao, 18 May 1966

4 : Rise of Chen Po-ta and Lin Piao;
Revolutionizing of the Army

Growing opposition between Maoists and Revisionists

The events of 1958–9 centre on a few important political meetings.

5–23 May 1958: Second meeting of the Eighth Party Congress. The plans for the Great Leap Forward were decided upon; the country was to be organized in accordance with the principle of the people's communes; it was decided to attempt a Twelve-Year Programme for Agriculture (a programme that turned out to be too ambitious and was twice revised). One of the key figures in the planning was Chen Po-ta, previously one of Mao's secretaries. Modelling himself ideologically on Stalin and Mao, he was especially important as a prominent exponent of Mao's radical ideas in the field of agricultural politics. In 1955 he became director of the Rural Work Department of the Party. In 1956, together with Lin Piao, he was elected to the Political Bureau of the Central Committee.

25 May 1958: Fifth Plenum of the Eighth Central Committee. Chen Po-ta, who was also acting as deputy director of the Propaganda Department of the Central Committee, was appointed chief director of the new theoretical party organ – *Red Flag.* Lin Piao became vice-chairman and member of the seven-strong Standing Committee of the Political Bureau of the Central Committee. Lin Piao, from the beginning of the thirties, had been one of the most brilliant guerrilla and war experts (army leaders) of the communists. From 1938–42 he had been in Moscow for medical treatment and military education. After the Liberation poor health kept him in the background. Since 1954 he had also been Chairman of the Chinese/Russian Friendship Association, in which Chen Po-ta also played an important role.

27 May–22 July 1958: Extended meeting of the (important)

Military Commission of the Central Committee. Marshal Lin Piao, known to be a Maoist, was one of the sternest critics of the 'revisionist' policy of the army leadership. In Chen Po-ta's *Red Flag*, revisionism is also criticized, firstly in the form of criticism of Yugoslavia.

28 November–10 December 1958: Sixth Plenum of the Eighth Central Committee. The difficulties around the Great Leap and the forming of the people's communes constituted the main problem. Mao Tse-tung announced that he would retire as President of the Republic (although remaining Party Chairman) 'in order to have more time for theoretical work'. Shortly afterwards he was succeeded in the Presidency by Liu Shao-chi.

2–5 April 1959: Seventh Plenum of the Central Committee, and following that, the first meeting of the second National People's Congress (the parliament). Here, too, the problems surrounding the Great Leap and the people's communes were the order of the day. The position of the Maoists at the top was strengthened by the appointment of Lin Piao as vice-chairman of the National Defence Council, by which he acquired equal status with the Minister of Defence, Peng Te-huai. After a journey to Eastern Europe, the latter wrote an open letter to Mao in July, declaring himself to be the spokesman for those who saw proof of the mistakenness of the new political developments in the economic problems of China. At the same moment, Khrushchev began to make similar criticisms.

2–16 August 1959: Eighth Plenum of the Central Committee. The party leaders conceded that serious mistakes had been made, but turned against the Chinese and foreign critics who had claimed the development programme to be a complete failure. Mao launched a heavy counter-attack against Peng Te-huai and the latter's Chief of Staff, Huang Ko-cheng. Shortly afterwards they were replaced by Lin Piao and Lo Jui-ching respectively.

September 1959: Extended sitting of the Military Commission of the Central Committee. The new army leaders drew further conclusions from the conflict. Lin Piao appeared as new Vice-Chairman (under Mao) and sharply criticized his predecessor, Peng. According to Lin, Peng's revisionist political standpoint lay behind the continuing revisionist military leadership. That would not be the case in the future, he announced.

The situation of the army in 1959

Since its formation in 1927, the Chinese Red Army had been occupied for a quarter of a century in continuous fighting in isolated territories; its role had involved a constant intermingling of military, civil, ideological and productive tasks; for its privileges and upkeep it was pretty well completely self-reliant, and in practice Party and army tended to act together. Only after the Liberation and after Korea did there come a change in the status and character of the army; this was largely due to the support and influence of the Soviet Union, which helped China in the modernization and professionalization of the army. This brought the whole structure of the armed forces into question – both horizontal (the division of the country into military regions), and vertical (the organizational structure of the army sub-divisions). This transformation needs to be examined for a moment, before Lin Piao's use of the army before and during the Cultural Revolution can be properly understood.

The existence of relatively independent political-military units before 1949, the separate 'armies', led to the division of the People's Republic into a sextet of military and political regions: north, north-west, south-west, central-south, east and north-east. It was quickly apparent that the control of the capital over the regional governments was too limited to be able to guarantee national unity in situations of conflict. This was true in particular for the industrialized north-east, which in the previous twenty years had undergone a development rather different from the rest of the country, first under Japanese occupation, and later through the strong influence of the U.S.S.R. on this region. It was the only region where the functions of First Secretary (Party) and military commander-in-chief were united in one person – Kao Kang, who attracted suspicion of trying to establish an 'Independent Kingdom', as it is called in Chinese terminology. The tensions led in 1953 to a conflict that was resolved to Peking's advantage in 1954–5. Apart from Kao Kang, the strong man of the eastern region, Jao Shu-shih, was also obliged to give up his functions. A solution to the regional problems was sought by abolishing the *military* regions. In their place a complicated system was introduced of 11–13 regions of a primary or secondary category, that were divided yet again into 23–26 districts, sub-districts and town garrisons. A large number of the military region leaders were promoted to the capital.

The six *political* regions were only later, and then only partially, abolished as a number of their powers were transferred to the party committees of the provinces, which were naturally autonomous national areas (through isolation), and the few large towns that came directly under central government. When later, during the Cultural Revolution, the Government's grasp was to relax, it became apparent, however, that the regional problem had not been solved, in spite of the reorganization.

As far as the army was concerned, besides the regional units which comprised about one-half of the manpower, there were also a number of central units – thirty-six 'army corps'. After 1953, development and modernization took place, particularly in these units. 'Technological' divisions were formed within the land forces, and a navy and an air force established. Weapons and technology came principally from the Soviet Union, with consequent influence on military thought. When Lin Piao moved to the forefront and opened his attack on revisionism, these central army divisions gave him every reason for his position: but the direct control of the central army leadership and the charges were naturally also the strongest there. The result – far-reaching for future developments – was that political Leftist indoctrination was to advance furthest where it was least expected: in the centrally-led, modern, trained army divisions.

Then Lin really began to concentrate on the business with which he was principally preoccupied as a military and political man.

The main problem is: is it still important for politics to be in command in the stage of modernization of the army? Concretely speaking, what place has political and ideological work? What attitudes should members of the armed forces adopt toward the country's economic construction and the mass movements?[1]

The theoretical answers to these questions are given by Lin Piao in the conclusion of the article, and the practical answers in a series of campaigns mounted from 1960–61, and aimed at political re-mobilization of the People's Liberation Army and a return to its social involvement. In typical Chinese jargon these campaigns were named (among others): the campaign for the three–eight work style (aimed at devotion to the people) – the campaign for the four and five perfections (aimed at improvement of the conduct of the individual soldier and the company), and the campaign for the four 'Firsts'. The last, in particular, is important. It is based on a system of priorities: Men before weapons; political thought before military thought; ideological renewal before political routine; practical application before sterile book knowledge.

Besides these campaigns, there were also changes in organization which will show themselves to be of great importance during the Cultural Revolution. The General Political Department of the army was restored. Although this Party-organization-within-the-army was officially dependent both on the heads of the Party (Military Commission of the Central Committee) and on the army command, the Department expanded within a few years to what was in fact an independent organ. From the first campaign to the expansion and the strengthening of the Party organization of the army (mid-1960s), a steady growth of power took place in stages of six to twelve months, always ending in a national conference (March 1961–January 1964).

The character of a People's Army was re-established by altering the nature of its authority from authoritarian/hierarchical to democratic/communal, a development which began in 1961 with the announcement of 'Regulations governing the People's Liberation Army's work at communal level', dealing with mutual criticism, self-criticism, and the functions of men and officers. The rank and distinction system (built up after the Liberation on the Soviet Union's example) was abandoned, and in 1965 conscription was abolished – just ten years after it had been introduced by Peng Te-huai.

Meanwhile, an intensive campaign was in progress within the army to further the study of the thought of Mao Tse-tung; this also served as a starting-point for the expansion and populariz-ation of Maoism among the civilian population. Thus, precisely one year after the publication of Lin's article, quoted above, the 'long-awaited fourth volume of the *Selected Works of Mao Tse-tung* was presented to the people, and in the following years (also at Lin's instigation) the Little Red Book of *Quotations from Chairman Mao Tse-tung* was distributed. This was distri-buted within the army from 1964 onwards, and outside the army from the end of 1966 (with an introduction by Lin), in an edition of many hundreds of millions.

The Party organization of the army was consolidated during 1964 under the leadership of Hsiao Hua, a former comrade of Lin Piao. The last stage had thus begun: henceforth, in addition to the civil Party apparatus, the army would also start to exer-cise political influence on society. A national campaign was organized under the slogan, 'Learn from the People's Liberation Army'. Party secretaries in the provinces were called up to act as political commissioners of their military districts. Thus, on the eve of the Cultural Revolution, eleven of the thirteen military regions and eighteen of the twenty-three military districts were linked to the civilian Party organization, through the personnel of the General Political Department. After a national confer-ence in January 1966, Hsiao Hua declared explicitly [2] 'The sys-tem of dual leadership by the military command and the local Party committees – under the united guidance of the Central Committee of the Party – must be enforced.' In other words, the General Political Department of the army was ready to take over the job of the party bureaucracy, if the latter were to be seen to fall short of requirements during the forthcoming mass-mobilization campaign of the Cultural Revolution.

Imperialism, Revisionism and the People's War

The escalation of American involvement in Vietnam in the latter half of 1965 lent further support for the new interpretation of the nature and duties of the army. The U.S. had in the so-called Tonkin incident given itself an excuse to bomb North Vietnam and to step up its military presence in the south. Both China and the Soviet Union were faced with the problem of how to react to this intensification of the undeclared war on a small 'fraternal socialist country'.

The Soviet Union found itself in a delicate position. It was difficult to avoid becoming involved at all, especially since the Soviets had been under very heavy critical fire from the Chinese for supposed revisionism. The Soviet Union was also the only country which could conceivably be a match for the United States in military terms. At the same time, however, the tendency of Soviet policy had been towards peaceful coexistence with American imperialism, and a limited joint action with the Chinese probably seemed the ideal solution to the dilemma.

This possibility was also hinted at by, among others, Lo Jui-ching, Lin Piao's Chief of Staff. The twentieth anniversary of the surrender of Nazi Germany gave him the opportunity of drawing a parallel between the United Front and its resistance to Fascism, and contemporary events; this article by Lo did not fail to arouse the opposition of the Maoists. Four months later, on the anniversary of the surrender of the Japanese (3 September), appeared an article by Lin Piao, which was to become his best-known theoretical work: *Long Live the Victory of the People's War*. Lin concluded, from the experiences of the Second World War, that a joint action with the Soviet Union was out of the question.

How was it possible for a weak country finally to defeat a strong country? How was it possible for a seemingly weak army to become the main force in the war? The basic reasons were that the War of Resistance against Japan was a genuine people's war led by the Communist Party of China and Comrade Mao Tse-tung, a war in which the correct Marxist-Leninist political and military lines were put into effect, . . .

Today, the U.S. imperialists are repeating on a world-wide scale the past actions of the Japanese imperialists in China and other parts of Asia. It has become an urgent necessity for the people in many countries to master and use people's war as a weapon against U.S. imperialists and their lackeys. In every conceivable way U.S. imperialists and their lackeys are trying to extinguish the revolutionary flames of people's war. The Khrushchev revisionists, fearing people's war like the plague, are heaping abuse on it. The two are colluding to prevent and sabotage people's war.[3]

Further paragraphs discuss: 'the principal contradiction', 'the correct application of the line and policy of the united front', 'reliance on the peasants and the establishment of rural base areas', 'the building of a people's army of a new type', 'the carrying out of the strategy and tactics of people's war', and 'adhering to the policy of self-reliance'. Then follows a paragraph on 'the international significance of Comrade Mao Tse-tung's theory of people's war.' The most important concept in this theory is seen to be the following:

It must be emphasized that Comrade Mao Tse-tung's theory of the establishment of rural revolutionary base areas and the encirclement of the cities from the countryside is of outstanding and practical importance for the present revolutionary struggles of all the oppressed nations and peoples in Asia, Africa and Latin America against imperialism and its lackeys . . .

Taking the entire globe, if North America and Western Europe can be called the 'cities of the world', then Asia, Africa and Latin America constitute the 'rural areas of the world'.

Then follow two other paragraphs, the first a call to arms: 'Defeat U.S. imperialism and its lackeys by people's war'; and the second: 'The Khrushchev revisionists are betrayers of people's war.'[4]

The message is clear: those who advocate joint action with the Soviet Union are preparing the ground for revisionism.

During the autumn, the conflict between Lo Jui-ching and Lin Piao became increasingly acute. In December 1965, Lin made a number of serious accusations against Lo during a meeting of the Standing Committee. It was decided that a special working group of the Central Committee should investigate the accusations. By the time of the national conference of the General Political Department, the next month, Lo's name was no longer being mentioned. A few months later, when the working group had handed in its report, he was relieved of all his functions. He was succeeded by Yang Cheng-wu as chief of staff. Like his eventual successor, Huang Yung-sheng (and the director of the General Political Department, Hsiao Hua) the new chief of staff was a former comrade-in-arms of Lin Piao's from the 115th Division of the Eighth Route Army. They were all strong advocates of a positive role for the army in politics, and all of them were to be loyal allies of Mao during the initial phase of the Cultural Revolution. All of them, however, later went beyond the bounds of the powers conferred on them and were eventually removed from office for 'Leftist deviationism'; Hsiao Hua in 1967, Yang Cheng-wu in 1968, and Lin Piao and Huang Yung-sheng in 1971.

5: Chiang Ching and Chen Po-ta; Revolutionizing of Culture

Mao Tse-tung goes over to the offensive; the rise of Chiang Ching

At the Central Work Conference, which ended in Peking in September 1962, Mao managed to halt the retreat from the ambitious economic aims of the Great Leap Forward. The retreat had started in 1959, when serious faults were discovered in the planning of the campaign. During the next two years the falling away from the aims of the campaign was further accelerated by poor harvests, caused by bad weather conditions, which further undermined the credibility of the plan. Nor was Mao in a position, at that time, to convince the Party leadership of the rightness of his views. These setbacks did lead to some subdued criticism of Mao and there was a certain amount of undercover pressure to rehabilitate Mao's most important critic, Peng Te-huai.

On the first signs of recovery of the economy, however, Mao launched a counter-offensive. He did not confine himself simply to strengthening the measures already taken, but issued a dramatic and significant appeal not to forget the class struggle. At the Tenth Plenum of the Eighth Central Committee, at the end of September 1962, Mao's proposal, dating from 1957, for the start of a new campaign was accepted: the Socialist Education Movement was under way. After the revolutionizing of the base of the social system, this movement was intended to see through the completion of the revolutionizing of the superstructure in order to solve the problems which had caused difficulties in the Great Leap Forward. The incompleteness of the political education of the rural population had made it possible for mistakes to be made by administrative personnel, which went uncorrected by their own people. This inequality between the mass of the population and the administrative classes was what, according to the Maoists, had led to Stalinism in the Soviet Union.

In addition to a constant tendency towards the stagnation of the revolutionary process in the rural areas, there was also a serious 'weakening in revolutionary morale' among the population in the big cities (a minority in terms of the total population, but still amounting to about a hundred million people) which further slowed down progress. This was especially the case in important groups of leading officials, intellectuals and artists. Their ideas weakened the morale of the new generations, thus endangering the continuation and future of the revolution in its entirety. Subversion was particularly rife in intellectual circles during 1959–62. Mao, however, was absolutely determined that revisionism should not take hold.

The Socialist Education Movement finally got under way in the rural areas with the co-operation of a half-hearted Party organization and an increasingly enthusiastic army; meanwhile, during 1963, Mao Tse-tung prepared his offensive against 'bourgeois' intellectuals and artists. On 12 December of that year he wrote:

The social and economic base has changed, but the arts as part of the superstructure, which serve this base, still remain a serious problem. Hence we should proceed with investigation and study and attend to this matter in earnest.

Isn't it absurd that many Communists are enthusiastic about promoting feudal and capitalist art, but not socialist art? [1]

Just under two weeks later the Theatre Competition for East China began in Shanghai; the competition was to last for four weeks, during which several new 'socialist dramas' were to be produced. The sponsor of the festival was Chiang Ching, who had had a successful career as a theatre and cinema actress in the same town thirty years earlier. In 1937 she went to join the Communists in Yenan, where she married Mao Tse-tung in spite of some opposition – according to some accounts – to a third marriage for Mao from within the Party. As far as is known, her first appearance in an official capacity only came in September 1962, when she acted as official hostess for President

Sukarno's visit to China. In the same month, during the Tenth Plenum, Mao put forward the first proposals for a Cultural Revolution. During the following year, Chiang Ching began to appear more and more in public. Her first appearances were made distinctly as the wife of the Party Chairman, but there is reason to believe that she developed an increasingly independent role in the fields of culture, politics, and culture-politics.

On 27 June 1964, Mao again spoke out very strongly against the 'popes' of culture in the Party:

They have acted as high and mighty bureaucrats, have not gone to the workers, peasants and soldiers and have not reflected the socialist revolution and socialist construction. In recent years, they have slid right down to the brink of revisionism.[2]

The timing of this attack was not accidental. During the same summer, Chiang Ching's *avant-garde* drama group took the most traditional stage in the capital by storm with its 'Festival of the Peking Opera on contemporary themes'; at the same time, rectification campaigns in art and literature and the reformation of the Peking Opera were officially inaugurated. Emperors, generals and ministers were replaced by workers, farmers and soldiers as the principal characters. The revolution, the War of Liberation and the national effort were to be the new main themes. It was certainly a step forward, but not final victory. The time had now come to launch an all-out attack on the 'feudal and capitalist' elements which had already been denounced, especially those who had tried to use the difficulties encountered in the Great Leap Forward to discredit the whole campaign.

Criticism of Wu Han's 'Hai Jui Dismissed from Office'

A perfect example of what was happening at the time is provided by the reception of a work by a modern author, Wu Han, about an enlightened sixteenth-century mandarin who stood up for the farmers against a despotical emperor, and was relieved of his functions because of this. The work was published in 1961, with the slogan, 'Learn from Hai Jui'. The publication of the work had been preceded by two years of discussion. The historical hero showed a striking similarity to Peng Te-huai, who had been deposed in 1959 from his post of Minister of Defence, after his fierce criticism of collectivization in agriculture and of Chairman Mao.[3]

The criticism of Wu Han took seven or eight months to prepare, during which time it was rewritten several times by Chiang Ching and her two collaborators. The elder of these was Chang Chun-chiao, third secretary of the Shanghai Party Committee; the younger was Yao Wen-yuan, a journalist on *Wen-hui Pao*, one of the two big Shanghai daily papers. (The reason given for the important part the latter was to play in the Cultural Revolution – he became the youngest member of the top echelon of the party – was that he had married a niece of Mao's. According to informed sources, however, this marriage could only have taken place after the Cultural Revolution.) The continuing collaboration of Chiang Ching and these two probably dates from the revolution she initiated in the Shanghai theatre.

Although the critique of Wu Han was a collective work, it was decided to publish it under the name of the least-known author, Yao Wen-yuan. The reaction of the propaganda apparatus would thus be 'unprejudiced' and any judgement appear that much more open. Wu Han, after all, was by no means unknown; this became apparent after 10 November, when the criticism was published in *Wen-hui Pao*, and was ignored. Although the tone of the piece was unusually sharp, and its content of sufficient importance to attract national attention, its publication passed without comment by the mass media in Peking and elsewhere.

The Peking media were the responsibility of the city council headed by Peng Chen, the Mayor. Wu Han, and two other similarly criticized authors, Teng To and Liao Mo-sha, were among Peng's closest collaborators. Peng Chen was also a powerful man in the Party at national level, with considerable influence in the propaganda division of the Central Committee. The national mass-media were the responsibility of the director of the division, the Minister of Culture, Lu Ting-i. Both Peng and Lu were members of the Group of Five for the Cultural Revolution which had in the meantime been formed at the highest level.

All five had come to the fore during the campaign against Lin Piao's predecessor, Peng Te-huai. Kang Sheng was the only one of the five destined to play a progressive role in the developing situation. The Group of Five, like the party secretariat, was then very much under the influence of conservative and moderate elements and Peng Chen was very much in control of the situation.

Wu Han's critics were therefore forced to find other ways of publicizing their criticism. Which sections of the media were not under the direct control of Peng Chen and Lu Ting-i?

1. The Shanghai group could turn to other local and regional authorities via the relevant local administrative apparatus (Chang Chun-chiao was still third secretary of the local Party committee). The local authorities do have certain areas of responsibility in propaganda over which they are not obliged to consult national authorities.

2. Contact could be made with sympathizers with responsibility for specific sections in the media. An obvious member of this category seemed to be Chen Po-ta, an acquaintance of Chiang Ching, who had replaced Lu Ting-i as editor of the *Red Flag*; the eminent position enjoyed by Chen in the social-intellectual world made him an ideal contact with the sections of the media for that sector.

3. Last but not least, there was the propaganda apparatus of the army, as opposed to that of the Party. Chang Chun-chiao had excellent contacts there in his position as political commissioner for the military district of Nanking, which also entailed his membership of the General Political Department of Hsiao Hua.

The first way was through the critics' own contacts within local organizations. The article was sent out, probably from the East China bureau of the Party, to all mass media in the provinces, where it received a lot of attention. It was then circulated in the form of a pamphlet by a local publishing house and offered telegraphically to institutions throughout the whole country. Within half a year, circulation had reached half a million copies. At the beginning of December 1965, the *Wen-hui Pao* published a survey of the controversy as it had developed up till then,

placing a localized attack within a broader frame of fundamental cultural criticism.

The second way involved an attempt to influence a sector of
the national propaganda apparatus. An approach was made to
Chen Po-ta and, thanks to his influence, the article appeared in
a special academic supplement to the *People's Daily* at the end
of November. The attack was taken up in January in a monthly
magazine published by the Department of Philosophy and
Social Sciences of the Academy.[4] The author was a certain Kuan
Feng, who, with several other supporters of Chen Po-ta, such as
Wang Li, Chi Pen-yu and Lin Chieh, was later to form a group
of radical publicists around Chen in much the same way that
Yao and Chang had come to the support of Chiang Ching in
Shanghai. (These two ideological vanguards were later to join
forces and form the Cultural Revolution Group – the successor
to the Group of Five.)

The third way was aimed at circumventing the propaganda
apparatus of the Party. At the end of November the original
article by Yao Wen-yuan appeared in the *Liberation Army
Daily*. During the following weeks the General Political Department began a vigorous campaign of culture criticism. At the
beginning of February 1966 Lin Pao offered the group around
Chiang Ching a 'free place' within the army, thus enabling the
group to escape from the direct control of the Party secretariat
in Peking. The group was given *carte blanche* to carry on with
their activities from inside the army. Chiang Ching was asked
by Lin to set up a 'Discussion group on work in literature and
art in the armed forces'; she was provided with facilities and
personnel for this task. When members of the upper echelon of
the General Political Department went for a number of weeks
to Shanghai, Lin announced:

Comrade Chiang Ching talked with me yesterday. She is very sharp
politically on questions of literature and art, and she really knows
art. She has many opinions, and they are very valuable. You should
pay good attention to them and take measures to insure that they
are applied ideologically and organizationally.[5]

The reaction of Peng Chen to the criticism of Wu Han

A situation had now been created in which the group around Peng Chen could no longer keep silent. His tactics were to snatch the initiative and to divert attention in other directions. These were the tactics constantly used – often successfully – by conservative elements during the Cultural Revolution to protect their positions.

In mid-December the daily paper in Peking (under the control of the city committee) published a pseudonymous article dealing with the attack on Wu Han. The criticism confined itself chiefly, however, to the academic-historical aspects of the disputed play, disregarding its real political implications. It turned out later that the author of the article had been Teng To, a colleague of Wu Han's from the top level of the Party in Peking and co-author with him of a number of other disputed publications during the period 1959–62. A few days later the *People's Daily* published a résumé of the whole discussion – less, it appears, to give an account of events to date than to suggest that the matter could now be considered closed. This impression was further strengthened by the organization of a session of criticism on Wu Han behind closed doors among the top officials of the Party in Peking. The result of this was an article of self-criticism by Wu Han in the *People's Daily* at the end of December. The following week, the Shanghai *Wen-hui Pao* was already calling the self-criticism insufficient and intensified its attack, with the support of critics in Peking. The top officials of the Party in Peking then organized another session of criticism on Wu Han, which produced a new, more comprehensive self-criticism by the author. But the cultural critics in Peking and Shanghai were still dissatisfied. This time, however, Peng Chen decided to counter-attack. At the beginning of February the *People's Daily* issued a sharp criticism of Yao Wen-yuan's 'gossip', while 'incriminating' material was assembled against Kuan Feng at the same time. Peng then called a meeting of the Group of Five in order to decide on the lines of action for further culture criticism; he insisted that this be confined to academic-historical discussion, and that it should be kept in the hands of 'qualified' ideological authorities, instead of political polemics being set 'before the whole nation'. He succeeded in obtaining a majority in the Group of Five and his proposals were pressed through with little opposition. A similar thing happened at a subsequent meeting of the Standing Committee from which Mao was absent and which was chaired by First Vice-Chairman Liu Shao-chi. By the middle of February, Peng's proposals had been approved and were soon being propagated within the Party. Pei-ta University was then invited by the Peking city committee to make an 'expert study' of the figure of Hai Jui; the national propaganda organ also made it quite clear that all 'demagogical parallels' with the Peng Te-huai affair had to be avoided. It now appeared that the central Party bureaucracy had succeeded in diverting this piece of Maoist culture criticism into a dead end. The 'pens' – Chiang Ching and Chen Po-ta – seem to have got the worst of the exchange. The 'gun' – Lin Piao – was thus finally forced to come to the rescue.

The fall of Peng Chen; dissolution of the Group of Five

Another meeting of the Standing Committee and of the members of the Political Bureau was called in mid-March. This time the meeting was chaired by Mao, and not held in Peking, but in Hangchow: that is, within the area controlled by the reshuffled East China bureau and very close to the Maoist power base of Shanghai. The first important item on the agenda, proposed by Chen I, Minister for Foreign Affairs, was the rejection of the invitation to attend the Twenty-third Congress of the Communist Party of the Soviet Union. Joint Soviet-Chinese action over Vietnam now seemed more unlikely than ever. In the context of the continuing argument between Lin Piao and his chief-of-staff, Lo Jui-ching, this meant a further weakening of the latter's position, with a consequent strengthening of the former's. It also represented a considerable victory for the Maoists among the Party leaders, and confirmed them in their feeling that they were now strong enough to contemplate a confrontation with the conservative Party bureaucracy. This resulted in the second important decision of the meeting.

Mao Tse-tung now made himself responsible for the criticism of Wu Han by Yao Wen-yuan, and delivered an even sharper rebuke to those who had opposed it:

Wu Han and Chien Po-tsan (vice-rector of Pei-ta University) are members of the Party, but in reality they are still part of the Kuo-mintang (reactionaries). The bourgeois academic authorities must be criticized on these grounds. We should form the young people ourselves, without the fear that they will offend against the so-called 'King's laws'. Their articles must not be withheld.[6]

The attack on Wu Han thus reached a new stage, with widening implications. Peng Chen was obliged to beat a retreat, while Liu Shao-chi, who had allowed Peng's proposals to be passed in February, had to dissociate himself from them. Helped by a 'centre group' in the Party secretariat, however, Liu was able to prevent Peng Chen's position from being affected for the time being. Relationships within the Political Bureau were still confused; but the decisive battle was to be fought after this meeting of March 1966.

At the end of March Mao Tse-tung is reported to have said to one of his collaborators:

Wu Han has published so many articles, without having to seek anyone's permission. But when it comes to Yao Wen-yuan, permission has to be asked. Why is this so? Articles from the Left are suppressed, while the great despots of the academic world are protected . . . the department of propaganda has become the court of the king of hell; but the little devils must now be released. For a long time now I have begged all local authorities to rebel against the Central Committee, if those in power there have done their job badly. We need more rebellious spirits among the local authorities who will create disorder in the Temple of Heaven. Peng Chen, the Peking Party Committee and the propaganda branch of the Central Committee have been responsible for protecting bad people. The propaganda branch of the Central Committee, the Cultural Revolution Group, must be dissolved.[7]

However, the Maoist group still did not feel sure enough of

itself to place the entire matter on the agenda. Another detour had to be made, but one which brought the whole weight of Lin's army apparatus into play.

Two days after the end of the meeting of the Political Bureau, a résumé of the proceedings of the February discussions of the Chiang Ching group was sent by Lin Piao to the members of the Military Commission of the Central Committee. The fall of Lo Jui-ching in December 1965 had left this important body almost completely under the control of the Maoists. At the end of March, then, the Military Commission of the Central Committee, in its turn, decided to put Lin Piao's report to the Party secretariat and the Political Bureau. This unexpected move broke the stalemate among the Party leadership. Peng Chen and his supporters were now confronted with the power of the Military Commission.

By mid-April the movement had already started, which was to gather momentum during the following weeks and months, to bring Wu Han and his protectors down. Some days later, Teng To began to retreat from his position (followed later by Liao Mo-sha), by publishing a self-criticism in the *People's Daily*; this was again rejected by his critics as insufficient. Peng Chen then tried to dissociate himself from his compromised collaborators on the city council. Supported by Kang Sheng and Chou En-lai, Chen Po-ta launched an attack on Peng Chen during a meeting of the Party secretariat; the reorganization of the Group of Five was announced. During the second half of April and the first part of May, the Standing Committee and members of the Political Bureau met again in Hangchow and Shanghai, where the conflict seems to have been finally resolved in favour of the Left wing.

On 1 May, however, the Party leadership (including Peng Chen) still appeared united in public, but political events had in fact already reached the point of no return. This can easily be seen from the accompanying campaign in the press, during which a series of increasingly critical leading articles were published in Lin Piao's *Liberation Army Daily*. On 18 April (at the beginning of the decisive meeting), the headlines ran as follows, 'Hold aloft the great red banner of Mao Tse-tung's thought!

Take an active part in the Great Socialist Cultural Revolution!'
By 4 May the headlines had become even more militant: 'Never
forget class struggle!' (Mao's appeal of September 1962).
And on 8 May (when the confrontation within the Party leadership had reached a decisive point) the headlines screamed:
'Open fire on the evil anti-socialist and anti-Party line!' The
other mouthpieces of the radical Left wing also began to bestir
themselves. Chen Po-ta threw his *Red Flag* into the battle, while
Yao Wen-yuan published a more violent and extended critique
than ever in *Wen-hui Pao*. During the meeting itself Peng Chen
was accused of having been the 'brain' behind the cultural and
political reaction of 1959–62, and, with the help of supporters,
to have held a secret meeting in 1961 to criticize systematically
all documents issued by the Central Committee on the Great
Leap. Accusations of the withholding of cultural criticism was
thus extended to the more serious accusation of faction-
forming. These accusations not only linked Wu Han with Peng
Chen, but also Peng Chen with other members of the Group of
Five. The Group was actually dissolved, and not reorganized,
as had been announced. It was not immediately replaced by
another group.

According to a later communiqué from the Yugoslav Press
Agency Tanjug, special commando units were placed on an
emergency footing at critical times during the April–July period,
to pre-empt any possible move towards rebellion by the opposition. After a decisive meeting of the Party leadership in April,
according to the Yugoslav report, the secretariat of the Peking
Party Committee was placed under military control, and on
17 April, Peng Chen left, accompanied by two bodyguards,
while another ten officers were posted in front of his offices.
After these events, but before the reorganization of the garrison
in Peking and the military district, Lin Piao is said to have
brought some centrally-commanded army corps from the provinces to the capital to prevent any possible mutiny. About the
middle of May, Mao gave up his idea of returning to the capital
at the last moment, because he was not satisfied that his security
was adequately guaranteed there. It was only in the middle
of July – in a politically tense situation – that Mao is re-

ported to have returned, and only then after his new chief-of-staff Yang Cheng-wu had increased the number of troops in Peking. This version of events from Tanjug has not gone uncontested,[8] but it does seem likely, after the event, that displays of military power were used by both the Left and Right at decisive moments at the beginning of the Cultural Revolution to intimidate the opposition and prevent any hostile moves being made. It is even open to question whether the confrontation between the Maoists and the central Party bureaucracy would have been decided so swiftly in favour of the former if the central army units had not supported them. The army played a decisive role in the Cultural Revolution from the very beginning of events in 1966.

Although Mao was to become increasingly opposed to the army's playing a permanent leading part in events after the Ninth Party Congress in 1969 ('The Party must control the gun, the gun must never be allowed to control the Party'), it is certain that Mao lent his support to the ambitions of the politically-oriented soldier, Lin Piao, during the first half of May 1966. On 7 May Mao sent a 'private' letter to Lin. Three months later, on 7 August (the anniversary of the People's Liberation Army), the contents of this letter were presented by Lin as a call to the 'whole country' (following the example of his army) to form 'a school of the thought of Mao Tse-tung'. Initially, this provided justification enough for the influence of the army (it was in effect filling the temporary political gap caused by the ossification of the Party bureaucracy) on the rest of Chinese society and its important role in popularizing Mao's thought. After the Cultural Revolution, however, it seems to have become the base of a movement towards a semi-military administration and a personality cult which had then outlived its use.

6: Mao between Determination and Doubt; Three Documents

Circular of the Central Committee of 16 May 1966[1]

A decisive move was finally made in the first round of the Cultural Revolution on 16 May 1966. The Standing Committee and/or the Political Bureau issued a circular in the name of the Central Committee, which had been drafted with Mao Tsetung's authority and which gave a final answer to Wu Han and Peng Chen. The circular was addressed to all the regional bureaux of the Central Committee, the Party committees of the provinces, the autonomous regions and the centrally-administered towns, the departments and commissions of the Central Committee, groups of leading officials in the Party, the Party committees in government institutions and mass organizations, and the General Political Department of the Army.

The Central Committee has decided to revoke the Outline Report on the Current Academic Discussion Made by the 'Group of Five in Charge of the Cultural Revolution' which was approved for distribution on 12 February 1966, to dissolve the 'Group of Five in Charge of the Cultural Revolution' and its offices, and to set up a new Cultural Revolution Group directly under the Standing Committee of the Political Bureau. The so-called Outline Report by the 'Group of Five' is fundamentally wrong. It runs counter to the line of the socialist cultural revolution set forth by the Central Committee and Comrade Mao Tse-tung and to the guiding principles formulated at the Tenth Plenary Session of the Eighth Central Committee of the Party in 1962 on the question of classes and class struggle in socialist society. While feigning compliance, the Report actually opposes and stubbornly resists the Great Cultural Revolution personally initiated and led by Comrade Mao Tse-tung, as well as the instructions regarding the criticism of Wu Han which he gave at the working conference of the Central Committee in September and October of 1965 (that is, at the session of the Standing Committee of the Political Bureau of the Central Committee which was also attended by the leading comrades of all the regional bureaux of the Central Committee).

The so-called Outline Report by the 'Group of Five' is actually the report of Peng Chen alone. He concocted it according to his own ideas behind the backs of Comrade Kang Sheng, a member of the 'Group of Five', and other comrades. In handling a document of this kind regarding important questions which affect the overall situation in the socialist revolution, Peng Chen held no discussion or exchange of views at all with the 'Group of Five'. He did not ask any local Party committee for its opinion, nor did he make it clear that the Outline Report would be sent to the Central Committee for examination as an official document, and still less did he get the approval of Comrade Mao Tse-tung, Chairman of the Central Committee. Employing the most dishonest methods, he acted arbitrarily, abused his powers and, usurping the name of the Central Committee, hurriedly issued the Outline Report to the whole Party.

There then follows a summing-up of the ten most serious mistakes in the Proposals: they failed to make clear that the central theme of Wu Han's play on Hai Jui was the question of dismissal from office (thus recalling the case of Peng Te-huai); the essentially political nature of the discussion (returning to the reaction against the Great Leap) had been overlaid by 'academic' and 'theoretical' considerations; the proposals contained a number of bourgeois concepts, such as 'freedom of expression', 'impartial truth', 'scientific expertise', 'positive criticism', 'academic freedom', without drawing proper attention to the class aspect; they laid unnecessary stress on the need for 'guidance' in the Cultural Revolution, whereas the whole point of this phase was to mobilize the masses unrestrainedly. The circular concludes:

In short, the Report opposes carrying the socialist revolution through to the end, opposes the line on the Cultural Revolution pursued by the Central Committee of the Party headed by Comrade Mao Tse-tung, attacks the proletarian Left and shields the bourgeois Right, thereby preparing public opinion for the restoration of capitalism. It is a reflection of bourgeois ideology in the Party; it is out-and-out revisionism. Far from being a minor issue, the struggle against this revisionist line is an issue of prime importance having a vital bearing on the destiny and future of our Party and state, on the future complexion of our Party and state, and on the world revolution.

Party committees at all levels must immediately stop carrying out the Outline Report on the Current Academic Discussion Made by the 'Group of Five in Charge of the Cultural Revolution'. The whole Party must follow Comrade Mao Tse-tung's instructions, hold high the great banner of the Proletarian Cultural Revolution, thoroughly expose the reactionary bourgeois stand of those so-called academic authorities who oppose the Party and socialism, thoroughly criticize and repudiate reactionary bourgeois ideas in the sphere of academic work, education, journalism, literature and art and publishing, and seize the leadership in these cultural spheres. To achieve this, it is at the same time necessary to criticize and repudiate those representatives of the bourgeoisie who have sneaked into the Party, the government, the army and all spheres of culture, and to clear them out or transfer some of them to other positions. Above all, we must not entrust these people with the work of leading the Cultural Revolution. In fact many of them have done and are still doing such work, and this is extremely dangerous.

Those representatives of the bourgeoisie who have sneaked into the Party, the government, the army and various spheres of culture are a bunch of counter-revolutionary revisionists. Once conditions are ripe, they will seize political power and turn the dictatorship of the proletariat into a dictatorship of the bourgeoisie. Some of them we have already seen through, others we have not. Some are still trusted by us and are being trained as our successors, persons like Khrushchev, for example, who are still nestling beside us. Party committees at all levels must pay full attention to this matter.

Lin Piao formulates his ideas[2]

On 18 May 1966, the Party leadership met once again. Mao was absent, and the first to speak was Lin Piao. Amid the sudden changes in the balance of power, Lin had begun to emerge as a key figure, and he took advantage of this occasion to make an extended speech – the most important of his career. What he said on this occasion throws considerable light on his thoughts, which were now beginning to play an important part in events. He began by saying that the accusations against Peng Chen also applied to two other members of the Group of Five: Lu

Ting-i and Yang Shang-kun. He again mentioned Lo Jui-ching, the chief-of-staff with whom he had had very considerable differences of opinion on national defence policy, and who had ceased to play an important role in public affairs since December. His accusations now extended beyond those stemming immediately from deep political differences to accusations of a military threat to the security of the régime in the preparation of a 'counter-revolutionary *coup d'état*'. Although this extension of the number of the accused and the escalation of the accusations themselves did not come as a complete surprise to the people present at this meeting, several of them were probably taken aback by the sheer directness of the delivery. Lin Piao then went on to develop his theme by talking about *coups d'état* in general and the possibilities of a putsch in China at that particular moment. He then went on to talk of the great role played by Mao Tse-tung, his thought and how it should be spread. At this point, however, he began to simplify the problem again, and, instead of talking about the correct political line, he began to extol Mao's particular genius, which outshone the geniuses of Marx, Engels and Lenin; similarly, China's 'revolutionary experience' would never be surpassed by that of other countries. He concluded by saying that his decision to issue the Little Red Book of *Quotations from Chairman Mao Tse-tung* for the ideological education of the army was correct and should be followed.

Many of the half-truths and obvious exaggerations uttered here were to develop an independent life of their own in the coming years. At the time, however, no one in the Maoist camp spoke out against them openly. It was accepted that a simplifying of propaganda was unavoidable during the mobilization of opinion, and that the might of the central army corps and the General Political Department was in any case indispensable in the confrontation with the Party bureaucracy. It was also probably thought that this kind of rigidity would give way to a more flexible approach as the movement developed. During the course of 1970–71, however, it became clear that this was not going to be the case and that Lin had remained the same – a person who would reduce deep political differences to head-on military confrontation. By 1971, Lin had got himself into the position in which literally almost all the accusations he had made against his opponents in May 1966 could be made against him, and with greater justification.

It would be better if other members of the Standing Committee made their speeches first. Since I am asked to speak first, I am going to say something. I don't have a prepared text, therefore I shall speak without it. At times, I may read some material.

This is the enlarged meeting of the Political Bureau. Not long ago, the enlarged meeting convened by Mao Tse-tung concentrated on and took the initiative in the solution of the Peng Chen problem. Now we will continue our efforts to solve this problem. The Lo Jui-ching problem has already been solved. The problem of Lu Ting-i and Yang Shang-kun was exposed during the investigation of underground activities and has been fermenting for some time. Now we are going to solve it. The problems of these four are connected with each other and bear certain similarities. The worst is the Peng Chen problem, and the others are less important. The exposure and solution of these problems are of grave concern to the whole party, the insuring of continuous development of revolution, the prevention of capitalist restoration, and the prevention of revisionist usurpation of political power, a counter-revolutionary *coup d'état*, and subversion. It is an important measure for China's advancement. It is also Mao Tse-tung's wise and resolute decision.

Here the greatest problem is the prevention of a counter-revolutionary *coup d'état*: the prevention of subversion, and the prevention of *coup d'état*. The fundamental problem of revolution is the problem of political power. Once they obtain political power, the proletarian class and the labouring people will have everything. Once they lose it, they will lose all . . . Using my own words, political power is the power to suppress. Of course, suppression is not the only function of political power. The political power of the proletarian class should also reform the peasants and small owners of property, enhance economic reconstruction, and resist foreign aggression. Of these numerous purposes, suppression is the most essential. Reactionaries in the society and representatives of the exploiting classes who have infiltrated into the Party should be suppressed. Some should be sentenced to death, some should be imprisoned, some should be controlled through labour reform, some should be expelled from the Party, and some should be dismissed from public office. Otherwise, it means that we don't understand the fundamental views of Marxism regarding political power; we are going to lose political power and become fools.

In recent years, especially last year, Chairman Mao has reminded us of the problem of preventing revisionism, inside and outside the Party, on every front, in every area, and at high and low levels. I understand that he refers chiefly to the leading organs. Chairman Mao, in recent months, has paid particular attention to the prevention of a counter-revolutionary *coup d'état* and adopted many measures. After the Lo Jui-ching problem, he talked about it. Now the Peng Chen problem has been exposed, and he again summoned several persons and talked about it, dispatched personnel and had them stationed in the radio broadcasting stations, the armed forces, and the public security systems in order to prevent a counter-revolutionary *coup d'état* and the occupation of our crucial points. This is the 'article' Chairman Mao has been writing in recent months. This is the 'article' he has not quite finished and printed, and because of this, Chairman Mao has not slept well for many days. It is a very deep-penetrating and serious problem. This is the work of Chairman Mao we ought to learn from.

Coups d'état have today become a fad. Generally speaking, the change of political power results from either people's revolution, which starts from below – such as Chen Sheng and Wu Kuang's rebellion (in the Chin dynasty), the Tai Ping rebellion (in the Ching dynasty) and the Communist Revolution of our Party –; or counter-revolutionary *coups d'état* – which include *coups d'état* from the Court, from within, collusion of the high and low, collusion with the subversive activities of foreign enemies or with armed invasion, and combination with natural calamities. This has been so, both historically and at present. Concerning *coups d'état* in the world, we may put aside those in the distant past. According to incomplete statistics, there have been sixty-one *coups d'état* in the capitalist countries in Asia, Africa and Latin America since 1960. Of the sixty-one *coups d'état*, fifty-six were successful. Eight chiefs-of-state were beheaded, seven were kept as puppets, and eleven were deposed. These statistics were compiled before the *coups d'état* in Ghana, Indonesia, and Syria. During the course of these six years, *coups d'état* averaged eleven per year ...

Now let us examine the problem from the standpoint of our national history. There are many examples in which we see that political power was lost through *coups d'état* before a dynasty was established for 10, 20, 30 or 50 years. The following examples illustrate this point ... The Republican Revolution of 1911 made Sun Yat-sen

President of China. Three months later, Yuan Shih-kai seized political power from him. After another four years, Yuan was also overthrown. Then came a period of over a decade of civil wars among the warlords: two Hopei-Manchu wars, and one Hopei-Anhwei war. These reactionary *coups d'état* should have terrified us and heightened our vigilance. Our seizure of political power has already lasted sixteen years. Will this régime of the proletarian class be overthrown and usurped? If we are not careful enough, we shall lose our political power. Soviet Russia was overthrown by Khrushchev ... Now Chairman Mao has noticed this problem to which we seldom paid attention. He has several times summoned responsible comrades to discuss the problem of preventing a counter-revolutionary *coup d'état*. Did he do this without any reason? No, there are many clear indications confirming it ... I am not going to talk in detail of these phenomena and source materials. After experiencing the anti campaigns, you may have smelled it – the smell of gunpowder. Representatives of the capitalist class infiltrated into our Party and into the Party's leadership organs, became the faction of authority, and controlled the government machinery, the political power, military power, and the headquarters of the ideological war front. They united to undertake subversive activities and caused much trouble ... Chairman Mao said that we had not occupied the ideological front for the past sixteen years ... Seizure of political power depends on gun barrels and inkwells. These deserve our attention ... Otherwise, once the opportune time comes, a counter-revolutionary *coup d'état* will occur; once we have a natural calamity, or once a war breaks out or Chairman Mao dies – this political crisis will come and this vast country of 700 million people will be in disorder and chaos ...

We should struggle against them, and at the same time unite ourselves, taking Chairman Mao and Mao Tse-tung's thought as the centre. These people have something in common – anti-Chairman Mao and anti-Mao Tse-tung's thought. It is alike with Peng Chen, Lo Jui-ching, Lu Tingi-i, and Yang Shang-kun as well as with Teng To, Wu Han, and Liao Mo-sha. The materials against them are too numerous to be listed. They either ostensibly or by insinuation opposed Chairman Mao and Mao Tse-tung's thought maliciously in different languages, with different styles and different methods. Chairman Mao is the founder of our Party and nation, and the greatest contemporary Marxist-Leninist. Chairman Mao has ingeniously, creatively and in an overall fashion inherited, guarded and glorified Marxism-Leninism, promoting it to a brand-new stage.

Mao Tse-tung's thought is Marxism-Leninism in an age when imperialism moves towards total collapse and socialism moves towards world victory. Mao Tse-tung's thought is the guide line of all works of the Party and the nation . . . Many bad elements opposed the study of Chairman Mao's works and these are anti-party elements. The Ministry of Propaganda of the Central Committee controlled by Lu Ting-i opposed the study of Chairman Mao's works, saying contemptuously that they are elementary, vulgar, and pragmatic. They propagated not Mao Tse-tung's thought but capitalist ideology, not revolutionary thought but reactionary thought; they did not push the revolution forward but dragged it backward. When others propagated Mao Tse-tung's thought, they laughed and sneered, suppressed, attacked and opposed it by all means . . .

The Marxists should at least know that existence determines consciousness, material is primary and spirit secondary, and consciousness has a great pushing capability. Material and spirit can be exchanged. Chairman Mao said: 'Where do correct ideas come from? Do they drop from the skies? No. Are they innate in the mind? No. They come from social practice, and from it alone; they come from three kinds of social practice, the struggle for production, the class struggle and scientific experiment . . .' Chairman Mao has experienced much more than Marx, Engels and Lenin. Of course Marx, Engels and Lenin were great figures. Marx lived 64 years, Engels 75 years. They possessed abundant vision, inherited the advanced ideology of mankind, and predicted the development of human society. Unlike Chairman Mao, they did not have the experience of personal leadership in proletarian revolution, personally commanding so many political battles, especially military battles. Lenin lived only 54 years and died in the sixth year after the victory of the October Revolution. He never experienced so many long-term, complicated, violent and many-sided struggles as Chairman Mao has experienced. The population of China is ten times greater than that of Germany and three times that of Soviet Russia. China's rich revolutionary experience cannot be excelled. Chairman Mao commands the highest prestige in the nation and the whole world and he is the most outstanding and the greatest figure. Chairman Mao's sayings, works, and revolutionary practice have shown that he is a great proletarian genius. Some people don't admit genius but this is not Marxist. Engels said that Hegel and Saint-Simon were geniuses of the eighteenth century and Marx was the genius of the nineteenth century. He said that Marx stood higher than all others; he could see further than others, and his observation was richer and keener; therefore he was a genius. Lenin also accepted genius; he said there had to be more than ten leaders of genius and then Russia could be led to win the victory of revolution. Chairman Mao is a genius. What is the difference between him and us? We undertook struggle together – some are senior to him in age. We are not as old as he, but we have as much experience. We also read books, but we understand either nothing at all or don't understand fully; but Chairman Mao understands. I saw many people make small circles and dots on the books they read, sometimes a book was full of such circles and dots; these betrayed that the reader did not understand them, not knowing the centre nor the main or secondary points. Decades ago, Chairman Mao understood the nucleus of dialectics, but even now we don't; he not only understands it but can utilize it skilfully . . .

It was not meritorious but a 'must' that the P.L.A. should take Chairman Mao's works as the textbook for cadres and warriors. Using Mao Tse-tung's thoughts to unite the armed forces and the entire Party can solve any problem. Every sentence of Chairman Mao's works is a truth, one single sentence of his surpasses ten thousand of ours. I have not read Chairman Mao's works enough and would study harder from now on . . .

A letter from Mao to Chiang Ching[3]

It is not surprising that Lin Piao's ideas encountered some resistance, which came not only from the discredited Right-wing (from Lo Jui-ching and Peng Chen) and the conservative centre (Liu Shao-chi and Teng Hsiao-ping) but also from the more moderate Left-wing elements (such as Chou En-lai.) It is even less surprising, perhaps, that anyone who had not yet been discredited should not have wanted to take the risk of becoming so, by raising his voice against Lin's ideas at this delicate moment. Mao, too, had serious reservations, but hesitated at the time to express his opinions to anyone but members of his immediate entourage. While developments in Peking were entering a new phase, he retired to the country to consider the situation. It was from there, after an interval of two weeks, that he sent a confidential letter to his wife, Chiang Ching, in Shanghai, in which he expressed his reservations. There were obviously a small number of people who were familiar with the

Party Chairman's opinions, as expressed in the letter, even during the Cultural Revolution. But it was only after the fall of Lin Piao, during the information campaign of 1972, that the letter was circulated within the Party. Mao is said to have written the letter on 8 July 1966.

I have received your letter of 29 June. You would do well to follow the advice of comrades Wei and Chen [secretaries of the Party Committee of Shanghai] and to remain where you are for a little while longer. I shall be receiving two visits from foreign guests this month. I will keep you informed about my activities when these visits are over.

After leaving Wulin [near the town of Hangchow in the province of Chekiang], on 15 June, I spent more than ten days in the West, in a foxhole of a place in the mountains, where news penetrates only with some difficulty. It is ten days since my arrival in Pai-yung Huang-ho [a mountain area to the south-west of the town of Wuhan in the province of Hupei]. I spend every day reading documents, which is a very interesting way of passing my time. Chaos on earth has given way to order. In seven or eight years, chaos will return. Evil spirits will spring up again. It cannot be otherwise, since their nature is determined by the nature of their class.

The Central Committee is in a hurry to circulate the speech made by my friend [he is referring to the speech by Lin Piao reported above]. I am prepared to give my approval. In this speech, he draws particular attention to the problem of the *coup d'état*. No one has spoken like this before. I would never have thought that the few books I have written could have such magic powers. Now he has sung the praises of my works, the whole country will follow his example. This reminds me of the old woman who was selling melons and who exaggerated the quality of her wares. My friend and his colleagues have presented me with a *fait accompli*. It looks as if there is no other course left open to me than to give my approval.

This is the first time in my life that I have had to agree with other people about an essential problem against my wish. This is what is called changing course without wanting to!

Yuan Chi, from the Chin dynasty, was against Liu Pang. He made the journey from Liyang to Chengkaotao and declared: 'The world has not known many heroes, and this makes it possible for somebody like Liu Pang to make a name for himself.'

Lu Hsun [Mao's favourite modern author, 1881–1936] made some correction in his satirical writings. His soul and mine are in harmony. He said: 'I am often much stricter with myself than with other people.'

After stumbling several times, I often do what he did. But the comrades do not always believe that I trust myself, while at the same time doubting myself. I always believe that when there is no tiger in the mountains, the monkey becomes king, and have I that way become such a king? But this is not being eclectic. I have a bit of the tiger in me, which is the most important thing, and also a bit of the monkey, which is secondary.

I have already quoted sentences from the letter which Li Fu, from the Han dynasty, wrote to Hiang Chung: 'What is high, bends easily. What is white, becomes dirty quickly. The more difficult the song, the fewer people will be able to sing it. When one's fame is great, it is difficult to show oneself worthy of it.' These last two sentences describe my case exactly, and I have quoted them at a session of the Standing Committee. Man's dignity lies in the fact that he has the intelligence to know himself.

At the Hangchow conference, in April of this year, I expressed ideas which differed from those of my friend. But what could I do? He repeated the same things at the Peking conference in May. What is more, the papers show they have a high opinion of what he says and inflate it in the most extraordinary manner. In these circumstances, I cannot do anything but let myself be carried along. I suppose they intend to drive away the evil spirits with the help of Chung Kuei [an exorcist in Chinese mythology]. Thus, in the sixth decade of the twentieth century I have become the Chung Kuei of the Communist Party. Everything always goes from one extreme to the other. The higher one rises, the harder the fall. But I am prepared to break all my bones if I fall. And what does it matter? Matter is indestructible; it can only be pulverized.

There are more than a hundred communist parties in the world today. The majority of them do not believe in Marxism-Leninism any longer. They have reduced Marx and Lenin to the status of dust. Why could this not happen to us? I think you too should think carefully about the problem. You must not be intoxicated by our victory. One must continuously try to pick out any weak points, failures or errors. I do not know how often I have talked to you on this subject. I mentioned it again in April, in Shanghai. What I have said may seem a little like pessimism. After all, isn't this what the enemies of the Party are saying? This way of looking at things does not seem very right to me. But the difference between me and that black band [Peng Chen and his supporters] is that I am talking about my own personal reactions, while the black band is trying to overthrow our Party and myself.

What I have said here cannot be made public for the moment. At present, all Left-wing groups speak the same language. If what I have just said were to be made public, it would be as if cold water had been thrown in their faces, and this would inevitably help the Right wing. Our task is to bring about the partial overthrow of the Right wing (not complete, because that would be impossible) in the whole Party and the whole country.

In seven or eight years a new movement will be started to drive away the evil spirits. This movement will subsequently be repeated many times. We still cannot know when what I have said here can be made public, because it will not please the Left wing or the majority of the masses.

Perhaps the contents of this letter will be made known by the Right wing after my death, if they have seized power. If they do this, then they will have a surprise. Since 1911, when the emperor was overthrown, a reactionary régime has not been able to hold China for long. If there is a Right-wing, anti-communist *coup d'état* in China, then I am certain that those elements will not know a moment of peace.

It is very possible that they will be able to retain their dominance for a while. If the Right wing seizes power, it will be able to use my words to retain power for a time. But the Left will use other quotations of mine, and organize themselves, and overthrow the Right wing.

The Great Cultural Revolution, which is now taking place, is a great and serious movement. In certain areas, like Peking, certain organizations, like Pei-ta and Tsinghua Universities, which have uncertain foundations, will immediately fall apart when the revolutionaries appear again. While the Right is the most arrogant, the Left is the most tenacious. This movement is a great movement on a national scale. Left, Right, and the wavering centre will learn valuable lessons from it.

Part Three
The Cultural Revolution

So many deeds cry out to be done,
And always urgently;
The World rolls on, time presses.
Ten thousand years are too long,
Seize the day, seize the hour!
The Four Seas are rising, clouds and waters raging,
The Five Continents are rocking, wind and thunder roaring.
Away with all pests!
Our force is irresistible.

Second stanza of Mao Tse-tung's poem
Reply to Comrade Kuo Mo-jo, 9 January 1963

7: From Conflict at the Top to Mobilization at the Base; the Student Movement

The revolt of the students in Peking

Since his pronouncement of September 1962, 'Never forget the class struggle', Mao had been preoccupied with other problems, in addition to those of culture criticism – those of youth. In 1964, when the campaign to continue the revolutionizing of the superstructure of society had started to yield results, the following remarks by Mao were being quoted within the context of the disagreements with Khrushchev:

Basing themselves on the changes in the Soviet Union, the imperialist prophets are pinning their hopes of 'peaceful evolution' on the third or fourth generation of the Chinese Party. We must shatter these imperialist prophecies. From our highest organizations down to the grass-roots, we must everywhere give constant attention to the training and upbringing of successors of the revolutionary cause. . .[1]

In the same year Robert Guillain noted:

Mao Tse-tung is said to have presented a document of the first importance to the Central Committee of the Party, concerning Chinese youth . . . In this document the Chairman analyses the nature and role of youth; he indicates the methods by which youth can be won over to socialism, and gives detailed instructions for giving youth a sounder education for the carrying on of the revolutionary struggle.[2]

The statements made by Mao to the Party leadership gradually reached the lower levels of the Party organization. Two developments took place in 1964–5. The youth programme of the Party was considerably expanded, which can be seen from the more or less indiscriminate admission of eight million new members to the youth movement. Discussion began to take place at all levels on the existing forms of education, although

there seems to have been little clear idea of possible alterna-
tives. It was during this period that the first stirrings among the
students began to appear, especially in the universities. The reaction of the academic authorities varied from the imposition
of disciplinary measures (forced 'productive' labour in the
rural areas), to the establishment of so-called workgroups of
Party officials (whose task was to 'guide' the movement). The
atmosphere in institutions of higher education was such that
'one single spark could start a prairie fire'. Especially when culture criticism began to appear in 1965 and at the beginning of
1966, this description of the situation began to look apt, and
student opposition to academic authorities made its appearance
again.

At the beginning of February the philosophy department of
Peking's Pei-ta University opposed a motion by the university
board (closely connected with Peng Chen's city council) to start
an extensive historical investigation into the origins of the historical figure of Hai Jui in Wu Han's play, since this would
have transformed a fundamental political discussion into a
purely academic debate. During the following months the conflict gradually deepened. As the authorities were compelled to
give ground in relation to the Party leadership, their attitude towards the rebellious elements became more intransigent. And on
25 May the conflict burst out into the open.

On that day, at two in the afternoon, a number of teachers
and students from Peking University put up a big-character
poster on the wall outside the refectory, challenging the university authorities to justify themselves: 'What are you up to in
the Cultural Revolution?' Eleven days earlier, on the eve of
the publication of the 16 May Circular, the authorities of the
University had expressly forbidden such manifestations. The
poster aroused mixed feelings. Small groups of students, arriving for lunch, read the text in silence or commented on it in
subdued voices:

At present, the people of the whole nation, in a soaring revolutionary spirit which manifests their boundless love for the Party and
Chairman Mao and their inveterate hatred for the sinister anti-Party,
anti-socialist gang, are making a vigorous and great cultural revolu-

tion; they are struggling to thoroughly smash the attacks of the reactionary sinister gang, in defence of the Party's Central Committee and Chairman Mao. But here in Pei-ta [Peking University] the masses are being kept immobilized, the atmosphere is one of indifference and deadness, whereas the strong revolutionary desire of the vast number of the faculty members and students has been suppressed. What is the matter? What is the reason? Something fishy is going on. Let's take a look at what has happened very recently! [3]

At this point there follows a summing-up of the lines of action laid down by the university authorities on 14 May concerning the Cultural Revolution, which stressed the necessity for 'correct guidance' and not 'the unlimited mobilization of the masses'. Large-character posters were also forbidden, only small-character ones being allowed; there were to be no mass meetings, only gatherings of small groups of people, so that culture criticism would once again be reduced to the level of theoretical debate. The poster was signed by about seven rebels under the assistant professor Nieh Yuan-tzu. She had been a critic of the university authorities since the unfavourable reaction to the formation of the communes and the Great Leap Forward. In 1961–2, she had been elected as Party Secretary in the Department of Philosophy in opposition to the official candidate. Since then, she had regularly clashed with the academic authorities.

It seems likely that she knew that the radical 'Pen' and 'Gun' had already gained the upper hand in their confrontation with the Party bureaucracy. This knowledge could have come to her through a number of channels: she was a niece of Lin Piao's old comrade-in-arms General Nieh Jung-chen (who was responsible, among other things, for military interests at the Academy of Sciences); through her relationships at work, she was in contact with Chen Po-ta's Department of Philosophy and Sciences at the same university; and as a middle-level Party Secretary she was probably acquainted with the Circular of 16 May. She was thus taking a 'calculated' risk in putting her signature to the poster.

Nevertheless, the reaction to the poster was predictably strong. The same evening the university authorities mobilized the youth movement for a counter-demonstration. The poster was covered up and criticized in another poster. A meeting of the rebels in the evening was taken over by the 'loyalists', the authors of the poster were called upon to justify their position, and some of them were sent to the rural areas for 'productive' labour (as 6,000 others had been on previous occasions). But this time the rebels knew that they could not be silenced for long, and they appealed to Mao Tse-tung and the radical Left among the Party leadership, thus carrying the matter to the level at which it ultimately had to be decided: the city of Peking. According to some sources, the text of the poster was offered to local media for publication, but it is probable that, at the time, no one in the media dared challenge the academic authorities and the city council. According to other reports, however, the local newspaper, printing offices and radio stations had already been placed under the control of the centrally-commanded army units by Lin Piao to prevent all further resistance in the media. At the same time Mao is said to have issued an order via Kang Sheng whereby the text of the poster was to be generally distributed as an example of the rebels' initiative. One of the outcomes of this was a favourable commentary in the *Peoples' Daily* of 1 June on the events at Pei-ta University, which said,

The revolutionary struggle of the great mass of teachers and students at Peking University against the representatives of the bourgeoisie will be crowned with victory. A new, flourishing and genuinely socialist University of Peking will soon be established in the capital of the nation.[4]

The dismantling of the rigid Party bureaucracy of Peking was also beginning to take place on other fronts: the reorganization of the North China bureau was clearly the beginning of an imminent spring-cleaning of the city council – which was also to bring the academic authorities of Pei-ta under close scrutiny. The student revolution had begun to gain ground. While the city and university administrations were forced to abandon their positions time and time again, the revolutionary enthusiasm of a small group of rebels had gripped the whole Department of

Philosophy, the whole of the Pei-ta University, the neighbour-ing, and much larger, technical university of Tsinghua, and the secondary school affiliated to it, as well as other universities and secondary schools in Peking and outside. The main organs of the mass-media, (the *People's Daily*, the *Liberation Army Daily* and the *Red Flag*) launched a furious propaganda offen-sive against the Party bureaucracy, and disruptive action among students and in the schools finally brought education to a halt.

Meanwhile, Mao Tse-tung had retired to the country to con-sider the next steps in the situation, the radical Left in the capi-tal was making further advances against the Right, and the Centre-Right group had started to organize its next line of defence to stop the further spread of 'wild actions'. The two main members of this group were important figures in the Party secretariat: the First Vice-Chairman and President of the Re-public, Liu Shao-chi, and the First Secretary, Teng Hsiao-ping, who had been protecting the academic authorities of Pei-ta for the past few months. At the beginning of June they again tried to bring the movement under control by sending work-groups of party officials to the rebellious institutions to give 'guidance' to the Cultural Revolution. The arrival of the work-groups on 7 June signalled the end of a week of carnival for the students, during which those banished earlier to the rural areas were welcomed back triumphantly, and a massive outpouring of a hundred thousand posters criticizing the academic authorities was distributed. Initially the Party officials were recruited as reinforcements, but it was soon evident that they were simply trying to contain the spontaneous rebellion, as the academic authorities had tried to do earlier. Criticism of the University administration was neutralized and the campaign against Nieh Yuan-tzu continued. The difficulties thus created appeared on an even larger scale at Tsinghua University, where a work-group of 500 Party officials arrived on 19 June to lead the move-ment of 40,000 students 'along the right paths'.

The arrival of the work-group led to an unnecessary polariza-tion of the opposition, not only between the university adminis-tration and the rebels, but also between the work-groups and the rebels, and the work-groups and the University administration.

This escalation in reciprocal animosity was even further increased when a session of the Standing Committee and members of the Political Bureau in Shanghai on 20 June confirmed the complete elimination of the group of Peking bureaucrats led by Peng Chen. The outcome of this session gave the rebels at Pei-ta and Tsinghua new hope, and they abducted important members of the University administration to take them to mass meetings for criticism and self-criticism. They cited Mao as an authority for using such methods, quoting one of his first works in which occur the well-known words, 'A revolution is not a dinner-party'. The work-groups, however, claimed that circumstances were no longer the same as those prevailing when Mao uttered those words, and launched a counter-attack against 'anti-socialist' agitators. This situation developed into a direct confrontation between the 'loyalist' students, who had gathered around the work-group leader, Yeh Lin, and the rebels, who had grouped themselves around Kuai Ta-fu, the author of the first poster at Tsinghua, which had been put up on 1 June. The situation came to a head on 23 June. Kuai made a direct attack on the work-group in a heavily sarcastic poster, which opened with the words, 'What's all this about, Comrade Lin?' The loyalist students launched a counter-attack at a mass-meeting. Their spokesman was – very significantly – the daughter of the second figure in China, Liu Shao-chi. In the heat of the debate she let slip the following, 'My mother also thinks that the work-group is right!' Calls from the public: 'Where is your mother, then?' 'Here on the campus!' 'Let her come herself, then.' A telephone conversation ensued off-stage, and Wang Kuang-mei, the wife of Liu Shao-chi, who had a number of important functions, did indeed appear. She confirmed what her daughter had said, declaring that this was her opinion.[5] The position of the loyalists was understandably strengthened by this personal intervention, and the large centre group began to show signs of hesitation. But the rebels were more than ever determined to expose the ways in which the 'loyalists' were being protected. Their resistance became more determined during the following weeks, while the discipline in Wang's work-group also became tougher. In the resulting deterioration of the situation (Kuai had been placed under house arrest and was on hunger strike), some of Kuai's friends again tried an appeal to the radical Left in the Party leadership. At the end of June, Chen Po-ta came with his two closest supporters, the younger Kuan Feng and Wang Li, to visit Tsinghua University to acquaint himself with the situation there. They concluded that the work-group had gone beyond all acceptable limits, and while Kuai held out with his last supporters, Chen informed Mao Tse-tung of the machinations of the Party secretariat. According to some sources, Liu Shao-chi, realizing the precariousness of his position, tried to call an emergency session of the Central Committee in Peking, thus taking advantage of Mao's absence (he was said to be ill or even undergoing an operation) and the presence of a large number of members of the non-Maoist regional bureaux who were in Peking for a solidarity meeting on the events in Vietnam. Determined administrative intervention by Chou En-lai and similar action by Lin Piao in the military sphere prevented this premature session of the Central Committee from taking place.

The return of Mao Tse-tung to Peking

On 16 July 1966 Mao perpetrated an incredible *coup de théâtre*, which was to be a turning point in the situation. He engaged in an impressive (considering his 73 years) swimming marathon in the Yang-tzu-chiang near the town of Wuhan. The event was publicized in the whole country. The meaning of this demonstration was absolutely clear: the Party Chairman was still full of vitality, not at all ill, and certainly not on the way out politically. The next day, after his long absence, he returned to the capital. Some reports claim that Lin Piao had recalled special army units from the provinces to Peking to prevent any possible moves by Mao's enemies. His closest colleague, Yang Cheng-wu (who was to be the official replacement for Lo Jui-ching, Lin's rival, as chief-of-staff two weeks later), was given the responsibility for Mao's personal security.

The first task for the Party Chairman was to acquaint himself with the activities of Liu Shao-chi and Party Secretary Teng

Hsiao-ping, especially as they were concerned with the organization of the work-groups against the student rebellion. His most important source of information on those events were undoubtedly Chen Po-ta and his supporters; though, according to some unconfirmed reports, Mao himself got in touch with the universities directly as well. Mao was also writing a poster, the cryptic text of which is a fair indication of his feelings at the time: on the one hand he found it absolutely unacceptable that the Right-wing Party bureaucracy should try to check the relatively spontaneous student rebellion, but on the other he disapproved as much of the methods and principles of some of his colleagues among the leadership.

'What shall we see after the revolution?' In the eyes of many, the words 'we shall see that later' are like an atom bomb.

These are the words used to threaten 'a handful of rebels', so that they will surrender without resistance.

It appears that I have to give personal thought to the end of the revolution. Do I stand on the Right? No!

Shall China no longer be proletarian at the end of the movement, but bourgeois? Certainly not!

What am I afraid of? Have we not seen what they wanted after the opening period?

Intrigues, threats, 'black evidence' ...

Hats are flying in the air and cudgels are roaming the land. We have already sustained blows and lumps on the head. We have already heard the principal reasons for rejecting a general.

When one has dived into the sea, one is no more than a drop of water. There can be no more clouds on top of the range of mountains.

Those who were accused of being counter-revolutionaries and scoundrels in the first period, don't fear death. Now that the people do not fear death any longer, why the threat of death?

What shall we see in the last period of the movement?

The sky has been cleaned of dust.

The surface is full of sunlight and flowers.

And as the mountain flowers open up, the plum-tree blossom laughs with them.

And if you do not believe me, just watch and wait a little.[6]

On the day that this poster was written by Mao, the rebels

were freed. A few days later, the trio which was to form the senior nucleus of the new Group in charge of the Cultural Revolution, Kang Sheng, Chen Po-ta and Chiang Ching, arrived at the two universities. From 22 July to 26 July they carried out an investigation which vindicated the actions of the rebels, who were called together to form a broader movement, while the work-groups were to be dissolved. Chiang Ching herself led the attack on Wang Kuang-mei, the wife of the President, who had to undergo self-criticism and apologize to the students. She also reported to the refectory during the following days to perform 'humble tasks'; she was later reproached with having favoured friends while handing out food.

This phase itself came to an end when Premier Chou En-lai arrived on 30 July to draw his conclusions from the investigation and to take the relevant measures; the final settlement with the Liu Shao-chi group was to take place on another level.

The phenomenon of the Red Guards

At this point the rebellion of the students entered a new phase, in which it became the catalyst for a much wider anti-bureaucratic movement. A great variety of political societies had been formed among the students some months earlier, when culture criticism had first become bitter. Some of these were semi-official in character; branches of the Communist Youth League, for instance, had in turn formed smaller groups at the instigation of the Party bureaucracy. These consisted at first only of the sons and daughters of 'proletarian' and party milieux. It was intended that these groups should serve as the *avant-garde* of a much wider youth movement. Other groups were almost semi-illegal; these were the rebel student groups which had been forced to ally themselves in a number of underground secret societies since their confrontation with the work-groups.

The retreat of the work-groups was accompanied by an appeal to the students to become more independent and to found political youth clubs on a larger scale. This relatively spontaneous process of mobilization led to the formation of tens of thousands of independent groups all over the country, which designated themselves with a variety of revolutionary names drawn from the history of the socialist movement; their collective name, though, at least as far as school and university students were concerned, was 'Red Guards'. A great deal has been written about the ways in which the Red Guards were organized, and various 'sponsors' of the movement have been named. In fact, however, no major part of these societies ever belonged to one national network. Such alliances as existed were usually local, temporary, and probably influenced by a number of national institutions, without being directly controlled by them.

The groupings of the national institutions can be divided into three: the traditional complex of Youth League–Party bureaucracy–trade union organizations; the central army apparatus, especially the General Political Department; and the Cultural Revolution Group.

At the beginning of the Cultural Revolution the grouping of traditional interests – the Party organization and its institutional extensions – spared no pains to turn the new mass movements into a classical campaign guided from above. Although this trend was quickly checked in the centre, it continually recurred in new forms during the following years at regional and local levels, where the traditional Party organization maintained its influence and remained relatively immune to criticism.

The central army apparatus and the General Political Department had been prepared for several years by Lin Piao to take over the commanding role from the Party in the event of a renewed revolutionizing of society. That time had now come, and the army corps provided material support in the form of transport, clothing and shelter, while the political commissioners added their moral support in the form of ideological education, or personal presence on long journeys.

The most important influence on the Red Guards, and later on the revolutionary worker-rebels was, however, the newly constituted Cultural Revolution Group, with its subsidiary bodies and organizations. This Group had replaced the Group of Five and was now under the direct control of the Standing Committee.

It was only at the end of July 1966 that the shape of the Group became clear. Only one member of the old Group of Five was included in the new Cultural Revolution Group; this was Kang Sheng, who had denounced Peng Te-huai in 1959 and Peng Chen in 1966. His part in events was, however, relatively minor. The most important members of the Group were: Chiang Ching as vice-chairman, her allies from Shanghai, Chang Chun-chiao and Yao Wen-yuan; furthermore Chen Po-ta, who now became chairman with the support of his associates from Peking. The trio of Wang Li, Kuan Feng and Chi Pen-yu were added after a few months. Throughout June and the early part of July (the so-called 'fifty days' of the work-groups) these radical intellectuals and artists were hardly seen in the foreground of events, though they were prudently keeping in touch with the rebel students. But as soon as the work-groups had been removed from the scene, they began to make good use of their knowledge of the situation by organizing the rebel students for mass-mobilization. A secretariat for the Cultural Revolution Group was established in Peking to keep in touch with the revolutionary liaison centres at the various universities. It was from these liaison centres that the three national Red Guards' headquarters (Rightist, moderate and Leftist) were to develop later.

The sixteen points; the first corrections

On 1 August 1966, the Thirty-ninth Anniversary of the People's Liberation Army, the *People's Daily* published a leading article under the heading, 'The whole country should become a Great School of Mao Tse-tung thought.'

It contained Lin Piao's version of the letter which Mao had sent to him 'privately' on 7 May, in which he was reported to have appealed to the army to become skilled in 'politics, military affairs and culture', 'to engage in industry and agriculture', 'to participate in each struggle of the Cultural Revolution', and in that way 'to play a very great role indeed'.[7]

On the same day, the Eleventh Plenary Session of the Eighth Party Committee started; this was the first plenary session for four years! A number of members who had been discredited in the meantime were absent. A considerable number of army personnel were present in and around the meeting hall, and there was also a delegation of 'revolutionary teachers and students' from the Peking universities. The session had only just opened when Mao held up the actions of the students as an example to the rest of the audience in his new poster, 'Bombard the Headquarters', the title of which refers to the Civil War, when the guerrillas threatened to mutiny if their commanders tried to compromise with the enemy.

China's first Marxist-Leninist big-character poster and Commentator's article on it in *Renmin Ribao* [People's Daily] are indeed superbly written! Comrades, please read them again. But in the last fifty days or so some leading comrades from the central down to the local levels have acted in a diametrically opposite way. Adopting the reactionary stand of the bourgeoisie, they have enforced a bourgeois dictatorship and struck down the surging movement of the great cultural revolution of the proletariat. They have stood facts on their head and juggled black and white, encircled and suppressed revolutionaries, stifled opinions differing from their own, imposed a white terror, and felt very pleased with themselves. They have puffed up the arrogance of the bourgeoisie and deflated the morale of the proletariat. How poisonous! Viewed in connection with the Right deviation in 1962 and the wrong tendency of 1964 which was 'Left' in form but Right in essence, shouldn't this make one wide awake? [8]

Influenced by this attack of Mao's, a breakthrough was finally achieved in the Party leadership. The Central Committee agreed to the expansion of the Cultural Revolution into a wider anti-bureaucratic movement.

Lin Piao also made a speech which threw remarkable light on his reading of the situation. On the one hand, he took the greatest trouble to praise Mao and to present himself in the humblest light possible: 'I have no talents; I rely on the wisdom of the masses and do everything according to the directives of the Chairman.' On the other hand, he reduced the very complicated struggle against bureaucratic tendencies in the Party to the simplest possible proportions:

We demand an overall examination and overall readjustment of cadres. In this connection, in the light of the five principles for the achievement of success in the proletarian cause, as set forth by Chairman Mao, we have proposed three measures, to which the Chairman has agreed: (1) Do they hold high the Red Banner of Mao Tse-tung's thought? Those who fail to do so shall be dismissed from office. (2) Do they engage in political and ideological work? Those who disrupt it and the Great Cultural Revolution are to be dismissed. And (3) are they enthusiastic about the revolution? Those who are entirely devoid of such enthusiasm are to be dismissed.[9]

Although Lin had, by this time, developed into the strong man of the Left, his ideological analysis was not rated highly. It was a much more subtle view of developments (formulated under Mao's influence) which became the starting point for any steps forward. On 8 August the Central Committee adopted a kind of charter which laid down a complete programme for the future of the Cultural Revolution. The resolution was popularly known as 'The Sixteen Points', which can be summarized as follows:

1. The socialist revolution has entered a new phase: the Great Proletarian Cultural Revolution;
2. The chosen direction has been correct from the beginning, but opponents will always try to sidetrack the movement;
3. However, one must not be afraid; one must have the courage to mobilize the masses without restraint;
4. That is why one must not try to act for the masses in everything: they will indeed educate themselves in this movement;
5. At the same time, the class line of the Party must be firmly applied: the reactionary Right must be completely isolated, the left must be developed and try to gain the centre, so that the movement will achieve the unity of a large majority of the masses and a large majority of the cadres;
6. So that contradictions among the people can be handled correctly, the difference between antagonistic contradictions (with the class enemy) and non-antagonistic contradictions (among the people themselves) must be recognized; differences must be resolved through discussion and not through force; the minority is often right, but even when

     this is not the case, it must conserve its right to express its opinion – this right must be upheld by everyone;

7. Beware of those who brand the revolutionary masses as counter-revolutionary;

8. When approaching the problem of cadres, we must distinguish between four groups: the good, the relatively good, those who can be improved, and those who cannot; the first groups are in the great majority;

9. The organization of congresses on the Cultural Revolution and the formation of committees and groups to carry it out must be encouraged;

10. One of the most important tasks for the Great Proletarian Cultural Revolution is to carry out a radical reform of the educational system and of methods of teaching;

11. The question of criticizing by name in the press must be decided by the Party Committee at the same level;

12. Scientists, technicians and managers who have made important contributions must be helped gradually to transform themselves politically;

13. The Great Proletarian Cultural Revolution must add practical momentum to the already existing socialist education movement;

14. The Great Proletarian Cultural Revolution must not hinder the development of production;

15. In the armed forces the Great Proletarian Cultural Revolution and the socialist education movement must be carried out in accordance with the instructions of the Military Commission of the Central Committee of the Party and the General Political Department of the People's Liberation Army;

16. The thought of Mao Tse-tung is the guide to action in the Great Proletarian Cultural Revolution.[10]

The ideological landslide among the Party leadership was also reflected in personal relations. Mao moved to the foreground and began to play a more active role as Chairman; Lin became much more than simple Minister of Defence at this point, and appeared as Mao's deputy and possible successor. The former First Deputy Chairman of the Party, Liu Shao-chi, and the

Secretary of the Party, Teng Hsiao-ping, receded into the background. Only the position of Chou En-lai remained roughly the same. He was one of the first to declare himself behind Mao, and he now had the task of solving the innumerable administrative problems arising from the expansion of the Cultural Revolution.

The development of the student movement had not been limited to Peking; it had now also reached the provincial capitals. A few days after the end of the Plenum, Chen Po-ta, Chairman of the Cultural Revolution Group, was already making a first speech to the students who had come to Peking from all over the country to 'exchange revolutionary experiences' and to receive 'instruction' on the further development of the movement. On 18 August he was again among the speakers on Tien An-men Square, where the first of many mass-meetings of the Red Guards from the provinces took place. Other speakers were Lin Piao and Chou En-lai. Chairman Mao was also present, and allowed one of the younger members of the audience to tie a Red Guard band on his own arm. On the same day there was an outbreak of iconoclasm in Peking, which soon spread to other towns. Names of streets and buildings which were not revolutionary enough were changed. Processions of schoolchildren and students marched through the town with drums, red flags and banners, warning the old and new bourgeoisie to beware. Slogans were painted everywhere, posters put up, pamphlets distributed and mass-meetings organized. The huge mobilization soon spread to young workers, and from Peking to the provincial towns, and from there to the rural areas. As the action became more violent, so the first excesses began to occur. This may partly have been the result of a declaration made by Lin Piao at the meeting on Tien An-men Square, where, among other things, he had said:

Under the leadership of Chairman Mao, we must launch fierce attacks on bourgeois ideology, old customs, and old forces of habit! We must thoroughly topple, smash, and discredit the counter-revolutionary revisionists, bourgeois Rightists and reactionary bourgeois authorities, and they must never be allowed to rise again![11]

Arbitrary house searches of 'bourgeois' families were organized, and all the valuables found in the houses, foreign currency or Kuomintang documents were shown to an indignant public at enormous exhibitions. The destruction of antiquities was later to be stopped, when it was pointed out that they did not only represent the wealth of the exploiting classes, but were also the results of the craftsmanship of poor artisans. At the end of August, Lin Piao himself found it necessary to remind some Red Guards specifically and repeatedly of the limiting clauses in the Sixteen Points, referring also to the army practice of the 'three points of discipline' and the 'eight points of attention', which had been observed during the Civil War and which had been restored at the beginning of the sixties.

At the beginning of September the need to redress the situation became even more emphatic. Four (later six) 'freedoms' were proclaimed, with special emphasis on the freedom of expression; yet by way of contrast, strong warnings against 'anarchism' were being issued at the same time.

In the meantime, the flow of young people from the provinces to the capital, and in the opposite direction, had continued to grow. Travel had been declared free, and large reception centres were organized in Peking. There were mass meetings almost every week on Tien An-men Square, where the young people hoped to catch a glimpse of Mao Tse-tung, or hear speeches by Chen Po-ta, Lin Piao or Chou En-lai. Before the end of the summer, the capital had been visited by about ten or eleven million young people. The intention was that these young people, together with the Peking students who had already spread throughout the country, should return home to break down the monopoly in the dissemination of information held by the local Party organizations, and to spread the movement among the rest of the population. This also led to a certain number of excesses being committed; to many of the young people who had been brought up in a closed society this new freedom appeared as an unexpected luxury, and many of them took advantage of the situation in the name of ultra-revolutionary principles. Millions of young people remained in the capital or travelled throughout the country, making incessant demands on the available resources. One example of what happened in this situation is given in the book by Gordon Bennett and Ronald A. Montaperto about a Red Guard who later fled to Hong Kong (*Red Guard: Political Biography of Dai Hsiao-ai*):

There was much singing of revolutionary songs. One fellow said exultantly, 'Even when dreaming I never imagined being able to go to Peking without spending a cent!' Another remarked hopefully, 'When we get to Peking we can see snow!' . . . A few even had great expectations of sampling Peking's famous cuisine. . . . I cannot remember anyone proposing that we exchange revolutionary experiences in the capital.

The same source reports on another occasion:

Upon entering we saw ten or so Red Guards confronting two of the staff:
  'Rotten egg! Call out the secretary of the Party committee!'
  'If we don't obtain money today, you gentlemen will not be permitted to leave!'
  'Do you know how you will be punished if you fail to support the activities of the Red Guards?'
  One staff member whined: 'It's not that I don't give support, it's just that we are in financial difficulty; I offered to lend you one dollar each but you refused to take it.'
  'Of course we did! I want five dollars!'
  'I want ten dollars . . .'[12]

The initial attempts to put a stop to this kind of occurrence were little more than friendly exhortations, coupled with a promise that it would be possible to resume travelling in the spring. The next step towards controlling the situation was to reduce aid for staying in the capital to a bare minimum; only the return fare remained free. Then the first threats were made that places in educational institutions would be cancelled if the intending student did not report on time. There were, however, a large number of people who managed to disregard these threats and to continue to circulate freely. This phenomenon was not without importance in the later phases of the Cultural Revolution during the formation of ultra-revolutionary groups. Slowly, however, the centre of gravity of the movement was shifting from Peking to the other towns; the rebellion was spreading.

8: From the Vanguard to the Main Force; the Workers' Movement

The 'January storm' in Shanghai

While the Red Guards from the provincial towns had gone to Peking, the vanguard of the Peking students had taken to the rural areas. Everywhere they went they organized liaison centres; political youth groups sprouted like mushrooms. One of their first targets was Shanghai, the largest city in the country, with approximately ten million inhabitants, a first-class harbour and a prosperous industrial centre. On 31 August 1966, Red Guards from Peking and from Shanghai itself laid siege to the city hall, when they were refused an audience with the city administration. The Mayor called the Red Guards counter-revolutionaries, and mobilized groups of workers through the trade unions. After a few days of serious fighting, the workers relieved the town hall. In reply, the rebels extended their agitation to the rest of the town, and called for reinforcements from Peking. These reinforcements arrived in the persons of two heroes of the very first hours of the revolution: Nieh Yuan-tzu (assistant professor at Pei-ta University) and Kuai Ta-fu (the student leader from Tsinghua University).

During October the movement began to take a firmer hold on the country; in addition to the hundred or so groups of Red Guards which had been formed at academic institutions, contacts had also been established with sympathetic young workers. A headquarters to co-ordinate the rebels was set up in November, with branches in the hundreds of factories in the city.

At the same time, however, the city administration was itself forming groups with revolutionary names, though these groups were clandestinely supported by the old Party organization and the trade union organizations. When a second demand for an audience with the city administration was refused, the rebels sent a large delegation to Peking to acquaint the leadership of the Cultural Revolution with the situation. But the train which they had requisitioned for the journey was diverted on to a branch line some miles outside the city and abandoned by the railway workers. The rebels reacted furiously and the confusion which this created in the city could no longer be ignored. In mid-November, on the demands of the rebels, Chang Chun-chiao arrived in Shanghai; he was a member of the Cultural Revolution Group and Third Secretary of the Shanghai Party Committee. The promises he managed to extract from the Mayor were soon forgotten after his departure. The rebels then tried to mobilize public opinion via the local press, to strengthen their position in the city. They wanted to have their own newspaper included as a supplement in one of the larger newspapers, but this request was refused. A demonstration of protest sparked off a counter-demonstration by conservative elements. This confrontation resulted in renewed fighting, in which there were several dead and dozens of wounded. The offices and printing works of the newspaper were taken over by the rebels. It was clear that Peking would again have to intervene to separate the two sides.

When Chang Chun-chiao arrived a second time in Shanghai, in mid-December, he was able to display his loyalties more obviously, since the signal had already been given in Peking for the expansion of the Cultural Revolution from education to industry, and to a lesser degree to agriculture. The rebels' demand to have their supplement distributed with one of the big newspapers was granted, and on 24 December the Mayor expressed self-criticism in public.

Chang had hardly turned his back before the situation had deteriorated again. The conservatives had now realized that this was the crucial struggle, and they set up a large counter-revolutionary movement. Many workers were allowed to take to the streets for counter-demonstration. A large group was given money to pay their fares to Peking, so that they could go and make a mass protest. The railways ceased to function; there were threats that water and electricity supplies would be cut off, and there were strikes in a large number of sectors. There were an increasing number of confrontations between mass organizations, which had formed alliances of almost equal strength, each group counting between 500,000 and a million members.

At the beginning of the new year the crisis looked as though it could very well assume the proportions of a civil war within the city. The 'January storm' in Shanghai, as this episode came to be known, had completely paralysed all public life in the city by the first week of 1967, and the number of bloody clashes was on the increase. Peking was obliged to intervene a third time, but this time the struggle had to be decided finally.

Chang Chun-chiao returned to Shanghai at the beginning of January. Links were established between the rebel headquarters and ten other organizations and, with the support of Left-wing journalists (among others, the Shanghai member of the Cultural Revolution Group, Yao Wen-yuan) the two largest local newspapers were taken over. An appeal to the population was published, asking for a return to work and an effort to combine revolution and production in accordance with the Sixteen Points resolution of the Central Committee. On 9 January, the rebels were joined by another twenty-one organizations, and the next day an 'urgent circular' was sent to all the followers, putting forward ten proposals for dealing with the state of emergency. On 11 January the rebels took over all the vital installations of the city to get things moving again. The Central Committee, the Cultural Revolution Group, the Military Commission, and the Council of State (the government) expressed their approval of this initiative in an open letter. This was in fact the decisive point in the struggle. On 14 January the rebels' alliance, after further increasing in size, finally took over the administration of the city.

The power of this new administration was gradually consolidated during the following weeks. Solutions had to be found for many practical problems, but close attention had to be paid at the same time to the theoretical problem of securing the gains of the Maoists. In addition to the necessity of changing the people in the administration, no one thought that the old Party structures should remain unmodified: the system had failed to operate adequately and was therefore wide open to discussion.

An alternative system, which would guarantee an effective and just administration was therefore sought in the history of the socialist movement. This was not a novel phenomenon: the Cultural Revolution had been permeated with a strong sense of history from its beginnings.

The Shanghai Commune

In March 1966, about a year before the revolution in Shanghai and the downfall of Peng Chen, an article appeared in Chen Po-ta's *Red Flag* on 'The Great Lessons of the Paris Commune,' on the occasion of its ninety-fifth anniversary. Chen Po-ta himself was known as a specialist in non-Chinese revolutionary history; together with the young, radical scientists and journalists among his group of culture critics from Peking, he was now deeply engaged in a philosophical and historical analysis of those cases in which the consolidation of newly acquired power had been at stake, and in particular of the Paris Commune, which was mentioned increasingly. Specific mention is even made in the Sixteen Points; in clause 9 it is stated:

It is necessary to introduce a system of general elections, like that of the Paris Commune, for electing members to the cultural revolutionary groups and committees and delegates to the cultural revolutionary congresses.[1]

At the end of August the electoral principles of the Paris Commune were published in *Red Flag*: 'All leaders must be elected by the people; the elected must be the servants of the people and be submitted to their supervision; the electors have the right to recall and replace the elected at any time.'[2] There then follows a detailed description of the electoral system, in which the negative lessons which Marx, Engels, Lenin and Stalin had drawn from the experiences of 1871 were passed over without mention. Lin Piao also associated himself with the appeal for 'extended democracy'. During one of the last mass meetings on Tien An-men Square, in the autumn of 1966, he said: 'The people's democratic rights are being fully instituted in accordance with the principles of the Paris Commune. Without such extensive democracy it would be impossible to initiate a genuine Great Proletarian Cultural Revolution.'[3]

However, the problem of maintaining the principles of the Commune during the phase of consolidation of power went unmentioned. On 3 February 1967, another article praising the principles of the Commune appeared in *Red Flag*; two days later, after a short meeting of revolutionary organizations in Shanghai, the 'Commune of Shanghai in the Sixties of the Twentieth Century' was proclaimed in the presence of a million people.[4] But like its predecessor in Paris, it was to be short-lived.

9: The Creation of the Revolutionary Committees; Intervention of the Army

The Revolutionary Committee of Heilungkiang

In the meantime, a succession of 'revolutions' had hit other provinces; between mid-January and mid-February there was some attempt to take over power in at least fourteen of the twenty-nine administrative districts. In most cases, however, the Maoists were too divided, too weak, or too inexperienced to gain sufficient support among the population to win the battle against the established bureaucracy. The radical example of the Shanghai Commune does not seem to have lent itself easily to imitation elsewhere.[1] A more moderate model had to be found, if the movement was to establish itself on a national scale. The first opportunity for this arose in another important industrial area, the north-eastern province of Heilungkiang. A few days after the assumption of power in Shanghai, local red rebels launched a large-scale offensive in the provincial capital of Harbin, during which they took over the local Party paper, the radio station and the police headquarters. They were almost immediately approached by the First Party Secretary (who had earlier expressed self-criticism) and the commander of the military district, to discuss terms for the formation of a new, joint, provisional organ of power. After a few weeks of fighting between the supporters and opponents of the plan, which finally ended on the intervention of the army, a 'Revolutionary Committee' was finally formed on 31 January. Within this framework, the rebels worked together with the old Party cadres, while the military authorities acted as a link between the two groups. The standing committee was composed of one rebel, one representative of the cadres, one military representative, while another military representative acted as chairman. The Heilungkiang model of assumption of power, the so-called 'three-in-one combination', had several advantages over the Shanghai model,

Events were less likely to get out of hand, and the risk of casualties was also considerably less. At the same time the army could prevent the movement from stagnating. The role of the army was thus one of protection as well as one of stimulation. It prevented bloody clashes between rival revolutionary groups, and guaranteed the reasonable functioning of the economy, which had suffered greatly during the previous few months. Vital production units (large factories), transport units (water, air and railway) and distribution units (such as department stores) were placed under the joint control of the Ministry of Public Security (the police) and the regional army units, who co-ordinated their services. The function of the army as a stimulant to the movement can be seen in the military and political instruction which it had provided for the Red Guards from the end of 1966, and in the fact that the army had made the local mass media (printing works for newspapers, radio stations) safe for the Left. Following a proposal by Mao Tse-tung and Lin Piao, the leadership of the Cultural Revolution decided to instruct the army to take sides openly and actively at the end of January. It had to support the new Left, but at the same time it was to act as a link between the rebels and the 'good' cadres in the existing Party and administrative institutions. It was thus hoped to make the process of power take-over easier and to bring this phase of the movement to a close.

Putting the final touches to the Cultural Revolution?

In the last week of February the future pattern of the organization of the movement began to take a more definite shape. The new provisional power structures were to be part of a national network of Revolutionary Committees. The rebels were also to play an important part in the setting up of this network, but the major part of the responsibility was entrusted to the army for the time being, while only a part of the old Party cadres were dismissed altogether.

Even Shanghai was going to have to conform to this national model to avoid becoming the exception. The province of Shansi, which had first followed the example of Shanghai, now based itself on the model of Heilungkiang. An opportunity for the reorganization to bring Shanghai into line with the rest of the country occurred on 26 and 27 February, when dissension flared up again in the city. The methods used by some students and school representatives were fiercely criticized by workers' representatives. From 28 February discussions were held towards the formation of a Revolutionary Committee, to consist of nine rebels, eight old Party cadres and six army representatives. Nothing more was heard of the Commune.

Only in a few out of the fourteen administrative units in which a power take-over had been attempted was the new power structure considered to be Left-wing enough by the leadership of the Cultural Revolution to be designated 'Revolutionary Committee'. Before mid-March only five such committees were recognized to exist in the twenty-nine centrally administered towns, autonomous regions and provinces; in addition to Heilungkiang, Shansi and Shanghai, there were Shantung and Kweichow. By mid-April Peking could be added to the list. Anticipating the future development of the movement, a considerable number of the commanders of the provincial military districts began to strengthen their control over the movement. This was especially the case in such strategic areas as the centrally-administered town of Tientsin and the provinces nearest the Soviet Union, India, Indo-China, Hong Kong and Taiwan. During the spring, power began to shift increasingly towards the army's representatives because of continued failure to agree by the rebels and the Party cadres. Faced with this situation, the leadership of the Cultural Revolution tried to aid the development of the movement in two ways. It appealed constantly to the military authorities to deal tactfully with their opponents, and not to deprive people of their liberty or to use force. From mid-February Mao issued a number of instructions which were intended to discredit the 'ultras' among the rebels and the 'incorrigibles' among the Party cadres, and to reestablish a sense of unity by bringing together the ordinary citizens, both young and old.

From the beginning of March, a number of measures were announced to speed the return to normality. During the first few days of the month the pupils of primary and secondary schools were asked to return to the institutions they attended. At the end of the first week the farmers were asked to put their spring programme in hand, so that the harvest would not be endangered. By mid-March the industrial workers were being encouraged to get any machines which were still idle back into production again. Where necessary, soldiers were sent to help restore production and to make up for the serious delays. At the end of the third week the students were asked to return to university. Everything seemed to suggest that the confrontation phase of the Cultural Revolution was coming to an and, and that normal social life had resumed its course. This, however, was not to be the case.

10 : Elimination of the Rightist and Leftist Dissidents

Problems on the Left

An important meeting of the central leadership of the Cultural Revolution was held in the middle of March 1967. This leadership now consisted of four component groups: representatives of the Central Committee, with Mao Tse-tung at its head in the position of Chairman, and Lin Piao as Vice-Chairman (wielding rather less influence in this group than in the following one); representatives of the Military Commission of the Central Committee, of which Mao was chairman, and in which Lin, as Minister of Defence, played an important part; representatives of the State Council, with Chou En-lai at its head, and a number of Vice-Premiers; members of the Cultural Revolution Group, with Chen Po-ta as Chairman and Chiang Ching as Vice-Chairman.

This meeting gave final shape to a number of important developments. Victory *seemed* to be in sight: the hard-core revisionists in Peking had been almost entirely defeated, and the mass movement of students and workers could take its time in dealing with the rest in the provinces. The pressure in the central army apparatus to rehabilitate Lin Piao's predecessor, Peng Te-huai, had ceased, and Lin's opponent, chief-of-staff Lo Jui-ching, had been replaced by Yang Cheng-wu. In the central Party apparatus the Group of Five of Peng Chen had been dissolved, and the new Cultural Revolution Group had been functioning as a Maoist nucleus for more than half a year. Finally, the 'cultural' sector of the central administrative apparatus had been substantially purged of conservative elements (such as minister Lu Ting-i), and a whole new generation of young radicals had come into positions of influence.

In the closely interconnected Party and public organizations, events did not stop at the dismissal of such figures as Peng Chen, but also involved Mao's opposite numbers at the highest level, Liu Shao-chi and Teng Hsiao-ping.

There were also successes at the lower levels. The mass movement spread from the students to the workers and farmers, and the revolution had already been crowned in several places with the successful take-over of power. Matters seemed to have been completely settled, since the army had come out resolutely in favour of the Left. Only a radical change in the political situation could have prevented final victory throughout the country.

It was just such a complication which had been threatening for some time. The complication was not, as might have been expected, a revival of the Right; it was, rather, the existence of serious problems among the Leftists which created a situation favourable to the Right and prevented the movement from being brought to a satisfactory conclusion.

From the beginning, the difficulties had a somewhat ambivalent character. The propaganda media (in which a large number of recently promoted personnel occupied key positions) had a tendency to reduce complex matters to the simplest outline. They found an all-too-ready audience in the students, who found it difficult to abandon their glamorous position as the vanguard of the movement, into which the main body of peasants and workers had been integrated in the meantime.

The heaviest responsibility for the propaganda policy which led to deviationism must be borne by Tao Chu, who had succeeded Lu Ting-i as chief of propaganda six months earlier. Tao Chu presents a strange case. In the past, he had not been particularly 'revolutionary'; he had been a typical Party boss, with an 'independent kingdom' in the south-central region. He owed his nomination in Peking to Teng Hsiao-ping. During 1967 he became the symbol of the ambivalence of the ultra-Left which played straight into the hands of the Right. When the ultra-Left had been later thoroughly discredited, the radical Yao Wenyuan wrote about him:

He shouted himself hoarse that 'in the great cultural revolution, it is correct to doubt anyone'. 'I am all for bombardment in general . . .

nobody knows what the headquarters really represent, and that goes for every headquarters.' 'You can oppose anybody.' He 'creatively' developed the bourgeois reactionary line of 'hitting hard at the many in order to protect a handful'. He appeared to be surprisingly 'Left', but in fact he was 'Left' in form and Right in essence.[1]

It was indeed Tao Chu's propaganda which caused a lot of revolutionary activity to become completely sterile by the beginning of the new year. For the time being, no one and no idea could escape the criticism of one or another group of ultras; even the Maoist Left wing and Mao himself came under attack. There seemed to be a distinct possibility that the movement would lose its sense of direction, thus permitting the Rightists to launch a full-scale attack under the disguise of a new radicalism. The indiscriminate attacks on everything and everybody tended to alienate the general public and the Party cadres from the movement, making alliances and the eventual taking-over of power less likely. Groups became smaller and more numerous, so that they were often too weak to produce any significant step forward in the revolution, and tended therefore to spend most of the time fighting among themselves. Internal battles and arbitrary commando raids (for instance, the abduction and 'judging' of important figures) led to increasing bloodshed.

In January Tao Chu was relieved of his functions, this move was followed by the first appeals for moderation. Some organizations were subsequently suppressed, while others had their activities curtailed. A number of high-ranking officials were given police protection, and meetings for criticism could only be organized after consultation with the leadership of the Cultural Revolution.

During the course of February there was a perceptible tendency among some of the leadership to restrain the still relatively spontaneous mass movement and to rehabilitate a large number of the discredited cadres. At a meeting of the leadership in mid-March, however, the 'ultra-Left' Tao Chu was condemned, together with the Right-wing revival which had resulted from his activities. The principal holders of this viewpoint, Vice-Premiers Tan Chen-lin (agriculture) and Po I-po (industry), were accused of wanting to discredit the whole movement, while simply seeming to condemn the excesses, as Peng Te-huai had done in the case of the Great Leap Forward.

The state of the nation in March 1967

How far, then, were the new groups in the power structure able to cope with the transformation? In the case of the Cultural Revolution Group, the older members of the leadership (Chen Po-ta, Chiang Ching and Kang Sheng) were reinforced with a lot of 'fresh proletarian blood' – mostly young academics and journalists. There was the group from Shanghai (Chang Chun-chiao, who was already somewhat older, and Yao Wen-yuan), and the group from Peking (Wang Li, Kuan Feng and Chi Pen-yu). The first two were closely linked to Chiang Ching, while the latter three were more closely associated with Chen Po-ta and the *Red Flag*, as were Lin Chieh and Mu Hsin, who were less prominent, but who were the first to have extensive contact with ultra-Leftist organizations. In fact, these latter five members of the leadership came to exercise considerable influence over all the most important organs of propaganda and over the mass media in Peking.

The other complex of organizations which began to play a more important role from this point on was the army, in which considerable developments had taken place since the initial breakthrough of the movement in July–August 1966. The balance of power within the army command had shifted towards the Left, as the movement as a whole progressed. When the principal army leadership made a public appearance with Mao in mid-October,[2] it consisted of, in addition to Lin, his closest colleagues, Hsiao Hua (director of the General Political Department) and Yang Cheng-wu (chief of staff). Taking a secondary position were two more moderate figures from other military institutions, which still maintained a certain amount of independence and which were very closely connected to the government apparatus: Yeh Chien-ying (inspection) and Hsieh Fu-chih (public security). Hsiao Hua's opponent in the direction of the General Political Department, Liu Chih-chien, had discredited himself on 1 October by adding a passage to the newly-issued directives of the Military Commission of the Central Committee, stating that the army should refrain from intervention in non-military matters,[3] just at the time when the army was beginning to assert itself in the Cultural Revolution. By way of contrast, Hsiao Hua strengthened his position during the same period by his increasing praise of Lin Piao: 'We must all learn from Comrade Lin Piao.' 'Follow Comrade Lin Piao's instructions.'

Comrade Lin Piao has always implemented Mao Tse-tung's thought and carried out his correct line most faithfully, firmly and thorough- ly. At every crucial turn in the history of the Chinese Revolution, Comrade Lin Piao has resolutely taken his stand on the side of Chairman Mao and carried out an uncompromising struggle against every kind of 'Left' or Right erroneous line and has courageously safeguarded Mao Tse-tung's thought.[4]

Towards the end of 1966 Liu Chih-chien disappeared from the political stage, while Hsiao Hua slipped into the prominent position of Vice-Chairman of the Military Commission.

The rise of Yang Cheng-wu continued, while the trials and tribulations of his predecessor, Lo Jui-ching, seemed never-ending. At the end of December he was abducted, interrogated and maltreated by a commando group representing the students of a large number of military colleges. A number of other high-ranking personalities, including several ministers, were to undergo similar treatment, until restrictive measures were introduced to prevent this in January and at the beginning of February.

At the same time as the resolution allowing the army to start participating in the Cultural Revolution had been taken, the army itself was undergoing considerable reorganization. The section of the army leadership originally responsible for the Cultural Revolution, which was under strong conservative influence, was dissolved. The part the army was to play in the Cultural Revolution now depended directly on the Cultural Revolution Group of the Party. Chiang Ching was to be especially important in this relationship (exactly a year before, she had been asked by Lin Piao to organize discussion groups on the role of art and literature in the armed forces); so also were some younger radicals in the propaganda apparatus of the army and the Party. In fact, most of the power in this area went to the General Political Department of Hsiao Hua and to Lin Piao's own Military Commission. The formal independence of the national police apparatus of the Ministry of Public Security was abolished at the same time, and the apparatus of that ministry integrated into the army.

However, the intervention of the army was not without its problems.[5] The lion's share of the army's new tasks fell to the regional units. This happened firstly because the central units had to maintain an alert in the face of the American (and the slowly growing Soviet Russian) threat of war; and secondly, it was quite natural for the regional units, districts and garrisons to be involved in all kinds of political and social questions during 'normal' times; this also meant, however, that the local units had already worked together with the old Party apparatus. And it soon became obvious in many provinces that the local military authorities were supporting the 'traditional' Party groups and were coming into serious conflict with the rebels. No measures taken by the central army command were successful in reversing this process, and by the end of March and the beginning of April, it had become obvious that things were going the wrong way in a large number of provinces. Numerous directives were therefore issued on 6 April which, among other things, removed a large number of powers previously held by the regional commanders. This did nothing, however, to remove the tensions in the provinces between the conservative high-ranking officers and the extremist Red Guards. This situation was to be at the root of the conflict which followed in 'the long hot summer' of 1967, during which a single incident threatened to involve the country in total civil war.

Part Four
A Revolution within the Revolution

Those with a 'Left' way of thinking magnify contradictions
between ourselves and the enemy to such an extent that
they take certain contradictions among the people for
contradictions with the enemy and regard as
counter-revolutionaries persons who are not really
counter-revolutionaries.

Mao Tse-tung, February 1957, quoted in the
Little Red Book

11: The Continuing Campaign against Revisionists in the Party

The Revolutionary Committee of Peking

In the meantime, events in the capital had not stood still. The political youth clubs, formed by pupils and students, had organized themselves into three liaison centres with nationwide ramifications: these were the 'first', 'second' and 'third' Red Guards Headquarters, which corresponded to three main political currents – the former 'loyalists', those who dissociated themselves from the loyalists as well as the rebels, and the original rebels. In the course of time a group with 'ultra-Leftist' tendencies broke away from both the first and last groups, partly as an over-reaction against Right-wing compromise, and partly from an excess of Left-wing enthusiasm. After an appeal for unity from the Cultural Revolution Group, the majority of members of the three headquarters regrouped in a single organization. The third (rebel) headquarters played a leading part in this move, though Left and Right wings soon developed in the new organization.

The situation on the radical and ultra-Left wings was thus relatively confused, when Tao Chu began to propagate his idea of 'distrust everything and everybody' during the winter of 1966–7. The reaction to these ideas was varied: the Right-wing Committee for Unified Action found them an occasion to organize 'ultra-revolutionary' acts, such as the occupation of the Ministry of Public Security; the Red Guards in the Left-wing Department of Philosophy and Social Sciences (with affiliations among the younger members of the Cultural Revolution Group) took the opportunity of searching for possible charges against leading figures in the dossiers of the Central Committee; and the Left wing of the third headquarters (led by Kuai Ta-fu's 'Chingkangshan' rebel regiment) took the opportunity of mounting fresh campaigns against real or imaginary revisionists.

By the end of December almost no one among the leadership had escaped criticism. Chou En-lai, Lin Piao, Chiang Ching and Chen Po-ta all became targets for criticism. During the January storm, the extremists began to take stronger action. Ministers who were especially susceptible to criticism were abducted and made to appear before people's courts. In some cases this ended in the serious maltreatment of the 'accused' or even his total disappearance. The intervention of the army at the end of January did not therefore prevent the occurrence of a Right-wing backlash in February. The partial elimination of this in March, however, again considerably encouraged the radicals and ultra-Leftists. Those groups that were mostly deviationist in tendency and the independent liaison centres were suppressed, and criticism limited to the members of the leadership who were known to have committed serious mistakes. But the attacks could be expressed in such a way that they could indirectly be turned against other targets. For instance, the full-scale attack made on the Vice Premiers of the Government was clearly aimed at creating a difficult situation for Chou En-lai himself. More and more anonymous posters against him appeared.

The enmity between Chou and the radical and ultra-Left interests was clearly not new. At the beginning of the year Chou had blocked an attempt to form a 'Commune of Peking', on the model of Shanghai. The Council of State had issued a statement to the effect that the take-over of power in the capital involved too many national interests to be entrusted to local Red Guards and worker-rebels. It was Chou who made himself responsible for organizing representative bodies which, together with the Government, were to lay the foundations for the stable administration of the capital. During January and February he succeeded in bringing the divided student organizations together. Tens of thousands of delegates chose their representatives, among whom were the rebel leaders Nieh Yuan-tzu and Kuai Ta-fu. Congresses of other groups were held at the end of March: 2,500 peasants from the surrounding thirteen districts, miners and industrial workers, and finally the most difficult of all, the pupils from schools. At the end of April the Revolutionary Committee of Peking was finally formed from representatives of these congresses. The Chairman of the Committee was – very significantly – Chou's Vice-Premier for Public Security, Hsieh Fu-chih. Nieh Yuan-tzu became Vice-Chairman.

The Party decides to continue the Cultural Revolution

The ideological confusion of these months gave rise to a number of contradictory sentiments about the various cross-currents in the situation. Officially, both Rightist and ultra-Leftist ideas were still considered as expressions of one and the same bourgois way of thought, and were therefore both considered prejudicial to the revolution. But while this type of criticism was easy to apply to a single person, like Tao Chu, it was more difficult to apply to the whole 'New Left' of the Cultural Revolution. There was some anxiety that the revolutionary ardour of the masses might be dampened. Official dissociation from Leftist extremism had occurred after the first, still relatively innocent, excesses of August/September 1966, and the later, more serious excesses of December/January. Suitable texts by Mao Tse-tung, such as his *On correcting mistaken ideas in the Party* (1929), were referred to as the theoretical validation of this attitude.

But this theoretical dissociation had only limited practical consequences. Only the 'ultra-Left' groups with obviously 'Right-wing' roots were dissolved, while those of radical origin retained considerable freedom of action (although even Chen Po-ta is reported to have been obliged to express self-criticism at the end of 1966). The elimination of people like Tao Chu and groups like the Committee for Unified Action (largely consisting of the sons and daughters of Party bosses) presented a good opportunity for laying down the policy for the correction of wrong ideas. This led to campaigns against the following deviations: liberalism and extensive democracy (insofar as it was in contradiction to democratic centralism and the dictatorship of the proletariat, and connected with the discussion about the Commune which took place during February in Shanghai); spontaneity and subjectivity (i.e. the wild actions of January in

Peking); (philosophical) idealism, schematism and apriorism (the *People's Daily* of 24 April 1967: 'When looking for the truth, we need to base ourselves on the facts and on class-analysis, and not on our preference for a kind of "left" over a kind of right'); lack of discipline, anarchy and individualism (Chen Po-ta on 5 February 1967: 'Anarchism and individualism are serious problems among the pupils of secondary schools. Certain schools had a party for every pupil, and formed a coalition between three.');[1] sectarianism, division of forces and factionalism (the *People's Daily* on 1 October 1966: 'Many Party leaders have unconsciously practised factionalism') – and what was true for the Party leadership was even more true for the rebels; Leftism in general, whereby non-antagonistic contradictions among the people were interpreted as antagonistic contradictions with the enemy (one expression of this was the refusal of the rebels to work together with 'reformed' cadres from the old Party apparatus on the Revolutionary Committees).

The persistence of the campaign clearly indicated the magnitude of the problem. During April, the leadership in the centre decided to abandon any attempt at forcing a conclusion of the Cultural Revolution in the short term; the time was obviously not yet ripe. Too many Right-wing and ultra-Left groups had taken advantage of the general confusion to acquire disproportionate influence over the development of the revolution. The masses themselves would simply have to separate the chaff from the wheat before a new national administrative structure could be formed. The series of proclamations of Revolutionary Committees was eventually suspended at the end of April, only to be taken up again much later and only then with the greatest caution.

The decision for this action seems to have been more or less unanimous within the leadership of the Cultural Revolution, although this unanimity probably sprang from very varied motives. Lin Piao, with his politicized supporters within the army, was easily able to ride out the intervening period and to create new organs of power. Chou En-lai and his supporters feared that any attempt to impose a solution on the situation would only have led to even greater administrative chaos. The duo of Chiang Ching and Chen Po-ta saw an opportunity to re-group their divided followers. And the trio Wang–Kuan–Chi, together with the younger co-members of the Cultural Revolu-tion Group, hoped to reopen discussion on the six Revolution-ary Committees which had already been formed, and which, according to them, should not keep their present composition.

The situation thus remained confused: beneath the apparent unanimity among the leadership, the radicals, like the ultra-Left, were busy looking for the opportunity of discrediting the moderates who were seen by them as Right-wing. While verbally dissociating themselves from 'ultra-Left' ideas, they remained alert for the slightest opportunity of intensifying their propa-ganda campaign without appearing to go against accepted policy. They were aided in this by the fact that their 'natural' followers in the capital were regrouping. This regrouping took place after the schoolchildren and students had been recalled to their institutions. At the same time, the influence of the radical group in the leadership was increasing: thus, in the publica-tions to mark 1 May, the Peking faction of the Cultural Revolu-tion Group was placed higher in the Party hierarchy than it had been previously. While workers of the centre demonstrated against internal acts of violence by the Left wing, and the *People's Daily* appealed again for the use of peaceful means, the radicals began massive mobilization campaigns, connected with such 'thought-provoking' issues as the commemoration of earlier events in the Cultural Revolution, and the further con-demnation of already discredited revisionists at home and abroad. On 18 May 1967, the anniversary of Lin Piao's Leftist speech of the previous year, the confidential circular of 16 May 1966 was published (which had originally been intended as a stimulus to the movement, and was now intended to have a similar effect). The wrath of the extremists continued to be directed against Liu Shao-chi, who in his book *How To Be a Good Communist* (written in 1939 in order to encourage Party members to apply the Confucian principle of self-cultivation) had devoted a whole chapter to Left-wing dogma-tism, in which he used a number of phrases which left him only too open to attack: 'an extreme attitude', 'the fighting mania', 'the habit of rejecting every compromise and creating a storm in a glass of water', 'those who condemn any idea of peace at the heart of the Party'.[2]

During the year, the Cultural Revolution had matured from being a struggle against a 'clique' (that of Peng Chen) to being a struggle between 'two lines' – the revolutionary line of Mao Tse-tung, and the revisionist line of Liu Shao-chi (who, it was claimed, had promoted a return to a capitalist system).

Just as the elimination of Peng Chen and his supporters had dragged on for four months, so too did the campaign against 'the top party person following the capitalist road', Liu Shao-chi, and his entourage, take a certain length of time to get under way.

He had already in fact exposed himself to criticism during the time of the Socialist Education Movement and the introductory phase of the Cultural Revolution; but it was only with the dissolution of the work-groups in July 1966 that his star began to wane definitively. During the Eleventh Plenum he was demoted. During October, criticism of Liu increased even further within the Central Committee, and his first self-criticism was made on the 23rd of that month. The ultras of varied political complexions seized avidly on this event. Kuai Ta-fu demanded that Liu and his wife Wang Kuang-mei should come and justify themselves 'before the masses'. He organized sit-ins in front of one of the gates to the Forbidden City, where Liu and Wang lived. On 25 December 1966 Liu expressed a second self-criticism. This second was more fundamental than the first, but it was still regarded as insufficient. Kuai repeated his request, and when Chou En-lai laid down definite conditions before it could be granted, Kuai used Liu's daughter (who was trying to rehabilitate herself for her former role as a loyalist leader) to tempt her mother outside so that she could be abducted and taken to Tsinghua University. After the intervention of Chou En-lai, Kuai promised that the President's wife would be treated well, but the mass meeting which followed this event was badly organized and the planned criticism and self-criticism therefore made little impact.

During the months of turbulence following the 'January

storm' the question of Liu was allowed to recede somewhat into the background. In spring, however, the campaign began anew with all its old intensity. At the beginning of April another mass meeting (200,000 people) was held at Tsinghua University. The meeting was much better organized this time and, instead of helping to calm the atmosphere, as moderate leaders had hoped, it became the signal for the outbreak of a fresh series of excesses in the campaign. This tendency was helped by the fact that a number of young radicals of the Peking faction of the Cultural Revolution Group had now become keenly interested in the matter. The debate had also got as far as the *Red Flag*, while the *People's Daily* became more and more involved in the demagogic confusion.[3] During May, public anger against the 'hidden traitor, renegade and scab Liu Shao-chi' took on such proportions, that an increasing number of Red Guards were encouraged to ask for him to be handed over to them. A fresh sit-in was held at Liu's residence with the support of Kuai's rebels and of several hundred organizations both inside and outside the third headquarters. The participants were finally encouraged by the young radicals of the Peking faction of the Cultural Revolution Group. A number of the demonstrators went on hunger-strike to make their protest more effective; the increasingly turbulent gathering did eventually grow into a kind of action-centre, while two further written self-criticisms by Liu were rejected. Feelings became even more heated by the rising in Wuhan against the progressive delegates from Peking (see below), and when on 1 August Lin Piao's ideas on the invincibility of the people's war were featured in the newspapers, and large crowds of people were present in the centre of the city for the anniversary of the People's Liberation Army, the demonstrators decided that the moment had come to issue an ultimatum. They demanded that Liu should come out and appear before them before 5 August (anniversary of his replacement as second in the leadership and of Mao's appeal to 'Bombard the Headquarters'), otherwise they would take active measures. Secret and frantic meetings took place between Kuai and members Chi and Lin of the Cultural Revolution Group. On the evening of 4 August a crowd numbering hundreds of thousands began to assemble on Tien An-men Square. The leadership of the Cultural Revolution found it impossible to accede to the demands of the demonstrators without running the risk of a lynching party. It was, however, just as impossible to refuse to satisfy their demands. A compromise solution was proposed by Hsieh Fu-chih, Minister for Public Security and chairman of the Revolutionary Committee of the capital, with the result that, on 5 August at noon, another criticism and self-criticism session took place with Liu Shao-chi within the Forbidden City. Only a select group of people was allowed to be actually present at the meeting, while the remainder of the demonstrators followed the proceedings with the help of loudspeakers. In addition, Chou, Chiang and Chen were also present, high on the rostrum, as a kind of guarantee that the agitators would disband peacefully at the end of the meeting. A large contingent of security troops was kept on the alert in the meantime – not, as later disclosures were to reveal, a superfluous luxury. William Hinton describes this particular meeting:

What most of the participants never knew was that under cover of this unprecedented demonstration a small group of ultra-left rebels had been mobilized to seize and hold Chou En-lai, should he come forth. Their theory was that if the demonstration was big enough and lasted long enough Chou would have to come out to calm things down. Then the militants would seize him. In the ensuing chaos others on the Central Committee, probably meaning Chen Po-ta, could make their move towards the seats of power.[4]

Thus, at the top too, the contradictions were hardly non-antagonistic ...

12: The Campaign against Revisionists, Reactionaries and Imperialists Abroad . . . and in the Government

Attacks on Chen I

While there was a certain lessening in the attacks on prominent members of the leadership (especially on ministers in the financial, economic and technical sectors), and the more enthusiastic members of the Red Guards were left with little more to do than renew their attacks on Liu Shao-chi, there was one area in which the Left wing could continue its activities unhindered: relations with other countries. No one could object to campaigns against revisionists, imperialists and reactionaries. Indeed, had not the prime target of the Cultural Revolution always been such groups? This shifting of attack also gave the radicals some leverage against the moderates in the centre.

There had already been a certain amount of trouble at the Ministry of Foreign Affairs at a relatively early stage in the Cultural Revolution. The minister, Marshal Chen I, had originally committed the mistake of introducing Liu's work-group system into his own rebellious departments. He had, it is true, recognized his mistake before the Central Committee in August 1966, but the affair did not end there. During the autumn of 1966, opposition to his policy began to grow again. Chen I himself was, in addition, a particularly good subject for criticism. Yet, in spite of being vulnerable because of past actions, this stubborn nonconformist indulged himself in making fun of the fanatics among his critics, and even continued to do so when he was at their mercy. Trouble really started when he asked the rebels in his ministry why 'they did not go to Vietnam' to carry out the revolution – a remark which was generally considered very much out of place. He was especially critical of his opponents' tendency to form cliques:

The Foreign Languages Institute is divided into two parts. Originally there were 21 units, but after a week there were over 50, and after

another week over 70. Over 4,000 people in over 70 units makes
over 70 cliques. The oceans are vast to behold: this is truly one
hundred flowers blooming and one hundred schools of thought
contending.

Finally he threw down this challenge: 'I shall be 66 this year,
and I am not afraid of facing difficulties. Don't forget that
grocers who try to take advantage of people in small ways usually come to grief.' [1] Chen I's refusal to take his critics seriously,
however, placed him in a difficult position. Not only was he
thought to owe an explanation – everyone did in the Cultural
Revolution – he had also committed serious mistakes during the
course of the movement. The leadership of the Cultural Revolution could do very little else but agree to meetings for Chen's
criticism. On 24 January 1967 10,000 people gathered in the
People's Palace. In the presence of his superior and friend, Chou
En-lai, and of Chen Po-ta, Chiang Ching and Wang Li, Chen I
outlined the basis of his self-criticism. The intention was to return to the matter in the future at a number of smaller meetings,
but little came of this idea. From the end of January, however,
Chen had every chance of proving his revolutionary tendencies.
A number of Chinese students had been expelled from the Soviet
Union, following an incident at Lenin's tomb. This incident pro-
voked violent demonstrations in front of the Soviet Embassy in
Peking; Kosygin recalled the women and children of the Soviet
legation and declared his sympathy for the opponents of the
'dictatorial régime of Mao Tse-tung'. Chen I found himself in
agreement with Chen Po-ta, who had stated shortly before that
revisionism in the Soviet Union had originated because, after
the October Revolution, no cultural revolution had followed (in
spite, it was added, of plans by Lenin and Stalin).[2] In February,
however, Chen I once again committed some serious errors.
He declared his support for Liu Shao-chi, with whom he had
developed a now 'unhealthy' association (due, among other
things, to the many trips abroad they had made together). It was
for this reason that the sudden revival of revolutionary activity
in March touched Chen, too. In the article by Chi Pen-yu, which
reopened the attack on Liu on 1 April, there was also extensive

discussion of foreign policy, arising from a number of comments praising the Boxer Rising; this played into the hands of the xenophobic elements among the Red Guards (the author later denied that he had intended this).[3] Attention was thus drawn again to Chen I, and although Chou En-lai was immediately responsible for Chen's ministry, it was Chen Po-ta who gave the go-ahead in mid-April for the resumption of the criticism of the foreign minister. The rebels, however, immediately extended this concession to include demands that Chen I be deposed, which went against the clearly expressed instructions of Chen Po-ta. The attack was also extended to include a number of Chen's important deputies, such as Chi Peng-fei (later temporary successor of Chen I) and Chiao Kuan-hua (the eventual successor of Chi Peng-fei).

A fresh diplomatic incident suddenly gave the rebels both extra proof of the failure of the current foreign policy and a leader in their fight against it. At the end of April, relations with Indonesia – already very bad after the 'abortive *coup d'état*' of September 1965 and the resultant persecution of communists – reached their lowest ebb. Indonesia expelled the Chinese *chargé d'affaires* Yao Teng-shan and the consul-general Hsu Yen. On 30 April they were welcomed back as true heroes by Premier Chou, minister Chen I, and a large crowd at Peking Airport. The next day, they were received by Mao and Lin Piao. However, far from being satisfied with the honours accorded them, they immediately launched a fierce attack on the foreign policy of Chen I. They accused him of having stood by and watched the Indonesian communists and the Chinese minority being bloodily persecuted without doing anything about it. Yao Teng-shan, as 'red diplomatic-fighter', soon became the champion of the radicals in the ministry; during the following weeks and months his influence gradually became felt more and more on government policy. This was especially the case after the rebels had occupied part of the ministry buildings (causing state secrets to be shown openly in public: 'What is so terrific about secrets? To hell with them!', one of the occupiers is reported to have said). The only person in any position to exercise a moderating influence on these new developments was Chou En-lai. But accusations of 'protectionism' against the Premier were still current, and he chose to remain in the background.[4]

On 7 August, the conflict seemed to have entered its last phase. Wang Li, whose position as a member of the Cultural Revolution Group was becoming increasingly strong, now indicated to Yao Teng-shan that he should definitely try to take over power from Chen I, hinting that there was nothing to fear from Chou En-lai: even he was not invulnerable. In the meantime, Chen I seemed to be morally unbroken. There were many anecdotes current about him. Joan Robinson writes:

... he had been sitting on a platform for some time wearing a dunce's hat, being criticized, when presently he looked at his watch, and said: Please excuse me, I have to go to the airport to welcome the President of Guinea. Or that, opening the quotation book, he intoned in the usual form 'Chairman Mao teaches us that Chen I is a good comrade.'[5]

He was, however, in the exhausting position of the one fighting against the many, and he began to give ground very quickly. Another mass meeting was held on 11 August, at which Chen I, under the supervision of Chou En-lai and in front of a crowd of ten thousand supporters and opponents, expressed self-criticism.[6] Chou En-lai opened the meeting by saying that Chen I had committed a number of serious mistakes, but insisting that these should be dealt with in a fair and objective way. The situation was no longer the same, however, as it had been six months ago; the extremists were present at the meeting in considerable numbers, and the scent of victory made them all the more violent in the pressing of their claims. Shortly after Chen I had been called to speak, the meeting degenerated into complete chaos; fighting broke out in the meeting hall and the army was called in to intervene. In the midst of the disturbance, an athletic young man leapt on to the platform and dealt the minister a resounding slap in the face. The young man was seized by security guards, while the minister was ushered behind the platform. A furious Chou En-lai came to the microphone to lecture the crowd on its behaviour. After some time the disturbance died down and the meeting could be continued. It was clear, however, that there would be more trouble from the rebels.

The storming of the British Embassy; Chou En-lai intervenes

From June onwards relations with foreign countries began to deteriorate increasingly because of the actions of the rebels. The working of the diplomatic service was disrupted both in Peking and overseas. All ambassadors were recalled from service abroad for 're-education' (except from Cairo, probably because of the Six-Day War). Sharp criticism – partly deserved – was expressed of the life- and thought-styles of the diplomats. The rebels now began to use Chinese embassies abroad on a large scale as propaganda centres (as a reaction to Chen I's remark 'These thoughts of Mao Tse-tung are really a Chinese product, we mustn't take them abroad'), politically activate friendship associations and Chinese minorities, and make the embassies of foreign nations in Peking the target of demonstrations. These actions unfailingly produced results which were almost catastrophic for China's diplomatic position in world affairs. Wang Li and Yao Teng-shan, however, chose to pursue their hard-line policy in diplomatic affairs. After the attack on the reactionaries (the generals' government in Indonesia), it was the turn of the revisionists. Demonstrations in front of the Soviet Embassy led to serious incidents on 17 August. Nor were the imperialists to escape attention. Britain had infuriated the rebels by taking action in Hong Kong against groups of sympathizers with the Cultural Revolution, and by closing down a number of pro-Peking newspapers. Wang and Yao issued Britain with an ultimatum: the measures had to be revoked by the 20th, otherwise ... The threats uttered could hardly fail to arouse the anxiety of Chou En-lai and Chen I: you do not deliver ultimatums if you do not intend to carry them out, and that was out of the question. The 21st and 22nd went by. Wang Li began to mobilize public opinion through the mass-media; he also began to assemble demonstrators for a 'protest' outside the British Embassy.

Events had developed thus far by 9 o'clock on the evening of the 23rd. At first it looked as though the demonstration was going to be a repeat of the ones held previously. During the last few months, embassies (like that of Burma) had been quite often besieged for days on end by hundreds of thousands of demonstrators. Chou En-lai had become worried about the situation, and, together with Chiang Ching, he went to remind the demonstrators that the territory of the embassy had to be respected. His intervention was in vain. A Red Guard (quoted by Hinton) recalled:

Actually, the break-in had long been planned by people who hoped to overthrow the Premier. The activists of the Anti-Imperialist Anti-Revisionist Liaison Station came up from behind with loudspeakers blaring. Some individuals in front jumped up and threw bottles of ink at the walls and windows of the building. This was a diversion. As the ink flew out front, others found their way inside the building from the back. They began throwing chairs and sofas out the windows. The loudspeakers behind us urged us to action. We pushed against the P.L.A. lines shouting, 'Back up! Let us in! People over there have already gone in!' There were eight lines of soldiers. Some youngsters tried climbing over their heads but they were thrown down. The soldiers' lines finally broke at one spot. We rushed through to climb the fence. Soldiers pulled some of us down but others got over.

At 11 we saw flames. First the oil barrels in the garage burned. Then the main gate opened. People rushed in. The cars began to burn, three Mission-owned cars burned. Fire engines came but armed people stopped the firemen. They had to withdraw. The flames rose higher. Fire engines returned, lots of them. The firemen pushed through the crowd to get near the building. About the time the fire started Chou En-lai and Chiang Ching sent an order to all of us to stop the assault, but it was not broadcast. We didn't hear it until later, but as soon as we did we all left the area. By then it was too late. We felt very bad.

When the P.L.A. lines gave way the British ran into the basement and locked themselves in. But people broke in and pulled them out. Police intervened and took the British across the street to the Albanian Embassy, but even as they crossed the street some of our people tried to tear their clothes off.[7]

At this point Chou could hesitate no longer. The Ministry of

Foreign Affairs was placed directly under his control. Wang Li and Yao Teng-shan were deposed and arrested shortly afterwards. Chou was taking a certain political risk in doing this, but Mao supported him: 'Wang Li has made more mistakes in the last forty days than Chen I in forty years.' Officially, though, the campaign of criticism against the Ministry went on as normal: another meeting took place on 27 August. Chou was not present, having requested Chen Po-ta to take his place. In addition, Kang Sheng had made it clear that criticism of Chen I's foreign policy amounted to criticism of the Central Committee – which did indeed determine policy. And although the discussion in the ministry continued far into 1968, from 1 October 1967 Chen I was again spoken of in normal terms as being the Minister of Foreign Affairs.

But his personal suffering during this period had been greater than during the whole Civil War. He had lost a lot of weight, and his physical condition was so poor that Mao later uttered this reproach to the rebels, 'I cannot show him in this condition to foreign guests!' Chen I was also in poor mental shape, and only Mao was able to convince him to attend the Ninth Party Congress: 'Come anyway. You can be the representative of the Right,' joked the Chairman.[8] Chen I, however, was in no condition to exercise his functions as before. He lived just long enough to see the actions of the extreme Left wing turn against their perpetrators. He also lived long enough to see the beginning of the end of Chinese diplomatic isolation – which he had fought for with Chou En-lai since Bandung. He died of cancer – as was very explicitly stated – in January 1972.

13: The Campaign against Revisionists in the Army

The mutiny in Wuhan

While the 'New Left' agitation in Peking rapidly accentuated the differences between the top and the base, it was developments in the provinces which ultimately brought the threat of civil war in the long hot summer of 1967. It was in the provinces that the responsibility for army intervention had fallen to the regional units, who were far less fitted for this role than the central army divisions. Instead of co-operating with the genuinely Left-wing rebels in their take-over of power, they often compromised with the apparently Left-wing, but really Right-wing, bureaucrats. The uniting of the various parties according to the three-in-one formula was a failure in many places, and led to increasingly violent confrontations between the various factions.

From the end of April the formation of the Revolutionary Committees had been blocked by the centre. Some attempt was made to strengthen control over the relatively autonomous regional commanders by changes in the command hierarchy. In the meantime, it had become increasingly necessary for the army to intervene in the situation, especially in the light of developments at home and abroad. The vital interests of the country had to be safeguarded. The large number of directives issued in the spring and early summer of 1967 by the Military Commission showed how complicated and incomprehensible the whole situation had become: by mid-July, it had become explosive. The conflict between the Red Guards and the worker-rebels on the one hand and the military and old Party cadres on the other was fiercest in the south-central region – the former 'independent kingdom' of Tao Chu. This is one of the most densely populated parts of the country, the backbone of which is formed by the provinces Kwangtung (capital: Canton), Hunan (capital: Changsha) and Hupeh (capital: Wuhan). The centre first concentrated on the conflicts in Canton and Wuhan – two towns of considerable strategic importance. Canton is right next to Hong Kong and Macao; Wuhan is at the crossing of the main east-west route (the river Yang-tzu) and the north-south route (with the only bridge over the lower reaches of the river). Furthermore, Wuhan is one of the chief industrial centres of the country, especially of the steel industry.

The struggle between the factions in Wuhan was increasing in intensity. A number of incidents in May and June produced dozens of deaths, hundreds of wounded, and thousands of arrests. Peking could hardly permit events to continue in this way for very much longer, especially since battles around the bridge blocked rail and road traffic for several days at a time. In mid-July a delegation was sent from Peking to conduct an inquiry. This delegation consisted of a group of Red Guards from the Aeronautical Institute; the Left-wing radical general political commissioner for the air force, Yu Li-chin; the deputy of Chen Po-ta, Wang Li; and the Minister of Public Security, Hsieh Fu-chih, a confidant of Chou En-lai, who had himself already made on-the-spot investigations. The main task of the inquiry group was to determine which of the two rival alliances of mass organizations represented the authentic Maoist Left wing: the 'One Million Warriors' or the somewhat smaller 'Three Commands'. The former alliance enjoyed the support of the former Party apparatus of Wang Jen-chung and of the commander of the military district, Chen Tsai-tao. The second alliance was connected with the rebel headquarters 'Kung Cheng', which had been dissolved by the commander of the military district. The group conducting the investigation talked to everyone concerned, but the radicals, according to later reports, soon began to show preference for the 'Three Commands', causing violent demonstrations to break out again, resulting in more dead and wounded. Nor was it the end of the affair when the investigation group announced its decision. Thomas Robinson summarizes:

By the 19th, Hsieh and Wang had evidently seen enough to arrive at some conclusions. Chou apparently approved their report and

authorized them to read out the verdict to both sides. After meeting
with the rebel factions, they called a meeting in the evening at the
Military District Headquarters, to be attended by all top leaders in
the area. The gist of the report was essentially equivalent to Chou's
earlier four-point statement: The Military District was mistaken,
the One Million Warriors was indeed a 'conservative' organization,
the *Kung cheng* case must in fact be reversed, and the 'Three Commands' (*San lien, San hsin* and *San kang*) were to be recognized as
genuine revolutionary rebel groups. At this point, Niu Hai-lung,
Commander of the 8201 Unit, became incensed, jumped up, announced his opposition to the four points, shouted 'I am prepared to
risk my life!' and stormed out of the meeting. Together with Chen
Tsai-tao and the local Party secretaries of the Tung hu (East Lake)
district of Hankow, Niu mobilized his troops and a large number of
the One Million Warriors converged on the Tung-hu Hotel where
Hsieh and Wang had now returned, and, despite the presence of a
guard platoon of the loyalist 8199 Unit, from 9 p.m. on laid siege to
the building. By early morning (about 1 a.m.) of the 20th, the district
was sealed off and soldiers of the 8201 were patrolling the streets and
had placed machine guns on the buildings.

At this point, Chen Tsai-tao appeared at the hotel, confronted
Hsieh and Wang, and said that the workers were now beyond his own
control, that there was nothing that he could do for them and that
they would have to cope with the workers as best they could. Although Hsieh and Wang apparently tried to reason with the workers,
the latter, together with Niu's troops, stormed the hotel, broke into
the rooms where the two were staying (overpowering their Peking
Aviation College bodyguards and reportedly stabbing to death
Hsieh's personal secretary), separated Hsieh from Wang, tied up
Wang and proceeded to kick and beat him.

In the city itself, the One Million Warriors and the 8201 Unit were
in full control. They replaced the regular guards at the District Military Headquarters, sealed off the area, blocked traffic from the
bridges over the Yangtse and Han Rivers (thus isolating the opposition in the three portions of the tri-city), seized the railway stations,
the radio station and the airport and garrisoned strong points
throughout the city. The workers' organization proceeded to carry
out forays against the Red Guards, to set fire to schools and to kill
and injure those who chose to oppose them.[1]

News of the 'mutiny in Wuhan' reached Peking during the
morning of the 20th. Chief-of-staff Yang Cheng-wu made com-

mander Chen Tsai-tao responsible for the safety of the delegation from Peking and ordered him to accompany them personally during their return. Lin Piao flew to Wuhan in person to
transfer military command to Yu Li-chin, who was already in
Wuhan as a member of the investigating group, and to the
deputy commander of the air force, Liu Feng. Chou En-lai also
flew to Wuhan, but was unable to land because the airport was
surrounded by mutineers.

A large-scale military operation was then mounted. Para-
troops were dropped to reinforce the Red Guards and take control of the bridge over the river. About five gunboats were
moved up the Yang-tzu, while central army units marched into
town to take control of vital points. As soon as control had been
gained of the local mass media, an extensive propaganda campaign was initiated. Pamphlets were dropped over the parts of
the town occupied by the mutineers. The central leadership told
the mutineers that they had been misled by anti-Maoist elements. Wang Li was apparently able to convince his guards of
this, since they allowed him to escape. Like Hsieh Fu-chih, who
had been freed earlier, he found safety at the airport, from
which operations against the mutineers were now being
organized.

Although it was only a matter of a few days before the town
was under control again (only the leaders of the mutiny were
detained, while their followers were urged to come to their sen-
ses), it was some weeks before life in Wuhan returned to
normal.

The 'drag out' campaign

In the meantime, Wang Li and Hsieh Fu-chih were welcomed
back to Peking by a crowd of millions on Tien An-men Square,
where they appeared in the company of Chiang Ching; Lin Piao
was also present. But in the same way that a similar reception
had seemed to go to the head of Yao Teng-shan, the 'red diplomat', so too Wang Li tried immediately to turn his newly-
acquired political capital into a platform for a Leftist agitation
campaign. His own propaganda branch made a film of his

triumphant return, with himself in the leading role. The message of the film's title to the rebels in the provinces was, 'Peking supports you!' The young radicals in the leadership, especially the Peking faction of the Cultural Revolution Group, which controlled most of the mass media, also made the incident at Wuhan the starting-point for a campaign supporting the opposition to the regional commanders. The left wing of the former 'third national Red Guards headquarters' was also asked to give support, and Wang Li told the rebel leader Kuai Ta-fu: 'The central task of this coming period is to drag out of the army a small handful of capitalist-roaders who have usurped military power.' [2]

Kuai immediately mobilized his national communications network into undertaking a large-scale drag out campaign. Informants in the provinces had been sending in reports of conflicts between the rebels and the local commanders for some time. The radicals in Peking now set up a military information service. 2,000 students were sent out into the field, 200 copies of a 'textbook for the collection of military information' were distributed, and about fifty liaison centres were set up. A variety of information began to come in, ranging from the composition and backgrounds of the regional commands to the military tasks performed by the units in the regions concerned. If they encountered any difficulty in obtaining information, the rebels invoked the authority of Kuai, or, if necessary, of the Wang–Kuan–Chi triumvirate of Chen Po-ta's Cultural Revolution Group, or even of Lin Piao's closest colleagues, Hsiao Hua and Yang Cheng-wu. As other Red Guard organizations joined the movement, the information began to be sorted in Peking. A headquarters was set up in Tsinghua University, complete with ordnance maps and filing systems, from which the action against the regional commanders could be co-ordinated. The radical-Left elements in the Cultural Revolution Group (Wang, Kuan, Chi and Lin Chieh and Mu Hsin) put out the following slogan to the nation, 'Drag out the small handful of capitalist roaders in the army!'

By the end of July this slogan was being seen and heard with increasing frequency both in the press and in radio broadcasts.

On 1 August, the *Red Flag*, the *People's Daily*, and the *Liberation Army Daily* all added their weight to the movement, quoting especially 'relevant' words spoken by Lin Piao. On 5 August, the first anniversary of Mao's poster, 'Bombard the headquarters', a further attempt was made to make the campaign more official by interpreting the poster more literally than had been intended when it was first issued. Attacks on already discredited revisionists in the army were resumed with unprecedented violence.

While it is true that Lin Piao never openly joined the campaign, he did give the impression of being sympathetic to it. Between 9 and 11 August, for instance, he described the Wuhan incident as something very bad which had turned into something very good. At the same time, however, he pointed out that not all the rebels who opposed the regional commanders were automatically good Maoists. All the regional commanders (who had been summoned to the capital) were told that under no circumstances were the rebels to be dealt with in an arbitrary fashion:

One must report to and ask instructions from Chairman Mao, the Central Committee and the Cultural Revolution Group. One must not think that you yourself have understood and need not report to the centre; you must not think that it is clear and that you can deal with it yourself. You must not think that you yourself are intelligent and do not need to report and ask for instructions. You need not fear that you are causing trouble to the centre. No matter whether it is a big or small affair, everything must be reported and instructions sought for. The Premier and the Cultural Revolution Group comrades are working day and night ... You can also fly and come here and be here in a couple of hours. You must not adopt the attitude of this must be so, assume yourself to be clever and act according to your own light.[3]

Lin's hesitant attitude in fact played into the hands of the organizers of the drag out campaign which gradually spread over the whole country. Red Guard commandos broke into the residences of high-ranking officers to search for incriminating evidence. Kuai Ta-fu himself travelled to Nanking where the campaign against the regional commander, Hsu Shih-yu, had turned into an interminable demonstration by hundreds of thousands of people outside the military headquarters, before it was finally occupied. A similar campaign was conducted in Fuchow against commander Han Hsien-chu; this campaign was encouraged by the radicals Wang and Chi, but was eventually slowed down from the centre by Chou En-lai and Kang Sheng. The movement was brought to a sudden halt when it was unexpectedly taken over by the propaganda media of neighbouring Taiwan. In Shenyang large-scale fighting occurred between the opponents and supporters of the local commander Chen Hsi-lien. The leader of the opponents was a close colleague of Kuai Ta-fu, and was also encouraged by Kuang Feng.

Throughout the country, demonstrators gathered at the gates of army camps demanding that 'revisionist commanders' should be made to come out. Arms depots were broken into by the rebels to add force to their demands. And although the military personnel generally acted with great restraint, the number of incidents involving bloodshed increased. Chou En-lai later told Edgar Snow that thousands of soldiers had died in the first half of the Cultural Revolution. And Chiang Ching said later:

You must not treat the army in that way. When you took their guns away, some soldiers were in tears. They knew you wanted to take their guns, but they could not fire on you because they, like you, belong to the revolutionary masses. If I were a soldier, I would certainly defend myself if someone wanted to take my gun away.[4]

One place in which Lin Piao was faced in a particularly painful way with the consequences of his hesitancy was Canton. From the beginning of 1967 the political confusion in that city had been greater than anywhere else, and the angry response to the intervention of the army inspired further agitation. According to the Red Guard cited by Bennett and Montaperto:

We had virtually succeeded in seizing power, in making a true revolution. Now the bastards had thrown it all away . . . I was actually being attacked and suppressed by the very authorities to whom I had dedicated my life. It seemed they had used me and then cast me aside when I had ceased to be of value to them. My bitterness knew no bounds . . .

During August and September the situation degenerated into complete chaos; robbery and violence became commonplace; and the endless series of demonstrations and confrontations resulted in a large number of deaths. In addition, it became clear during the month of September that a national organization was busy occupying strategic points, such as Canton station, and establishing guerrilla bases in the surrounding countryside and along the border with Hong Kong, in co-operation with other groups of similar persuasion, as a preparation for armed rebellion against the local military command. The international autumn fair in Canton had to be postponed for a month. It took until the beginning of November for the extremists to be isolated and for some of the other organizations to be brought together in a coalition for the formation of a Revolutionary Committee, so that the situation could again be normalized.

Reaction to the 'drag out' campaign

During the course of these events the leaders responsible began to realize that some of the radicals in the leadership had been guilty of bad faith. They had formed their own faction with its own policy, which contradicted official policy in more than one respect. The rebels could very well mobilize the masses for a purge of the Party, but only the Party could in turn purge the army. The armed conflict had by then brought the country to the brink of civil war; instead of advancing the Cultural Revolution, the latest campaign had caused it to retreat. On 7 August the Shanghai daily newspaper *Wen-hui Pao* published a statement to the effect that it was intolerable that discord should be caused between the army and the people. On 11 August the same newspaper published an announcement by Chang Chun-chiao forbidding the possession of arms (even under the pretext of self-defence) as well as the use of other weapons, such as chemical poisons. The Shanghai members of the Cultural Revolution Group thus set the ideological tone of the movement again, while the younger radicals of the Peking faction had clearly discredited themselves. Their political fate seems to have been sealed when it appeared that they had formed a secret co-ordination group, having direct links with the Left wing of the 'third Red Guards headquarters' and a new, ultra-Left 'fourth headquarters' of so-called 'May 16 groups', which had emerged in Peking at the beginning of August. It was but a short step to outright 'conspiracy'.

14: The Creation of the 'May 16 Movement'; Ultra-Left Offensive against Chou En-lai

The origin of the ultra-Left and the dissatisfaction with Chou En-lai[1]

The situation of the ultra-Left at this point can only be understood if we go back once again to the beginnings of the movement.

When the leadership of the Cultural Revolution had called for the students and pupils in the schools to unite their 'first', 'second' and 'third' headquarters under a single command in the autumn of 1966, two groups had refused to take part in the newly-created organization. These were the totally dedicated loyalists, and those rebels who were afraid that the Left wing of the 'third headquarters' (in which the 'first' and 'second' had been included) under the leadership of Kuai Ta-fu would begin to lose its influence, thus benefiting the moderate wing under the leadership of Nieh Yuan-tzu. Kuai was the leader of the rebel students of Tsinghua University, while Nieh was the rebel assistant professor of Pei-ta University.

The 'authentic' ultra-Left rebels who had remained apart from the amalgamation of the three headquarters recruited their followers chiefly among the carefully-selected student population of the national educational institutions in the capital, and among the younger cadres in the government services. Some of them feared that the revolution would somehow leave those of their chiefs (mainly ministers) who were revisionists untouched, if it became too moderate. In other words, the groups which later united in the 'May 16 Movement' drew the larger part of their membership from the many specialized colleges where cadres for the various departments and ministries received their education, such as the Economics College, the Trades College, the College of Finance, the College for the Iron and Steel Industry, the Forestry College, the Academy of Agriculture, the Academy of Medicine, the Aeronautical Institute, and especially the two Institutes for Foreign Languages. The Red Guard groups in those institutions had links both with 'ordinary' secondary schools and universities in Peking and outside, and with high officials in nearly all the important ministries and departments of the Central Committee. It was clear that this assembly of forces was capable of growing into a very powerful and influential organization.

Their task was made easier by the procedure which had been created during the Cultural Revolution whereby rebel groups could take over the political department of their work-unit by eliminating the old Party establishment, and by the fact that the influence exerted by the political departments on the work-units had increased during the Cultural Revolution. The result was that in some ministries (such as that for foreign affairs) policy-making fell into the hands of the rebels. Perhaps the situation would never have developed to this point, had there not been from the beginning a hard core of rebels whose firm intention was the unification of the various groups scattered throughout the different institutions under a common programme.

The 'heart' of the movement had its origins in the Department of Philosophy and Social Sciences of the Academy of Sciences, which was very much influenced by Chen Po-ta and already deeply involved in ideological developments. In October 1966 six rebels from this Department met to discuss their concerted plan of action: Pan Tzu-nien (head of the Department), Chou Ching-fang (his closest colleague), Wu Chuan-chi and Li-Yu-shih (chief editor and director of their journal *Philosophical Study*), and Hung Tao and Wang En-yu (both of the United Force of the Red Guards of the Department). Their idea was that a 'fourth Red Guards headquarters' should be created. 'We have grasped the struggle between the two lines earlier than Tsinghua' [the university of Kuai Ta-fu who had played such an important role in the 'third headquarters']. 'It is definite that premier Chou is the backer of Nieh Yuan-tzu. The reason for Nieh's opposition to Pan and Wu is that the Central Committee had eliminated many people who have referred to X (meaning Chou). To make events take another course Nieh has been appointed to make problems for Pan and Wu.'

Support for this line was found in the person of Tao Chu, who visited the Department three times during October and wrote his own poster there; it was short but clear: 'Support Wu!' However, when Tao Chu was discredited at the beginning of the year for 'Left deviationism' the leaders of the new movement swiftly dissociated themselves from him. They found new support among the Party leadership in the person of Lin Chieh, one of the younger radicals of the Cultural Revolution Group, who was soon joined by other colleagues like Mu Hsin.

Attacks on Chou En-lai via his ministers

Meanwhile, a plot to bring down the 'old' régime was set afoot. The attacks were to be concentrated on the Vice-Premiers, thereby implying attack on Chou En-lai. At the beginning of January 1967 a series of attacks was duly launched over a wide front on Vice-Premiers Hsieh Fu-chih (public security), Nieh Jungchen (strategic industry and Academy of Sciences), Chen I (foreign affairs), Tan Chen-lin (agriculture) and Li Hsien-nien (finance). There were systematic indications that Chou was regarded as the man 'behind the scenes'.

The critics were not particular about the methods they used: on 7 January a meeting was held to criticize the State Planning Commission under Vice-Premier Li Fu-chun and Yu Chiu-li. The latter was present at the meeting and expressed self-criticism. The former, however, was ill in hospital, but this was no obstacle for the organizers of the meeting. He was abducted and brought to face his audience. On another occasion a minister was held continuously for several days outside Peking and interrogated. Another disappeared without trace.

By the end of January, a group had begun to form in the Government which insisted that the extremist Red Guards should be restrained. The army was called in to protect high-ranking officials, and strict regulations to keep the situation in check were issued. Finding progress checked in one direction, the ultras promptly tried another way. On 15 January a number of them, led by Mu Hsin, obtained a considerable number of secret personal files from the archives of the Central Committee.

Incriminating evidence involving political friends was made to disappear, while that involving enemies was freely circulated. Other ultras occupied the Ministry of Public Security with the same intention, but they were expelled by the army at the beginning of February. Instructions were issued by the ultras to attack the Vice-Premiers to bring down the Premier, calling the whole group 'deviationists'. Chou was said to be in difficulties because of his protection of friends and because he was thought to have abstained from voting in the affair of the work-groups. Some of the ultras, however, began to be afraid of the consequences at this point. 'Now we have gone so far – what shall we do if the Central Committee hears about it?' 'There is nothing to worry about as long as we form an alliance', the leaders replied, and they ignored the suspicions of the Central Committee.

A number of previously sympathetic Red Guards began to dissociate themselves from the ultras. Students of the 'Revolutionary Rebel Commune' of the College for the Iron and Steel Industry handed one of its members over to the Bureau of Public Security for his connection with the group and his criticisms of the Premier. He later reappeared elsewhere, however, and finally became head of the important 'June 16 Group' of the Institute of Foreign Languages, which was active in the Ministry of Foreign Affairs. A number of students moved about in this way; having been excluded from one organization for 'counter-revolutionary activities', they would often reappear as 'ultra-revolutionaries' in another. In spite of continued resistance to them and doubts about their intentions, the campaigns against the Vice-Premiers enjoyed a certain amount of success. The first Vice-Premier to concede defeat was Tan Chen-lin of the Ministry of Agriculture. He had already compromised himself in connection with the Great Leap, and had discredited himself even further by calling for a complete halt to the Cultural Revolution during the so-called counter-current of February. The unmasking of Tan Chen-lin further encouraged the ultras. Hinting that they had been given confidential information by the Cultural Revolution Group, they issued the following statement:

The Central Committee has recently been preparing to expose a number of people. Perhaps the fourth man of the sequence Liu–Teng–Tao will also be exposed. You will be very surprised to hear his name. He has already protected a large number of people. The Central Committee has also prepared the unmasking of four Vice-Premiers, who are Li (Hsien-nien), Li (Fu-chun), Tan (Chen-lin) and Chen (I).

The ultras were very enthusiastic about their programme and decided to launch a large-scale offensive. Campaigns were thus initiated in all ministries and educational institutions. The attacks on Chou En-lai, which had hitherto remained relatively indirect, were now intensified.

Publication of the 'May 16 circular'; 'Bombard Premier Chou En-lai!'

16 May 1967 was the first anniversary of the confidential circular of the Central Committee which had initiated the Cultural Revolution; it was also a good opportunity for publishing the contents, which was done a few days later. It is not clear who actually took the decision to publish the text. But whether it was the Central Committee or the Left wing of the Cultural Revolution Group, the results were very much the same. The relatively violent contents of this document now made a very different impression than they had done a year ago. In the current phase of the Cultural Revolution there was far less need for radical mobilization – rather the contrary. However, the publication of the circular acted as the ideal stimulant for an intensification of the ultra-Left campaign.

A mass campaign was promptly mounted against the 'old' régime, against Premier Chou En-lai and against the leadership of the Revolutionary Committee of Peking, which had been set up at the end of of April, thanks to the efforts of Chou. Shortly afterwards, a small Leftist faction was formed within the Committee, the 'Group of the Peking Movement', which had close contacts with the ultras. The opening shots of the new 16 May offensive came from the students of the Institute of Foreign Languages. They put up posters bearing the slogan, 'See through a great conspiracy'. The Premier was not referred to by name

yet, but there was no doubt as to the implications of the poster:
'It is necessary to expose another Liu Shao-chi – an impostor
who plays with counter-revolution and who supports the conservatives to protect his tottering reactionary rule!'

Other groups chose their words less carefully. At the end of
May a poster was put up on the walls of the College of Com-
merce which left nothing to the imagination: 'Bombard
Premier Chou En-lai!' By this time the offensive had begun to
snowball and rhetorical, insinuating questions were asked of the
Premier on the posters, very much on the lines of the campaign
against Liu Shao-chi. This phase of the campaign started at the
end of May with the so-called 'ten whys'. At the beginning of
July the total had grown to twenty-three 'whys', and the
campaign had spread throughout the country.

The leadership of the Cultural Revolution forbids attacks on Chou En-lai

The leadership of the Cultural Revolution, which had no desire
to see this movement get out of hand, decided to intervene. On
3 June 1967, the delegates of the groups who had attacked the
Premier were summoned to a meeting for a discussion of the
matter. At the meeting they were faced with Hsieh Fu-chih,
Chen Po-ta, Chi Pen-yu (the most prominent representative of
the Left wing of the Cultural Revolution Group) and Yeh Chun
(probably representing the Cultural Revolution Group of the
army and, as the wife of Lin Piao, enjoying considerable prestige among the radicals). Chen presided over the gathering.[2]
From remarks made by Chi Pen-yu it was clear that the Cultural
Revolution Group felt very uneasy about the continuing attacks
on Chou En-lai: 'If you overdo it then foreigners will spread
the rumour that Po-ta has split with the Premier.' And 'The
imperialists and revisionists are afraid of the Premier and Comrade Chen Po-ta, and are spreading rumours about them every
day.'

Hsieh Fu-chih was the first to address the meeting:

'. . . Peking is the quarters of Chairman Mao and the Central Cultural Revolution Group and the birthplace of the Cultural Revolu-

tion. If events are developing well in Peking, the whole country will learn from Peking; if Peking fails to do a good job, the whole country will be affected. Now that you have engaged in creating splits – from small ones to big ones – the effect will be tremendous and will be very bad. The Premier works under the leadership of Chairman Mao and the Party Central Committee. What the Premier is attending to is important state affairs. The present struggle is aimed at Liu-Teng-and-Peng as well as a handful of power-holders taking the capitalist road in each unit. They are the main targets . . . If we exert our major effort in fighting a civil war and continue to write big-character posters to attack the Premier – the man who shoulders the major responsibilities of the country (!), we tend to disorganize our own camp. Comrades, please think about it . . . What you have been doing will disturb our orientation and affect our major targets. During our meeting today you may express your opinions. Last time I talked with your rebel group '616' [the ultra-Left June 16 Group of the Institute of Foreign Languages in the Ministry of Foreign Affairs] for six to seven hours but you were always of the opinion that I was not justified while you were. Now comrade Chen Po-ta, please give them a talk – as I am always despised by college students.'

Chen Po-ta: 'Every one of you believes that he has reason; however you never pay attention to big reasons . . . [Concerning the accusation that Chou-En-Lai always supports Chen I, he says:] I am the biggest royalist and I vouched for Chen I several times when the Premier did not. I protected Chen I, hence I am the biggest royalist. Why should the Premier be involved? You should think it over. However, I did not clearly say that I wanted to protect Chen I, but my statements implied that. I cannot serve as a Foreign Minister because the nominee was decided by the State. Can your school designate him? [There clearly followed hesitant confirmation at this point]. Whom do you represent? Don't you even have such small revolutionary sense?'

[There were probably objections here.]

Chi Pen-yu then said: 'Cut off your nonsense! You are too childish!'

Chen Po-ta: 'I'll cast my vote for comrade Chi Pen-yu, but one vote is not enough. You cannot be Foreign Minister even if I designate you, because you cannot even speak clearly . . . If you cannot talk reasonably, how can you serve as Foreign Minister? It won't do just to argue arbitrarily. You say you are concerned about state affairs, but one cannot be misinformed about state affairs. If you do not take the whole situation into consideration, you cannot say you are concerned about state affairs. You assert that I did not vouch for Comrade Chen I, but I said I did. Now tell me, did I really vouch or not?'

[A number still maintain their original position.]

'You talk nonsense! It is I who did. How can you impose it on the Premier?'

'Today I am prepared to be struck down by you!'

Chi Pen-yu: 'The Premier did not vouch. But I must make it clear that the Premier can do it. Comrade Po-ta can do it, and you can oppose Chen I. However, you cannot oppose the Premier just because he vouched for Chen I. You are wrong in opposing the Premier. Chen I has made mistakes and you can oppose him. However, the Premier has great prestige overseas and hence you cannot oppose him (!) We have said all this to you in the past; it is not my personal opinion but that of the Party.'

The exchanges continued in this fashion for some time, apparently without a satisfactory conclusion being reached. But although the students were by no means convinced, the attacks on Chou En-lai did diminish during the following weeks. The most that was achieved by this, however, was the terminating of only one line of attack on the much wider front of ultra-Left agitation, which had included the attacks on embassies, the 'siege' of Liu Shao-chi, and the events which followed the mutiny in Wuhan. This agitation had now begun to cause the upper leadership of the Cultural Revolution considerable anxiety.

Part Five
The Retreat of the Radicals

One-sidedness means thinking in terms of absolutes, that is, a metaphysical approach to problems. In the appraisal of our work, it is one-sided to regard everything as all positive or as all negative.

Mao Tse-tung, 1957, quoted in the *Little Red Book*

15: 'There Is No Fundamental Contradiction Within the Working Class'

The leadership condemns the May 16 Movement

The arrest of three ultra-Left student leaders in Peking on 10 August by Hsieh Fu-chih on charges of 'activities dangerous to the state, and conspiracy' could be considered a result of the decision to halt the attacks on Chou En-lai. And when Chen Po-ta and Chiang Ching addressed a delegation of Red Guards from Anhwei Province the following day, it had become clear that the leadership of the Cultural Revolution had launched a major counter-attack on the 'fourth headquarters' of the 'May 16 Groups'. Chen Po-ta went further and linked the campaign against Chou En-lai with the 'drag out' campaign:

There is also a 'May 16' . . . which is a secret and conspiratorial organization. Its spearhead is directed at XXX (Chou) but it actually is directed at the Central Committee, because opposition to XXX also means opposition to the Central Comittee . . .

If possible, the attack delivered by Chiang Ching was even fiercer:

I am not going to repeat what I have said in regard to the 'May 16' organization. In a nutshell, it will not be tolerated. You comrades must not be fooled by it. During the Great Cultural Revolution, there are bound to be some persons fishing in troubled waters . . . Some people want to sway the Central Committee from the 'Left' or the Right . . . Such an organization as the 'May 16' will not be tolerated. It is an act of sabotage.[1]

The attack on the ultras was limited for the time being to the leaders of specific closely-knit semi-secret Red Guard societies in Peking. By the end of August, after the campaign against Liu Shao-chi had got out of hand, the increasingly bitter and bloody clashes with the regional army units, and one day after the attack on the British Embassy, the offensive against the ultras reached the level of the Central Committee. The leadership was being gradually purged of extremists. Within the General Political Department, a number of people, such as Chao I-ya and Lin Piao's right-hand man, Hsiao Hua, now disappeared from public view. A major part of the younger members of the Peking faction on the Cultural Revolution Group were eased from their positions of power; these included Mu Hsin, Lin Chieh and Kuan Feng, and Chen Po-ta's right-hand man, Wang Li. Many sections of the mass media were reorganized, including the *Liberation Army Daily*, the *People's Daily* and the *Red Flag*. When another meeting of the Red Guards from Anhwei was held on 28 August, it was not, significantly, Chen Po-ta who addressed the meeting, but the 'moderate' Kang Sheng. Chen was obviously no longer considered the right person to talk about 'Left deviationism'.

A meeting of the Revolutionary Committee of Peking took place on 1 September, in the presence of a large part of the leadership of the Cultural Revolution. On this occasion Chiang Ching said:

The 'May 16' movement is superficially (!) opposed to the Premier. But it is actually divided into a number of area armies. It is a demolition squad seeking to sway the Party Central Committee headed by Chairman Mao from the 'Left' and the Right, and bring disorder to our setup. The 'May 16' is a counter-revolutionary organization!

And Kang Sheng added: 'The appearance of the "May 16" is by no means accidental . . . Some people have unconsciously been fooled by them and have come to their assistance. This handful of bad leaders must be firmly suppressed and arrested at once.'[2]

It is interesting to note that the major responsibility for the counter-attack remained in the hands of the Shanghai faction of the Cultural Revolution Group, Chiang Ching and Yao Wen-yuan. Like the Peking faction, they enjoyed considerable prestige among members of the Left wing, but were less compromised by their contacts with the ultras and their errors. On 8 September, in an article in the *People's Daily*, Yao Wen-yuan defined the relationship between the May 16 movement and

Tao Chu, and said: 'We have not as yet fully identified most of its members and leaders. For they only send their people out in the silence of the night to paste up broadsheets and to paint slogans. The broad masses are making investigations in relation to these people, and things will shortly be made clear.'[3]

The base takes over the counter-attack; Chou En-lai speaks out

The position clearly taken up by the leadership inspired a number of rival Red Guard groups to start a campaign against the 'May 16', whose members were now beginning to show some signs of panic. Their immediate reaction, on 11 August, was to try to contact their protectors. But the latter quickly severed all contacts with them. When the leader of the 'May 16', Chang Chien-chi, tried to telephone his contact in the Cultural Revolution Group (Lin Chieh?), the latter was not at home. Two days later, he made it known, as Mu Hsin and others had done, that contacts had to be temporarily suspended. During the days that followed, more and more groups began to dissociate themselves from the May 16 organization, starting with those who had previously had the closest contacts with it. To avoid being carried along with the downfall of the ultras, they hurriedly declared the matter closed; one of them pronounced very prematurely: 'The "May 16" has been uncovered, its ringleaders have been captured, victory has been won.'

The day after the meeting of the Central Committee held on 24 August, condemning the ultras, about 100 Red Guard groups in Peking organized a meeting, which was attended by thousands, to conclude the 'victory'. This action was again premature; on precisely the same day, Wu – the man behind the scenes – wrote an article under a pseudonym, which he was able to publish in the Peking intellectual journal *Kuang-ming Jih-pao*, with the help of his political supporter Mu Hsin; the journal was one of the main organs of the ultra-Left, which refused to change its course until the very last moment.

But the disintegration of the ultra-Left communications network could be halted no longer. When the debate was finally brought out into the open at the beginning of September, the radical rebel organizations, which had rivalled the ultras, decided to take action themselves. Their own account of events now follows.

I. HOW THE YOUNG PATHBREAKERS MAPPED OUT THE PLAN ON THE EVE OF THE BATTLE

After a long time of spying, we discovered that the 'June 16' of the Foreign Languages Institute of Peking was directly connected with the sinister hands and was also a key position for the important activities of the 'May 16 Corps'. We of the 'Revolutionary Rebel Commune' and the young commanders of the 'Red Flag' of the Peking Foreign Languages Institute and other fraternal organizations gathered under one roof on the morning of 6 September to study the plan of operations for storming and destroying this important stronghold.

The key position of the 'June 16' was located at the fifth floor of the main building of the Peking Foreign Languages Institute, and there were more than one hundred sinister soldiers. There is only a narrow staircase to the centre leading to the fifth floor. The place was closely guarded. The entrance to the staircase was blocked with tables, chairs and benches, and the narrow staircase was also shut off by a solid wooden door and was guarded by several persons. The terrain was nasty and ugly. They also stored a huge supply of lime, stones and sticks on the fifth floor and had spent a number of days to make preparations for the battle. The sinister soldiers vainly tried to hold the place.

Chairman Mao said: 'This army has an indomitable spirit and is determined to vanquish all enemies.' The young commanders coolly analysed the situation and pointed out that it was necessary to bring the absolute superiority of politics into full play. The operations plan to outwit the enemy and show courage in taking the place was formulated. It was also decided to launch the attack quickly. They planned to take the enemy by surprise during the lunch break.

II. HOW THE BRAVE AND CLEVER HEROES SEIZED THE KEY POSITION

The trucks laden with fighters sped towards the stronghold of the 'June 16'. When our Liangshan heroes arrived there by car, we found that the comrades-in-arms of nine fraternal units including the 'Red Flag' Battalion of the Peking Foreign Languages Institute, the 'Chingkangshan' of the College of Electric Power and the 'Red Flag' of the College of Economics had come to the place one after the other according to the original plan.

A comrade-in-arms of the 'Chingkangshan' of the College of Electric Power walked ahead. Disguised as one paying a visit to the 'June 16' and holding a letter of introduction in his hand, he mounted the staircase in the hope of taking the guards by surprise. We fighters waited on one side so that we could rush forward to subdue the two guards as soon as the door was opened, thus breaking their first line of defence.

Out of our expectation, the sinister soldiers of the 'June 16', on the strength of their counter-revolutionary scent, saw through our scheme. The only door closed with a bang. After that they put all kinds of tools and timber behind the door.

Since we were unable to outwit them, we began to attack by force. The comrades-in-arms of the 'Chingkangshan' of the College of Electric Power hit the door with a 12-lb hammer, and the door collapsed with a crash. We fighters quickly dashed right up to the fifth floor.

The hooligans on the upper floor were well prepared for this. Suddenly the whole staircase was scattered with lime. Our fighters could not open their eyes and were unable to see anything. They also found it difficult to breathe. To break the deadlock, the fighters sprayed water with the fire hose which they had brought with them. This cleared away the smoke in no time. The fighters stepped forward and drew closer to the other side.

Seeing that the situation was unfavourable, the sinister soldiers of the 'May 16' used stones to attack us rebels in a vain attempt to fight with their backs to the wall. Our fighters knew how to deal with this and they produced their weapons for fighting at close quarters ... the catapults. The first two missiles shot hit two sinister soldiers in the front, and the other flunkies, seeing that the situation was unfavourable, fought a retreating battle. Our brave men rushed forward and controlled the vantage point.

Our main forces quickly moved in to occupy the fifth floor of the main building. Fifteen hard-core elements headed by Chang X X, ringleader of the sinister soldiers, were caught, and an abundance of sinister materials, reactionary handbills, armbands, seals, banners and other propaganda materials were also captured. Even the sinister materials hidden in the ceiling could not escape the eyes of our heroic and mercurial fighters. The important sinister materials found and captured in this battle provided important clues and evidence for us to uncover completely the sinister corps and drag out its sinister backers.[4]

Just one week later, on 12 September, another meeting was held by the Red Guards in Peking, at which 10,000 members of the movement gathered to celebrate the real victory. But again, there were groups which saw this manifestation as just another manoeuvre:

Those burglars and clowns held a ten-thousand-man rally at the time when the majority of the members and leaders of the 'May 16 Corps' had still not been identified. They put up special posters all over the city, dragged out Chang Chien-ch'i, a minor leader of a counter-revolutionary group, for trial, and put up a show by noisily clamouring victory. They gave the impression that the 'May 16 Corps' had been uncovered and that Chang Chien-ch'i was its top leader. They attempted to benumb the fighting spirit of the revolutionary masses in this way. How wonderful!

However, after the manipulators of the 'May 16 Corps' – Lin Chieh and his ilk – had been dragged out by the proletarian revolutionaries, these 'rebels' who continuously claimed 'victory' in their 'first battle' and 'second battle' against the 'May 16' sinister corps, behaved in an abnormal manner and became hysterical. They published the notorious royalist statement branding the revolutionary action that exposed the anti-Party clique of Lin Chieh and Mu Hsin as a 'counter-revolutionary adverse current' and wanting to 'hit it in the head'.

This series of incidents, during which the rebels tried to outdo each other in the fervour of their revolutionary sentiments (n.b., the same phenomenon that had led to the extremism), showed how the atmosphere on the radical-Left wing had degenerated by this phase of the Cultural Revolution. It was high time for this destructive factionalism to be terminated. This would explain the publication of an important statement of policy by Mao Tse-tung in the *People's Daily* of 11 September.

There is no fundamental conflict of interests within the working class. Under the dictatorship of the proletariat the working class has no reason for dividing itself into two large, irreconcilable organizations. .

One last interesting aspect of the matter remains to be examined: the attitude of Chou En-lai. As the principal representative of the more moderate realists in the Cultural Revolution, he had been the main target for the attacks of the ultra-Left for the previous six months. At the same time, he had probably been the first to recognize the great danger of complacency on the part of the radical-Left wing. It was probably the Premier (with Vice-Premiers like Hsieh Fu-chih) who had mobilized the radicals at the beginning of August to dissociate themselves from the ultras. He was, however, enough of a tactician not to appear too much in the foreground of this movement. It was only on 17 September, when the critical phase of the conflict was over, that he made the carefully calculated gesture of talking openly about the matter in public, at a reception for Peking student delegates. Among other things, he said:

This group (the 'May 16' group) has brutally attacked our comrades of the central Party leadership ... As one of the responsible leaders of the proletarian headquarters, I will allow no one to cause trouble between the central group and myself ... The capitalists and revisionists are very pleased at this prospect ... It is fortunate that the 'May 16' group has been unmasked.

He was thus the first person to get directly to the heart of the situation; he later addressed himself to another sensitive area, by suggesting a cure for the 'Left-wing communist infantile disease': 'Young radicals who lack experience are easily misled ... I am telling you now that all students must return to their schools, or else they will be expelled.' (The report from which this speech is taken indicates an interruption by Chiang Ching at this point: 'Nor will they be given any help by the Government.')[5]

This problem, which became increasingly important from the end of 1966, could be summed up as follows. The intellectual youth of China, like its counterparts in other countries, had played an important role as the vanguard of the new mass movement; afterwards, however, it found itself incapable of uniting its efforts with those of the population at large, thus dooming itself to advance ever more swiftly into fruitless and damaging revolutionizing.

Chou's analysis of the ultra-Left problem was also interesting in its approach to problems among the leadership, as well as to the problems involving the social base. Too much complacency on the part of older radicals in positions of responsibility had created the opportunities for the arbitrary actions of the young ultras. Thus, he stated at a meeting held on 28 September that it was not simply a question of finding a few scapegoats: 'In this connection, we should first of all criticize ourselves. Our propaganda was wrong in that we simply called for dragging out a small handful in the army. It led to antagonism between the masses and the army, and this was exploited by bad men.'[6] By 'ourselves', Chou cannot have been referring literally to himself, since he had had no responsibility at all for the campaign in question. This was not the case, however, for other members of the leadership, such as Lin Piao and Chen Po-ta, who had allowed their collaborators sufficient leeway to carry out the campaign. Some responsibility for what had happened, though less, should also have been borne by Chiang Ching. However, her responsibilities in the actual development of the campaign had been less formal, and she had dissociated herself, together with her colleagues, from it at an early stage, finally playing an important part in bringing it to a halt. She and her colleagues[7] could thus afford to adopt Chou's view of the problem and to declare the matter still 'open'. The fact that people like Chou and Chiang Ching held this opinion on the shortcomings of the leadership (though soon to regard it closed as far as the base was concerned) created a kind of time-bomb in the leadership which was to explode when the right combination of circumstances occurred.

Attempts at illegal resistance

The course of events naturally confirmed the ultras in their opinion that another 'Thermidor' was in full swing. They tried to salvage what they could from the situation, so that the revolution could be continued underground. On 1 October, the anniversary of the People's Republic, an open letter appeared in the capital from a 'special central committee', which was taken up again two days later by the remaining supporters of the 'fourth headquarters' in an article entitled 'The snorting warhorse'.[8] Others, however, went further than a battle of words. After the arrest of all the important leaders of the 'May 16' group in Peking, Wang En-yu, the second-in-command to Wu Chuan-chi, encouraged his remaining followers with these words: 'Be prepared to fight a guerrilla war: the sites have already been selected! . . . Let us look again at things in ten years!'[9] Bands of guerrillas were still holding out in several places, urban as well as rural, after the end of 1967. Some of them persisted and proved troublesome until long after the Ninth Party Congress.

The continuation of the Leftist movement in the provinces

While some movement towards a solution of the problem of Leftism seemed to have been made in Peking, ideological confusion was still prevalent in a large number of areas in the provinces. 'Overground' organizations were still advocating extreme Leftist policies until the end of 1967; this situation arose firstly because of ignorance of developments at the centre, and later because of conscious opposition. When Mao Tse-tung made a tour of the provinces in September, he was brought into direct confrontation with this problem in, among other places, his native province of Hunan.[10] The ultra-Left was still very active in an organized form among the pupils of the secondary schools in Changsha. Mao attempted to introduce some calm to the situation, but, as usual, took no definite stand. When a large number of Left-wing groups came together to form the 'Provincial Proletarian Union',[11] it looked as though they were going through the usual preliminary steps for the formation of a Revolutionary Committee, for which unity was the first required condition. But when the Union announced its programme a few weeks later, it became obvious that the direction of its policies was completely different, and was guided by the opinion that the real revolution was still to begin. On 17 November a direct attack was made on the Preparation Group for a Revolutionary Committee, claiming that, while it wanted to replace 'the dynasty', it left the 'feudal system' untouched. At a congress of the alliance held on 21 December, one of the resolutions even remarked: '. . . at the moment, throughout the country, high and low, there is a counter-revolutionary adverse current, directed against the ultra-Left'.

An analysis of the whole Cultural Revolution, written in similar spirit, appeared on 12 January 1968, under the title 'Whither China?' It was said to be by a pupil of the No. 1 secondary school, and was accompanied by the note:

This is a project on which we should like your opinion. Should it be published now? Could it be used as a 'Declaration of the formation of Commune of the ultra-Left'? How should it be edited? After reading this project, please note your opinions in the margins left on both sides, and return it to the distributor before the 20th.

This document constitutes one of the most theoretically consistent, extensive and interesting analyses of the views of the ultra-Left. It is composed as follows:

I. 'SCIENTIFIC FORESIGHT'

Reference to the way in which Mao has outlined the 'vision' of a new society to Lin in his famous letter of 7 May 1966; the way in which he would have made an example of the political organization of the Commune of Paris to his people from June 1966 in Peking to January 1967 in Shanghai. The realization of this vision of the future cannot be brought about peacefully: 'The rule of the new bureaucratic-bourgeoisie must be overthrown by force in order to solve the problem of political power.'

II. 'STORM OF JANUARY REVOLUTION'

At the centre, power seizure was made in the Ministry of Finance, Broadcasting Affairs Administration Bureau, and other departments, and the power of Li Hsien-nien, Chen I, Tan Chen-lin and the like as well as that of Chou En-lai who represented them, also fell greatly. To whose hands did the assets go at that time? They went to the hands of the people, who were full of boundless enthusiasm and who were organized to take over the urban administrations and the Party, government, financial and cultural powers in the industrial, commercial, communications and other systems . . .

In that short period some places actually realized, though not very thoroughly, the content of the People's Commune of China and society was in a state of mass dictatorship, similar to that of the Paris Commune.

III. 'REVOLUTIONARY COMMITTEES'

The three-in-one combination is the concrete content of revolutionary committees. The putting forward of the three-in-one combination amounts to reinstatement of the bureaucrats already toppled in the January revolution. Inevitably it will be the form of political power to be usurped by the bourgeoisie, at which the Army and the local bureaucrats are to play a leading role ... Yet the January storm has not touched yet the vital problem of all revolutions, the problem of the Army. Thus it may be seen that the revolution lacked depth and remained at a low stage of development.

IV. 'FEBRUARY ADVERSE CURRENT'

Intoxicated by his victory of February–March, Chou En-lai – at present the general representative of China's Red capitalist class – hurriedly tried to set up revolutionary committees in all parts of the country. If this bourgeois plan had been fulfilled, the proletariat would have retreated to its grave. Therefore, without waiting for the establishment of all the revolutionary committees, the Central Cultural Revolution Group issued the order to hit back. After that the great August local revolutionary war in the country began to ferment.

V. 'LOCAL DOMESTIC REVOLUTIONARY WAR OF AUGUST'

August was the month when the power of the revolutionary mass organizations rapidly grew, while that of the bureaucrats again dropped to zero. A short-lived and unstable redistribution of 'assets and powers' took place for a second time. Once more society tried to realize the great 'People's Commune of China'. Once more people tried to solve the problem raised in the 7 May directive, namely, the Army should be a big school and workers, peasants and students should all learn military art.

VI. 'THE SETBACK IN SEPTEMBER'

But because the revolutionary forces of the proletariat have been greatly strengthened, the retreat has not ended in a 'rout' as the retreat in February had. The bourgeoisie cannot come near to swal-

lowing the revolution as they did in March. The revolutionary forces
in Hunan which bombarded Chou En-lai were not annihilated.
Instead, they have formed *Sheng-wu-lien* and have made progress in
certain respects.

VII. 'ENLIGHTENMENT OF THE POLITICAL THINKING OF THE WORKING CLASS'

Sheng-wu-lien was in fact born of the experience of the (people-
run) civil offence and armed defence command headquarters – a
form of mass dictatorship of the January revolution. It is a power
organ of mass dictatorship of a higher order than those of January
and August. It may be compared to the soviet of the January revolution in USSR when power was usurped by the bourgeoisie, while
the preparatory group for the provincial revolutionary committee
(*Sheng-ko-ch'ou*) is comparable to the bourgeois Provisional Government of that time ... *Sheng-wu-lien* is a newborn sprout comparable to the soviets. It is the embryonic form of a more mature
'commune' than that of January and August.

VIII/IX. 'REFUTATION OF THE REACTIONARY "DOCTRINE OF SECOND REVOLUTION": REFUTATION OF "LEFTIST" DOCTRINE OF ONE REVOLUTION'

We are for continuous revolution, but also believe in revolution by
stages. The commune of the 'ultra-Left faction' will not conceal its
viewpoints and intentions. We publicly declare that our object of
establishing the People's Commune of China can be attained only
by overthrowing the bourgeois dictatorship and revisionist system
of the revolutionary committee with brute force. Let the new
bureaucratic bourgeoisie tremble before the true socialist revolution that shakes the world! What the proletariat can lose in this
revolution is only their chains, what they gain will be the whole
world!

The China of tomorrow will be the world of the 'Commune'.

Long live the doctrine of Mao Tse-tung![12]

This document did not fail to produce a reaction. Confidence
in the masses (the May 16 Circular had said that they would
educate themselves) reached its limits a week later. On 18 January the official party paper of Hunan launched a fierce attack
on the ultra-Left wing. On 21 January a 'meeting for the study
of the thoughts of Mao Tse-tung' began, at which the Party

leadership itself sharply criticized the Union in the presence of a number of rebel delegates. Kang Sheng, Chiang Ching, Chou En-lai and Yao Wen-yuan were among the speakers.[13]

The fate of the ultras in Hunan was now also sealed. On 8 April the Revolutionary Committee was finally set up, consisting largely of members of the preparation group who had been so sharply criticized by the Union. The military commander who had initiated the counter-offensive became chairman.

16: The Calming Down of the 'Pens' and the 'Guns'

Chiang Ching weary

After a considerable number of their younger associates had discredited themselves as ultras, the older leaders of the radical Left wing now started to beat a swift retreat. The 'pens' and 'guns' which had initiated the anti-bureaucracy criticism by encouraging unlimited mass mobilization, now found themselves compelled to retreat to their former positions, so that the political atmosphere could cool. This was especially true in the case of the 'pens' Chiang Ching and Chen Po-ta, though they, as known radicals, had led the offensive against the ultras. Nevertheless, they were to some degree compromised by the purge which had now become necessary of their own Cultural Revolution Group. Chiang Ching, in particular, seemed 'depressed' by events. After leading the attack on the 'fourth headquarters' she more or less disappeared from public life for a long period. Only once did she figure prominently during this time, and that was at an occasion it would have been difficult to avoid: a reception for the revolutionary representatives of cultural organizations. Her speech on this occasion was, compared with her previous speeches, notable for its lack of vigour. She concluded it by saying, 'I am tired and was unable to prepare myself for this speech, so do not regard my remarks as being in any way definitive statements. I want to exchange ideas with you, and if I have been incomplete or wrong, you must criticize me.'[1]

After this she ceased for a long time to play a prominent part in public life, and, unlike Lin Piao, Chen Po-ta, Chou En-lai and Kang Sheng, she was not elected a member of the Standing Committee at the Ninth Party Congress of 1969.

Chen Po-ta brushes up his knowledge of agriculture

Chen Po-ta, whether of his own accord or not, was relegated to a position of secondary importance as well. All but one of his younger Peking colleagues from similar social and academic spheres, who had been in control of the mass-media organs in the propaganda division and in the Cultural Revolution Group, had been discredited because of ultra-Left deviationism. The services in which he had enjoyed greatest influence, together with the ultras, were all reorganized. Independent editorial work on the *Red Flag* was suspended for six months. In fact, it was not only his contacts with people who later discredited themselves which harmed his position, but also his direct or indirect support of the disputed ideas. It was his acquaintanceship with the history of the socialist movement which had suggested the model of the Paris Commune, which had been so comprehensively abused by his colleagues and himself. He now returned to his special field of study: the collectivization of agriculture,[2] where, according to Klein and Clark, he was the first to introduce the term 'people's communes'. Some time before this he had been heard to observe that the capital had become a very chaotic place where it was impossible to think clearly. He now retired to the country to take up his agricultural studies again. Basing himself on his new experience, he now recommended further collectivization of agriculture. Jean Esmein writes:

The official viewpoint, and the starting point for any commentary on the subject, appeared in a leading article published in the *People's Daily* on 23 November. This article probably reproduced the contents of the report put together by Chen Po-ta for the work meeting of the Central Committee, which had taken place from 21 to 27 October 1967. The article was militant in tone, criticizing the fatal policies of the past and urging the continuation of the revolution by 'new people'. It condemned revisionism in China and the bad influence on the socialist education campaign by the 'Chinese Khrushchev'. It appealed to the proletariat and the former poor and semi-poor peasants 'to seek refuge in the tremendous forces of the dictatorship of the proletariat, to strengthen and develop the socialist system of collective ownership of property and to set out on the way to collective prosperity'.[3]

It was hardly surprising that Chen's insistence on further collectivization (which entailed the abolition of all remaining forms of individual exploitation) and the taking-over of power by the radicals within the present organizational structure of the rural areas (which was to lead to much unnecessary division of opinion) met with resistance from the 'realists'.

There were other problems to be dealt with first in the agriculture of the country. The growing influence of radical-Left outsiders in some of the new temporary administrative bodies in the rural areas had led to all kinds of extreme measures being undertaken at very short notice: complete collectivization, abolition of private property, equality of wages, egalitarian distribution, and so on. The forced introduction of such methods, however, did the movement more harm than good. Many poor peasants had already become suspicious of the Red Guards because of the excesses which had taken place after 1966 (including destruction of traditional objects, forced assimilation of cultural minorities by introducing uniformity in clothing, usage, and so on). This resulted not so much in open resistance to the campaign, but rather in quiet sabotage or simple disregard for the new measures. In the meantime, agricultural production schedules fell seriously behind.

The realities of the situation could hardly be ignored by the senior members of the administration, and the programme of radical reform had to be suspended until conditions returned to normal. Discussion at grass-roots level, however, continued for years.[4] The radicals cited an earlier principle of Mao's to the effect that a difficult economic situation should not become an excuse for postponing changes in the production programme; on the contrary, the measures should be carried out immediately. Chen Po-ta wisely refrained from using this argument to defend his policies in public. According to some reports, he even expressed self-criticism during December 1967, though it is not clear what period was referred to in the criticism. What is certain, however, is that the last remaining member of his radical Peking group, Chi Pen-yu, fell from power in the spring of 1968.

It was thus that the wave of purges which followed the affair of the 'fourth headquarters' ended just before it reached Chen Po-ta.

And Lin Piao?

We thus come full circle and return to the person who, like Chen Po-ta, had come to prominence at the time of the Great Leap Forward and had since risen to the top: Lin Piao. Although no one would have thought of criticizing him,[5] let alone demanding his self-criticism, there was a risk that the elimination of the 'Leftist current' would weaken his position. He was forced to dissociate himself from two of his closest colleagues, Hsiao Hua, head of the General Political Department (the other was Yang Cheng-wu, chief-of-staff), because of the support given by the propaganda media and the political department of the army to the 'drag out' campaign. Several younger military propaganda specialists disappeared along with Hsiao Hua, among them the director of the *Liberation Army Daily*, Chao I-ya. And although it is true that Lin did dissociate himself from the discredited policies (he tried to re-establish himself in the political centre from mid-August onwards), there was no doubt that he had been closely associated with the drafting of those policies. His sympathy for the 'drag out' campaign had been apparent, and even now he still had his long-held aim in mind: that Left-wing control of the army apparatus (especially regional) had to be strengthened if the Cultural Revolution was to be crowned with decisive victory. A political working group was established by him within the army command during August. The working group was not dominated by conservatives, as the previous military Cultural Revolution Group had been, nor was it in the hands of the present Cultural Revolution Group of the Party. In fact, it was completely staffed by trusted members of Lin's own central army administration: his wife Yeh Chun (already *de facto* director of the secretariat of the Military Commission for some time past), Wu Fa-hsien (air force), and Chiu Hui-tso (logistics). After Hsiao Hua's elimination in September, the group kept a relatively low profile, while giving support to Mao's programme, which was aimed at solving the problems with the army by more subtle means than before.

Two lines of action developed from this policy. Firstly, the army was called upon to organize local study groups, and to get away from the stereotyped pattern of Left–Right representation. Secondly, it was asked to continue to lend its support to the Left, but no longer to any specific groups, which was an attempt to break up mistaken local commitments to the Right or ultra-Left, and to restore the role of arbitration in the three-in-one combinations. Lin's supporters, however, continued to use other means to bring the regional units under control. By the spring of 1967, the commanders of the military regions of Chengtu, Peking, Sinkiang, Lanchow and Inner Mongolia, and the commanders of the military districts of Liaoning, Kirin, Honan, Kiangsu and Chekiang, were removed from their posts. Immediately after the Wuhan incident, control of the four military districts of Honan, Hunan, Hupei and Kiangsi was taken over by the centrally-commanded army corps. According to other sources, almost half the total of the commanders of the military regions and districts were replaced by the central army command during the course of 1967. In addition, reorganization of the local military commands was reported to have taken place in a number of provinces, including Anhwei, Chekiang, Honan, Hopei, Hunan, Inner Mongolia, Kiangsi, Shenshi, Szuchuan and Chinghai.[6] Clearly, this policy could hardly fail to create strong opposition, especially since it was probably carried out with little tact or discrimination.

After the elimination of the 'Leftist current', some of the discredited or deposed commanders saw an opportunity of rehabilitating themselves. Complaints were made by them in a number of directions about Lin's closest colleagues. Complaints were lodged with the remaining regional commanders, the Party leadership and the government, and notably with the office of Chou En-lai, which had always maintained relatively good relations with the older military commanders. It was not long before complaints and reports began to accumulate in Peking. The climate seemed right for a discussion of the behaviour of the radical Left in the army leadership, especially after February 1968, when a renewed offensive against the 'Leftist current' seemed necessary and possible. Attacks on Lin Piao's closest associate, chief-of-staff Yang Cheng-wu, soon forced the Minister of Defence to dissociate himself from him, too. About three meetings of the Central Committee were held during March at which Yang was discredited. Kang Sheng – who was gaining influence as rapidly as the radicals were losing it and who often gave the impression of acting as spokesman for Chou En-lai – had this to say on 27 March about Yang's 'offences': 'These are only what is already known to us . . . In the future, when our comrades will continue to expose him, I believe that more serious problems will be found.'[7] Broadly speaking, the mistakes committed by Yang were considered to be the following:

1. He was reproached with being partly responsible for the misleading propaganda of the ultra-Left, and, in the discussions with his predecessor Lo Jui-ching, he was said to have limited himself to exalting Mao Tse-tung;

2. He was said to have encouraged Left-wing ultras like Wang Li to attack 'trustworthy Maoist military leaders' after the Wuhan incident;

3. He was said to have gone too far in replacing regional units with central ones, and to have replaced a number of local commanders with his own supporters.

4. During the Civil War and the Resistance against Japan, his influence had been divisive, he had tried to form a faction and had exaggerated his part in the revolution.

It is obvious that these criticisms could have been made with equal justice of Yang's immediate superior, Lin Piao. Hindsight makes it seem possible that some of the accusations were consciously intended for Mao's deputy. According to Lin's biographer, Ebon, certain Party papers called, during this period, for 'the exposure of the one who supports Yang'.[8] This would explain why, as Harvey Nelsen says,[9] Lin suddenly came out of his Olympian isolation, in which he had lived in the style of Mao, and took part himself in the campaign against Yang by delivering sharp personal attacks. He then made considerable attempts to have a conciliatory attitude towards the regional commanders adopted within the army command. A line of action was declared, which laid down that, 'It is utterly wrong to spread feelings of dissatisfaction with fraternal army units . . . Party committees within the P.L.A. at all levels must . . . foster unity between army units from outside regions and local armed forces.'

In addition, Lin set himself to deal personally with provinces such as Shansi, in which disputes between the Leftists and the regional commanders, or between the moderates and the central commanders, were still happening – which, considering Lin's position and personality, was a very unusual procedure.

What is striking about the situation is that the structure of the Lin Piao faction, which was to appear later, was identical to that of the present Yang Cheng-wu group. And the members of that faction were all to operate from positions they already occupied. The group surrounding the chief-of-staff, Yang Cheng-wu, had affiliations which extended in three directions: towards Lin himself (they had a past in common), towards the garrison of Peking and the North China region, and towards the most centralized army unit – the air force – from which Yang had come. The relevance of what was taking place at that time to the formation of future factions is such that it demands very precise understanding.

Yang Cheng-wu had caused the 'strong' regional commanders to be prejudiced against himself, especially the commanders in Nanking (Hsu Shih-yu) and Shenyang (Chen Hsi-lien). Yang's deposal was also achieved with the connivance of Chou En-lai. His successor appeared as a compromise choice between Lin's central army command and the 'strong' regional commanders; this was Huang Yung-sheng who was the regional commander of Canton, and also an old war comrade of Lin's. When the 'Leftist current' was revived within the army command of Lin and Huang, during 1970–71, causing a confrontation with Chou En-lai, they were opposed by Chen Hsi-lien and Hsu Shih-yu.

The second person to disappear from the scene during this period was Yu Li-chin. During the Wuhan incident he had opposed the local military commander Chen Tsai-tao in the name of Lin Piao. Yu was the first political commissioner of the air force and deputy commander. His chief was Wu Fa-hsien, an associate of Lin's, and the centre of the 'Lin Piao conflict' of 1971 was to be the air force. After the elimination of Wu Fa-hsien, Chen Tsai-tao was reinstated in 1972.

The third man to be removed was Fu Chung-pi. According to some reports, as garrison commander of Peking, he had been responsible for the arbitrary arrest of political opponents during that period. The matter seems to have been referred to Chiang Ching, who promptly got in touch with Hsieh Fu-chih, chairman of the Peking Revolutionary Committee, who in turn took the matter to Chou En-lai. Fu Chung-pi was succeeded by Cheng Wei-shan. The confrontation with the military Left wing was also to start in Peking in 1970: after the elimination of Chen Po-ta in the autumn of that year, Cheng Wei-shan and Li Hsueh-feng (from the Northern region) were deposed during the winter, leading to a reduction in Lin's influence and the reappearance at the centre of affairs of Hsieh Fu-chih and Chou En-lai.

Thus March 1968 was the prelude to September 1971. What, then, was the current position of the central figure of Chou En-lai? Although he had still not appeared in public as the accuser of the ultra-Left, there is no doubt that his support was for the regional commanders who were under attack. In April he made the following statement: 'Capitalist-roaders are of course found in individual army units; we cannot say that all army units are without capitalist-roaders. But such units are few and isolated . . . But capitalist-roaders infiltrated Party and government organs and so there are relatively more capitalist-roaders there.'[10] Similar remarks were made by Chou and Kang Sheng in July, on the occasion of a reception for the new military leaders of Wuhan. As far as Chou was concerned, the situation was still some way from being satisfactory.

17: The Proletariat in First Place

The students: from vanguard to rearguard

If the pupils of the secondary schools and the students had acted as shock troops in the opening phases of the Cultural Revolution, they had now become a rearguard which had lost touch with the main army. The corrections in the course of the movements which had been made in September 1967 and in March 1968 had had no effect on them – on the contrary. The universities of Pei-ta and Tsinghua, (especially the latter), which had led so courageously at the beginning of the Cultural Revolution, now lagged stubbornly behind. In the meantime, factionalism at Tsinghua had reached unprecedented proportions. The alliances which had been formed at the instigation of the leadership of the Cultural Revolution had again collapsed. From 14 April 1967 the campus had been seriously divided between the (older) Chingkangshan Regiment (called after the first area to become a Chinese Soviet in 1928–34) and the splinter 14 April Chingkangshan Regiment. The split had occurred because of the so-called cadre question. The Chingkangshan Regiment (led by the rebel of the first hour, Kuai Ta-fu) was of the opinion that virtually all the old Party cadres should be removed from positions of influence, while the 14 April Regiment supported the official standpoint that only a few need be dismissed. During the long hot summer of 1967 this division became confused again. Both groups tried to outdo each other in ultra-revolutionary activity; the first group was especially active during the 'drag out' campaign, while the second played a big part in the campaign against foreign embassies. Both groups also maintained close contact with the members of the ultra-Left wing of the Cultural Revolution Group. When the ultra-Left was denounced by Chiang Ching in September, the reaction of the two groups varied from outraged innocence (Kuai Ta-fu: 'What ultra-Left politics?'), to apparent co-operation in the shape of a cumbersome new alliance along the lines laid down by Mao Tse-tung.

By the end of December 1967, however, the intrigues had started again: Kuai Ta-fu mobilized his forces in support of Chi Pen-yu (at that time the last remaining young ultra of the Peking faction still in the Cultural Revolution Group) when the matter of his candidature came up again for discussion during the reorganization of the Peking Revolutionary Committee. At the same time, he tried to use Chi's prestige to bring about a resumption of his own propaganda campaign on the campus. On 21 December, the chairman of the Revolutionary Committee, Hsieh Fu-chih, finally summoned the rival groups to him, and urged Chi Pen-yu to denounce this move: ('This time I shall read out my speech, so that none of you will have the slightest reason for taking it as an excuse for faction-forming.')

Meanwhile, the political situation had again become as confused as it had been the previous year. On the one hand, the leadership of the Cultural Revolution had dissociated itself from 'Leftist excesses', while on the other it had to deal with a new 'February counter-current', which risked invalidating the whole movement. There was also a fear that the army might gain too great an influence over affairs, while at the same time there was continuing stagnation of the mass movement within the Party. This lack of headway explains why the Red Guards were still allowed so much freedom for their activities. While it was true that pupils and students had returned to their educational establishments, their fight was not limited to the educational field. Indeed, it was not aimed at education at all; the important thing for the students was the constant search for excuses to recommence the struggle all over again, both within and outside the educational institutions.

Guerrilla war and civil war in Tsinghua[1]

The elimination of such ultras as Chi Pen-yu and the trio of Yang–Yu–Fu about March 1968 did not put an end to the activities of the radicals like Kuai Ta-fu. On the contrary, since

such high-ranking 'Rightists' had been so successful in disguis-
ing themselves as 'ultra-Leftists', it was very necessary to be extremely vigilant – thus ran the reasoning of the radicals. To discover whether the 14 April Regiment harboured traitors, Kuai
Ta-fu caused two of his opponents to be abducted on the anniversary of the split. They were interrogated 'thoroughly', and
when this yielded no results, they were beaten up. When this
method also failed, 'confessions' were constructed from tape-
recordings. These 'confessions' were then used in the propaganda offensive against the 14 April Regiment to support
accusations that the regiment was composed of 'reactionary
supporters of Chiang Kai-shek'. In retaliation, the 14 April
Regiment abducted a leader of the Chingkangshan Regiment,
with similar intent.

No one taking active part in the conflict was safe. The most
committed supporters of each group barricaded themselves into
buildings, and the first ultimatums were exchanged. What had at
first been minor incidents soon became commando actions, and
small-scale guerrilla skirmishes escalated into tactical warfare.
Violence became more frequent along the perimeters of the
areas occupied by the two groups on the campus. The first fights
were fought with bare fists, but clubs, spears and swords soon
came into use. Hand-to-hand fighting was superseded by siege
tactics, during which bows and arrows and giant catapults,
using stones and bicycle tyres, were brought into the attack. Not
a week passed without its dead and wounded. On 23 April there
was a fight over an ambulance, on 29 April over two supply
trucks of rice, on 2 May over the violation of a truce, on 16 May
over a failure to exchange prisoners. On 30 May, the combat
entered a completely new phase, when the Chingkangshan Regiment stormed an isolated building held by the 14 April Regiment
– first using an improvised bridge between upper floors (which
failed), then with a tractor converted into a tank, and finally by
simply setting fire to the building. Thanks to the intervention of
people living close by, the outcome was no more serious than
the smoking-out of the beleaguered garrison.

The use of home-made tanks was countered by the use of
home-made anti-tank guns (and real ones, which had been

stolen in south China from a consignment of arms intended for Vietnam and brought to the capital via various illegal channels), revolvers, rifles, automatic weapons, 'rockets', a 'cannon', Molotov cocktails, dynamite, hand grenades and mines. Knowledge of arms manufacture is widespread in China, because of preparations for a possible people's war, and it certainly presented no problems at Tsinghua Technical University.

It seems almost superfluous to add that almost all the moderate students had withdrawn from the battle in the meantime. The situation had been thus reduced to a straightforward fight between the 200 students of the Chingkangshan Regiment and the 100 students of the 14 April Regiment, who were still holding out in one isolated building. About 100 outsiders of varied political loyalties took part in the battle on both sides.

The fighting spread to other universities and secondary schools, and finally to the town itself. During April and May, the bloody street battles claimed hundreds of victims. The student and workers' rebellion of May 1968 in Paris was an occasion for a closing of ranks for demonstrations of solidarity; it was also an opportunity to show that Peking was not to be outdone by Paris.

Appeals by the leadership of the Cultural Revolution to lay down arms were ignored. On 3 and 24 July there were appeals by the Central Committee itself, but the rebels claimed that these were addressed to the provinces of Kweichow and Shansi (where Revolutionary Committees were being organized), and not to Peking, where the fight was against 'Kuomintang agents'.

This was the situation on 26 July, when the workers and soldiers of the capital, with the approval of the leaders of the Cultural Revolution, decided to put an end to the violent faction-fighting between the students.

Workers and soldiers intervene

The universities of Pei-ta and Tsinghua had already been visited some days earlier by workers who had gone there to appeal to the students to stop the violence. They had, however, been forbidden entry to the grounds by armed students. Whereupon the workers of the Hsinhua printing works, known for their ideological sophistication, decided, after consultation with colleagues from about sixty other factories, to organize a demonstration of protest around the university grounds. As soon as the students heard about this, they blocked all access routes to the university. Together with the 'Thoughts of Mao Tse-tung Propaganda Teams' of soldiers, the workers now organized a much larger demonstration, which was to last until the students laid down their arms. On the morning of the 27th, seven groups of tens of thousands of workers and soldiers, accompanied by thousands and even hundreds of thousands of other followers, went to the grounds of the university. They were armed only with the *Little Red Book* and banners bearing appeals from the Central Committee and quotations from Mao Tse-tung, such as, 'Use arguments, not weapons!' In the face of such superior strength and after a short discussion, the students withdrew to two buildings, and the huge crowds flooded into the grounds, from where they called out to the students in chorus, 'Use arguments, not weapons!'

The first to respond were, obviously, the rebels of the 14 April Regiment, who were somewhat weary after a siege of 100 days. The workers and soldiers dismantled their stronghold, disarmed them and gave them safe-conduct to a less dangerous part of the campus. The Chingkangshan Regiment, however, refused to lay down its weapons, and while the workers and soldiers continued to demonstrate peacefully in the pouring rain, they were pelted with stones by the students. Three times, groups of 'lancers' armed with spears tried to break out. During the course of the day, about five demonstrators were killed, 731 wounded and 143 taken prisoner. Some demonstrators began to lose their self-control, but were held back by their comrades, and the demonstration continued simply to apply persistent moral pressure, a method of making one's point which is valued as much in the Confucian tradition as in Maoism as a means of solving internal social conflicts. Towards the evening, the students were ready to negotiate. Kuai Ta-fu appealed personally to Mao Tse-tung to condemn the 'intervention from outside'. That same night together with Nieh Yuan-tzu and three other prominent Red

Guards, he was received by the Party Chairman. But instead of welcoming them as rebels of the first hour, Mao expressed his disappointment about the way in which the rebellion had lost its way, and defended the right of the workers and soldiers to intervene. Early next morning, Kuai returned to Tsinghua to negotiate a surrender. However, he allowed his followers to remain under the impression that Mao approved of their actions and directed a number of them to other educational institutions. When the workers and soldiers came to clean out the building later that morning, they found that a large part of the incriminating material and much of the stock of arms had disappeared. What remained was, in any case, impressive enough:

5 semi-automatic rifles	2 home-made tanks
57 rifles	(armoured tractors)
31 pistols	50 bottles of poison gas
12 home-made rifles	185 bottles of acid and other
5 small-bore guns	caustic chemicals
5 air guns	15 large knives and bayonets
1,038 bullets	1,435 spears
688 hand grenades	380 short knives
52 home-made cannon	9 metal whips (made from
9 bags of explosives (used as	fine chains)
an anti-tank weapon)	25 cannon shells
168 home-made mines	2 type-59 semi-automatic rifles
16 packs of dynamite	1 type-56 sub-machine gun
	('tommy gun')

Some of the buildings housed complete workshops for the manufacture of weapons, communications control rooms, infirmaries complete with hospital equipment and wounded, cells which contained a number of prisoners who had been ill-treated, and even the rotting corpses of rebels who had obviously been dead for some time.

Proletarianization of education

When the moderates among the students returned to university, they were met by the workers and soldiers of the 'Thoughts of

Mao Tse-tung Propaganda Team', who were to work together with the students in drawing up plans for radical changes in education. 'Mao Tse-tung Thought' study groups, which had already been functioning in other sectors from 1967, began to be formed at the same time in educational institutions. These combined ideological education with attempts to better relations where these had become strained.

After Kuai Ta-fu had claimed that his actions had been approved, Mao emphasized once more that, on the contrary, it was the intervention of the workers and soldiers at the university which had been approved. He did this by sending a basket of mangoes, a present from the Foreign Minister of Pakistan, to Tsinghua at the beginning of August; the basket was exhibited almost as a religious relic at the university. This gesture attracted a lot of publicity, which also entailed giving more publicity to what was happening in the universities of Peking.

At the end of August there appeared an important article by Yao Wen-yuan which stated that leadership must be exercised by the working class in every field – therefore, in education as well. On a national scale, a radical reorganization of the educational system was initiated, to change it from an élitist system to a proletarian one. This involved fundamental changes: education not only became more practical and more condensed, but the possibility of a 'new mandarin class' being created also came under radical attack. Admission to university was to depend no longer on the possession of certain diplomas alone (and thus on ability to adapt to the values of university, automatically favouring particular milieux), but on the recommendation of the living- and work-units of the candidate students. In future, it was decided that all pupils leaving secondary school should go to work for a number of years; if they then displayed suitable intellectual capacities, a practical attitude, and the right social mentality, they might then be sent to university.

Proletarianization of the bureaucracy

In addition to the educational institutions, a number of administrative services were also placed in the hands of the workers, which produced considerable changes in this sphere. Methods of working were profoundly simplified and the size of the bureaucratic apparatus substantially reduced. Many of the public services in Peking eventually became no more than a fraction of their former size.

At the same time, on 7 May 1968, a new system of re-education was set up in the province with the oldest Revolutionary Committee, Heilungkiang. The old Party schools were replaced by 'May 7' schools for cadres, named after the famous letter sent by Mao to Lin on 7 May 1966 which had outlined the problems to be faced. The cadre schools were intended for all those in important positions, with the exception of the aged, sick and invalid, so that they could be transposed from their comfortable positions at least once every five years for between six and twenty-four months and confronted with the harsh realities among which the proletariat and the peasantry had to live and work. To this end, a number of spartan establishments were set up in which the daily life was an exact replica of the life of the poor peasants in the interior and where all the work (from hewing or baking building bricks, working in the kitchens, cleaning latrines, hoeing the fields, to the installation of electricity, etc.) was to be carried out by the officials there. The stay in such establishments also involved intensive self-examination and ideological study, so that alienation from work and the everyday life of the common man would be broken down.

There was also a parallel development on a strictly political level, which aimed at the rehabilitation of the principle of the 'dictatorship of the proletariat', to counteract 'ultra-democratic' tendencies. A considerable amount of difficulty was created by both the Left and the Right since the exaltation of the Paris Commune in 1966 and 1967 had led to the introduction of 'Western-style elections' in a large number of places. This, together with the use of Worker Propaganda Teams, meant that the system of general elections was once again combined with a system of consultation with the centrally-controlled preparation groups for the Revolutionary Committees. Control from the capital was also strengthened again, after a period in which it had been consciously relaxed. It was still fairly easy under the new system to propose someone as candidate for a particular function. But an election committee, controlled politically, could easily influence the final result through repeated rounds of an election, by offering support to some candidates and withholding it from others.

The two most important 'Leftist' groups (students and cadres) were thus brought back under social control, and the political reconstruction had started. The emphasis had moved from the first to the later phases in the triple process of 'struggle-criticism-transformation'.

Part Six
The Ninth Party Congress

Comrade Lin Piao has consistently held high the great red banner of Mao Tse-tung Thought and has most loyally and resolutely carried out and defended Comrade Mao Tse-tung's proletarian revolutionary line. Comrade Lin Piao is Comrade Mao Tse-tung's close comrade-in-arms and successor.

The Constitution of the Communist Party of China (14 April 1969), Chapter 1

18: The High Noon of Lin Piao

The Twelfth Plenum of the Eighth Central Committee

During the summer of 1968 China appeared to be regaining her political equilibrium. After a period of struggle and competition for power, the Cultural Revolution had now entered a phase of self-examination and reform. The various social forces were becoming more stable. This was also true of the Maoist mass organizations. Though they had of course squandered a great deal of goodwill because of the ultra-revolutionary activities of the Red Guards, they were now accepted as partners in the social structure in many places. The majority of the old Party and administrative cadres had also been able to rehabilitate themselves, although a number of them had disappeared for good. The movement towards stabilization was especially noticeable in the People's Liberation Army which had acted as arbitrator between the younger Maoists and the old cadres. During the summer of 1968 and for a long time afterwards, there were still clashes, sometimes bloody, between the ultra-revolutionaries and the military as the representatives of law and order, but these no longer occupied the centre of the stage. The role of the army, or of its various components, was no longer a subject for discussion. On the anniversary of the army, 1 August, a propaganda campaign was organized to help to strengthen confidence in the army: a sure sign that attempts were being made to restore normality. The conflict between the central and regional army commands disappeared beneath the surface for the time being.

The stabilization of the situation was expressed further in the extension of the Revolutionary Committees, although this was not achieved without some problems. On 7 September 1968 the last takeover of power became fact. On this occasion, speaking at a mass meeting, Chiang Ching stressed the fact that, in spite of the great achievements of the young people in the early and middle phases of the Cultural Revolution, the leadership of the movement finally depended on the workers. The military were also mentioned by her, but only in the context of their supporting role for the workers. This was some way away from being a true statement of the situation, since she must have been aware that the part played by the Maoist mass movements in the Revolutionary Committees had steadily diminished, while that of the army had increased.

The formation of the Revolutionary Committees had taken too long for the Ninth Party Congress to be held just after the anniversary of the People's Republic on 10 October, as had been originally expected from statements previously issued by the leadership. The Twelfth Plenum of the Eighth Central Committee was finally held, however, during the second half of October. Although the final communiqué was no less general than usual, it did confirm three obvious suppositions: Liu Shao-chi as 'hidden traitor, renegade and scab' was declared stripped of all his functions and expelled from the Party; Lin Piao became Mao's new deputy Party Chairman; both decisions were to be worked out in greater detail at the Ninth Party Congress to be held in a few months.

The Congress[1]

The Ninth Congress opened on 1 April 1969 – twelve and a half years, instead of the statutory five, after the Eighth. This fact, however, did not seem to carry any weight: the Congress finally confirmed Mao's triumphant victory in his efforts to prevent the sneaking restoration of the capitalist-type relationships after a lengthy battle in which he had been supported by a broadly-based mass movement.

Of the 1,512 delegates (a record number) many were newcomers to the national political scene. The lower average level of education among the delegates demonstrates the strengthening of the representation of the 'ordinary man' – peasants and workers – in contrast to previous congresses. But the majority of them were not chosen by the Party base, as they had been in the past, but 'selected democratically' by the Party leadership in consultation with the lower-level organizations, such as the Revolutionary Committees.

This procedure, coupled with the sharp reaction to the previous period of 'ultra-democracy' and the state of dissolution in which the old Party structure still found itself, meant that the army was able to exercise a disproportionate influence on the Congress. The only Party branches still functioning were those of the General Political Department of the army, which also controlled the key positions in the newly-formed Revolutionary Committees.

Olive green, then, was the dominant colour among the groups of delegates who made their way on the opening day of the Congress to the Square of Heavenly Peace, where, almost two and a half years ago, Mao had given the signal to one and a half million Red Guards to spread the Cultural Revolution from the schools and universities to the rest of society. In contrast, though, prominent Guards were very thinly represented at this Congress, which was characterized by a return to law and order after the efforts to bring the excesses of the movement under control.

The agenda consisted of only three items: the political report of Lin Piao, the project for the new Party statutes, and the election of a new Central Committee. Two weeks had been allocated for the discussion of the first two items, and ten days for the third. The Congress would then be declared closed and the new Ninth Central Committee would hold its first Plenary Session. This would involve fewer people than the Congress and would be able to come down to the practical consideration of the actual application of policy.

Lin Piao's political report

At 62, Lin was the youngest of the first generation of Chinese leaders; although it had been much thinned out, this generation still held the reins of power. His speeches were composed of strings of quotations from Mao; his own political thinking was not very advanced in a Marxist sense. Most important, however, was the fact that he had so far not made any attempt to encroach on Mao's position.

In discussing the course of the Cultural Revolution his report went back to the the publication of Mao's considerations *On the correct handling of contradictions among the people* in 1957. His main thesis was: the class struggle, especially in its ideological aspects, is far from finished in China, and can even take on violent forms at certain periods. This opinion had not been shared by the group around Liu Shao-chi, though the validity of it had been totally proved by the Cultural Revolution. Of the various 'Leftist' movements, Lin had this to say: 'After the fall of Liu Shao-chi, his revisionist supporters and agents in various places continued to change their tactics, shouting slogans which were "Leftist" in form, but "Rightist" in essence.'

Later – after his fall in 1971 – it was said that such passages had been added by Yao Wen-yuan, in the name of Mao Tse-tung, while others had been written by Lin and Chen Po-ta in the draft but had been removed from the public speech. Other passages, however, were retained by Lin. According to these reports, at the time of the Congress, there were already serious differences of opinion on how the Cultural Revolution and its consequences had to be judged.

In his comments on the tasks ahead, Lin emphasized the role of the army for which he had very warm praise; it was in this context that he quoted Mao's words: 'From a Marxist point of view the army is the most important part of the state.' As far as the problems connected with the transformation of the super-structure were concerned, Lin asked his audience to 'learn from past mistakes in order to avoid future ones'. He recalled the sixteen-point resolution of August 1966 which had placed strict restrictions on the arbitrary treatment of opponents. He then turned his attention to the theory that mass movements would damage production: 'The Great Proletarian Cultural Revolution is a powerful driving force behind the social production processes in our country', and warned against self-satisfaction, again quoting Mao:

According to the Leninist viewpoint, the final victory of a socialist country not only requires the efforts of the proletariat and the broad masses of the people at home, but also involves the victory of the world revolution and the abolition of the system of exploitation of man by man over the whole globe, upon which all mankind will be emancipated. Therefore, it is wrong to speak lightly of the final victory of the revolution in our country; it runs counter to Leninism and does not conform to facts.

It was to become apparent to Lin Piao two and a half years later that the ovation he received from the Congress at the end of his speech did not constitute final victory either.

The new Party statutes

The delegates had already had the outline project for the new Party statutes in their possession for several months. The document had been discussed 'chapter by chapter and paragraph by paragraph' in the schools and universities, in the mines and factories, in the agricultural communes, and in offices. The suggestions which were made following these discussions were then communicated to the delegates, who in turn had them placed on the agenda of the Congress. In comparison with their previous form, the statutes had been simplified, and now consisted of twelve instead of sixty articles. The fact that the two previous sets of statutes had been prepared respectively by Teng Hsiao-ping (in 1956) and Liu Shao-chi (in 1945) no doubt had something to do with the substantial difference between those and the new ones, as well as the fact that the influence of the 'revisionist' Soviet example had now disappeared along with its attendant bureaucratic mentality.

The part of the statutes dealing with regulations contained sections on membership of the Party, on the principles of its organization, and also contained clauses on the central, military and base organizations of the Party.[2] More interesting, however, was the general programme to which the first part was entirely dedicated. This started as follows:

The Communist Party of China is the political party of the proletariat.

The basic programme of the Communist Party of China is the

complete overthrow of the bourgeoisie and all other exploiting classes, the establishment of the dictatorship of the proletariat in place of the dictatorship of the bourgeoisie and the triumph of socialism over capitalism. The ultimate aim of the Party is the realization of communism.

The Communist Party of China is composed of the advanced elements of the proletariat; it is a vigorous vanguard organization leading the proletariat and the revolutionary masses in the fight against the class enemy. The Communist Party of China takes Marxism-Leninism-Mao Tse-tung Thought as the theoretical basis guiding its thinking. Mao Tse-tung Thought is Marxism-Leninism of the era in which imperialism is heading for total collapse and socialism is advancing to world-wide victory.

For half a century now, in leading China's great struggle for accomplishing the new-democratic revolution, in leading her great struggle for socialist revolution and socialist construction and in the great struggle of the contemporary international communist movement against imperialism, modern revisionism and the reactionaries of various countries, Comrade Mao Tse-tung has integrated the universal truth of Marxism-Leninism with the concrete practice of revolution, inherited, defended and developed Marxism-Leninism and has brought it to a higher and completely new stage.

Comrade Lin Piao has consistently held high the great red banner of Mao Tse-tung Thought and has most loyally and resolutely carried out and defended Comrade Mao Tse-tung's proletarian revolutionary line. Comrade Lin Piao is Comrade Mao Tse-tung's close comrade-in-arms and successor.

The preamble did go further, but the quotation given above is sufficiently eloquent. Many of the formulae employed were to be exposed as not entirely correct after the Second Plenum of the new Central Committee.

The new Central Committee

On 15 April the Congress finally came to the third item on the agenda: the election of a new Central Committee. The press communiqué on this particular question stated:

The Congress proceeded with the third item on the agenda from 15 April and the delegates have been working conscientiously and with a great sense of responsibility. In accordance with the rules laid down by the praesidium of the Congress, candidates for membership and alternate membership of the Central Committee were first nominated by the delegations freely. After collecting the opinions of the delegations, the praesidium proposed a preliminary list of candidates and handed it to the delegations and, after full consultation, a list of candidates was worked out. A preliminary election by secret ballot was then conducted. After such repeated, full democratic consultation from below and from above, a final list of candidates was decided upon, and it was submitted by the praesidium to the Congress for final election by secret ballot.

This was the stage which had been reached by mid-day on 24 April. The delegates walked past the ballot-box in front of the hall in a long procession. The election of the Central Committee and the division of the functions within it again produced a small number of changes. These all tended to operate in the same direction: Lin Piao succeeded in increasing his sphere of influence, while Chou En-lai had some difficulty in maintaining his position; and, while it was true that the remaining five of the Cultural Revolution Group retained their total representation in the leadership, it had lost some of its importance through losing some of its original supporters. And whereas the Party apparatus had not yet been rebuilt, Lin had the central army apparatus behind him, while Chou enjoyed the support of sections of the central state departments. The five of the Cultural Revolution Group had largely lost their close contact with the Red Guards, insofar as these still existed here and there. Besides these, there was the influence of a number of regional bodies (military as well as administrative), but they could hardly be recognized as a group at the time.

The new Central Committee was composed of 170 permanent and 109 deputy members, which meant that it was twice as large as its predecessor. Only forty per cent of the members of the previous Central Committee were returned to the new one, so that the Ninth Central Committee had only twenty per cent of its members who had previous experience of the working of the Committee. The most interesting aspect of the new Central Committee was that it included a large number of peasants, soldiers and workers, who had taken part in the revolution from the beginning, but whose access to the highest organizations had always been blocked by the bureaucrats. They now took up between a fifth and a quarter of the places on the Committee. For this reason the Ninth Party Congress and the new Central Committee were received with great enthusiasm by the population at large. This situation implied a curious paradox; in the past, when the election of congress delegates had been formally more 'democratic', the masses of the social base had been less well represented, because of administrative hindrance, than at the present Congress, where the delegates had been more or less co-opted by the leadership.

The composition of the new Central Committee[3]

Although half of the members of the new Committee were military personnel, the actual representation of the *People's Liberation Army* made up only one-third of the Central Committee – a considerable, but by no means homogeneous, group. Only about half of these (one-sixth of the total) represented the central military authorities. In addition to these, there were between two and five representatives for each of the military regions, who together formed another sixth. In addition to this direct representation from the People's Liberation Army, another sixth of the members came from a military background, but had been delegated by other authorities, such as the Revolutionary Committees.

The Political Bureau elected by the Central Committee during its First Plenum was made up as follows: the chairman and vice-chairman of both bodies (and of the Party as a whole) were Mao and Lin respectively; other members of the Standing Committee were (in 'Chinese alphabetical order'): Chen Po-ta, Chou En-lai, and Kang Sheng. The other members of the Political Bureau were Yeh Chun, Yeh Chien-ying, Liu Po-cheng, Chiang Ching, Chu Teh, Hsu Shih-yu, Chen Hsi-lien, Li Hsien-nien, Li Tso-peng, Tung Pi-wu and Hsieh Fu-chih. At first sight, these sixteen fall into four or five groups. The first, and by far the strongest and most united, was that of Lin's closest colleagues from the central military apparatus : Yeh Chun (his wife and the director of his personal staff), Huang Yung-sheng (his chief-of-staff), Wu Fa-hsien (deputy chief-of-staff and commander of the air force), Li Tso-peng (deputy chief-of-staff and commander of the navy) and Chiu Hui-tso (deputy chief-of-staff and commander of the logistics departments). They were all to be later involved in the faction of 1970 and the 'conspiracy' of 1971.

The second group, which is of mainly symbolical importance, was the personal Left-wing of Mao, consisting of Chiang Ching (who, although she was Mao's wife, was not the 'gatekeeper' over all outside contacts with her husband, as was the case with Yeh Chun and Lin), Chang Chun-chiao and Yao Wen-yuan.

The third group consisted of Chou and two colleagues he had succeeded not without difficulty in piloting through the Cultural Revolution: Li Hsien-nien and Hsieh Fu-chih, although their personal connections with him were not as strong as in the case of the groups around Mao and Lin. The distinctions between the different groups become rather more vague at this point, and the fourth and fifth groups tend to merge into one another. They consist of a number of military representatives with strong regional support and a number of older military and administrative figures, who had no distinct political allegiance. Hsu Shih-yu and Chen Hsi-lien were members of the first-mentioned of these groups, while the second was probably made up of Yeh Chien-ying, Liu Po-cheng, Chu Teh and Tung Pi-wu. A number of them had been sharply attacked in the past by the 'Leftists' in the central military apparatus, which later made them more receptive to pressure for a more moderate line from a number of regional commanders.

Finally, there remain some four deputy members of the Political Bureau: Chi Teng-kuei, Li Hsueh-feng, Li Te-cheng and Wang Tung-hsing. The first two were later to appear as supporters of Lin, and the last two as supporters of Mao.

It is important to look at the affiliations of the various groups; during the period from the Ninth Congress to the Second Plenum, one of the above-mentioned groups was to form a real faction which was only held in check by a broad coalition of the other groups. For the moment, however, personal relations remained very much in the background, and the main efforts of the groups were directed towards objective decision-making after the years of relative chaos.

Part Seven
The Threat of War

The Soviet Union was the first socialist state and the Communist Party of the Soviet Union was created by Lenin. Although the leadership of the Soviet Party and state has now been usurped by revisionists, I would advise comrades to remain firm in the conviction that the masses of the Soviet people and of Party members and cadres are good, that they desire revolution and that revisionist rule will not last long.

Mao Tse-tung, quoted by Lin Piao, April 1969

19: Soviet-Chinese Border Incidents

On the border in the north-east

On 16 February 1969, the C.P.S.U. paper *Pravda* published the following:

The more the extent of the failures of the policies of the leadership of the Chinese Communist Party at home and the fiasco of its foreign policy – which has brought the country into total isolation – becomes apparent, the stronger the anti-Russian campaign has become. The more this leadership has turned away from the principles of scientific socialism, the louder and more bigoted the propaganda from Peking, which has claimed that it was the Soviet Union which had abandoned these principles, that it was the Soviet Union which had betrayed the interests of the revolution and had restored capitalism. Shortly afterwards, Chinese propaganda began to be motivated by distinctly nationalist sentiments – they could even be called racist. The leadership of the Communist Party of China has laid claim to Soviet Russian territories to inflame even further the nationalist sentiments of the Chinese people . . .

The Cultural Revolution, and all its political and ideological implications had not made Soviet feelings for China any warmer. Attention in both capitals became increasingly focused on the borders, and border guards on both sides were instructed to take good care that their own territories were not violated. It was not clear everywhere, however, exactly where the territory of one ended and that of the other began. In the border rivers of the Ussuri and the Amur there are a large number of small islands, frequently no more than slightly overgrown sandbanks, which appear and disappear with the natural changes in the course of the river. The Ussuri lies to the north of Siberia's easternmost port, Vladivostock, and to the east of the industrial town of Harbin in the Chinese province of Heilungkiang. On 2 March 1969, fighting broke out around an island in the

Ussuri which both sides claimed as their territory. The Russians called it Damansky, and the Chinese Chenpao. In the past, such cases had never caused serious difficulty, but the situation was now completely changed, as the border guards of both sides watched each other in an atmosphere of mutual distrust. At about eleven on the morning of 2 March one of the small boats which navigate the river put ashore at that tiny island, and some of the crew went ashore. Warning shots were fired from one of the banks. All was quiet for a very short time, until a full-scale battle suddenly flared up. In a matter of a couple of hours heavier arms were brought up, including tanks and artillery. Before the afternoon was over 1,000 grenades had exploded on the Chinese side and there were dozens of dead and wounded. On 15 March another incident became transformed into an artillery duel, and the losses were probably considerably in excess of those suffered on 2 March. Peking and Moscow naturally accused each other of having been the first to violate the border and to use arms. The propaganda radio station of the Soviet Union, 'Radio Peace and Progress', threatened the Chinese openly with the full Soviet might of strategic rocket weapons, and said that if the provocation on the part of the Chinese continued, there could be millions of Chinese dead because of Mao's reckless policies.[1] Tempers were also beginning to rise on the Chinese side:

The days when the Chinese had the law laid down for them by others are over. You must be completely blind and deluded if you think you can treat the Chinese people with the same old-fashioned, underhand methods which were used by Russia in the time of the Tsars . . . The 700 million people of China and the Chinese People's Liberation Army – armed with the Thoughts of Mao Tse-tung and hardened in the Great Proletarian Cultural Revolution – are more powerful than ever. Anyone who dares penetrate our great socialist motherland will inevitably be thrown roughly back. Down with the new Tsars! Down with Russian revisionist social-imperialists!

At the Ninth Party Congress, Lin Piao had this to say about the incidents:

The Sino-Soviet boundary question is the product of Tsarist Russian imperialist aggression against China. In the latter half of the nine-teenth century when power was in the hands neither of the Chinese people nor of the Russian people, the Tsarist government perpetrated imperialist acts of aggression to carve up China, imposed a series of unequal treaties on her, annexed vast expanses of her territory and, moreover, crossed in many places the boundary line stipulated by the unequal treaties and occupied still more Chinese territory. This gangster behaviour was indignantly condemned by Marx, Engels and Lenin. On 27 September 1920, the Government of Soviets led by the great Lenin solemnly proclaimed: It 'declares null and void all the treaties concluded with China by the former Governments of Russia, renounces all seizure of Chinese territory and all Russian concessions in China and restores to China, without any compensa-tion and forever, all that had been predatorily seized from her by the Tsar's Government and the Russian bourgeoisie'[2] ... However, betraying Lenin's proletarian policy and clinging to its new-Tsarist social-imperialist stand, the Soviet revisionist renegade clique re-fused to recognize these treaties as unequal ...

Recently it has gone further and made successive armed intrusions into our territory Chenpao Island. Driven beyond the limits of for-bearance, our frontier guards have fought back in self-defence, dealing the aggressors well-deserved blows and triumphantly safe-guarding our sacred territory ...

On 29 March, the Soviet Government issued a statement still clinging to its obstinate aggressor stand, while expressing willingness to resume consultations. Our Government is considering its reply to this.

After the Ninth Party Congress, however, further skirmishes took place, not only along the Ussuri, but also along the Amur, to which the Ussuri is a tributary, over the right to possession of a large number of small islands and sandbanks, the adminis-tration of which had not been laid down clearly in existing treaties. Mutual goodwill was required to solve the problem, but this was clearly lacking at the time. After fresh incidents in May, the official Chinese reply to the Soviet note of 29 March was issued on the 24th of the month, though it did not contain anything of substance which was new. It was proposed, how-ever, to separate for the time being the problem of the use of the northern border rivers from the more fundamental dispute, and a meeting of the joint Sino-Soviet Commission on the navigation of border waters was held on 18 June. After a certain amount of argument, a limited settlement was reached. It began to look as though the escalation of the conflict had been brought under control. Nothing could have been further from the truth.

On Uighurs and atomic bases

The tension began to spread to other frontiers, and to territories of greater importance, where the considerable strategic interests of both sides could even have led to a serious possibility of war. This new dispute concerned the borders of the extreme northwest province of China, Sinkiang, close to the capital of Urumchi. This is a thinly-populated autonomous region, inhabited by Uighurs and nomads of Turkish-Islamic origin. Part of this community also lives on the other side of the border, again in a thinly-populated autonomous region. This people, however, continued to roam freely from one side of the frontier to the other for a long time after the border had been created. By the beginning of the sixties, when Sino-Soviet relations had begun to worsen, this had started to create problems. The Chinese accused the Russians of setting the Uighurs of Sinkiang against Peking by creating a separatist movement which played on religious and nationalist sentiments. In the *New York Times* of 2 March 1970, Harrison Salisbury reported that a 'Movement for a free Turkestan' bureau had been set up in the capital of Soviet-Uighur territory, directed towards Sinkiang. The accusation was thus not completely without foundation. The Soviet effort, however, had little success, even if 60,000 people were incited to cross the border illegally. A fierce exchange of notes followed. As tension increased, so did the number of incidents involving the use of arms along the borders, reaching a known total of 4,000 in barely seven years – an average of two per day. The fact that considerable areas along the borders of this province were not included in treaties only aggravated the conflicts.

The conflicts along the Ussuri and Amur obviously had repercussions on the situation in Sinkiang, where the incidents began to increase dramatically. The timing of the incidents was particularly unfavourable to the Chinese, as the previous period of increased unrest had been. Sinkiang had just undergone three years of the Cultural Revolution, which had created more difficulties than anywhere else in China, especially among the more traditionally-minded groups in the population.

There was still another aspect of the conflict which brought an even greater element of instability to the situation. Seven years before, the area had only held strategic importance for the Russians, because of the nuclear installations of Alma Ata, which were of vital military importance. In the meantime, however, the Chinese had also established a nuclear test area in the remote region of Lop Nor, where the most important (or at least a number of) Chinese uranium mines and their related conversion factories were located. By the beginning of 1969, China was on the point of putting into production rockets capable of delivering an atomic warhead. The possibility of 'limited action' against the Chinese atomic installations was the subject of open speculation in Russian army publications, so that Chinese nuclear power could be postponed for several vital years. These threats were not taken lightly in Peking; it would not have been difficult for the Soviet Union to justify a rapid 'Blitzkrieg' in the eyes of the world as a border incident which had got out of hand because of the Uighur minority. The shooting along the Sinkiang border continued throughout May and June, when heavy weapons made their first appearance on the Russian side, consisting of complete tank battalions and heavy artillery. By August the battles had become more extensive, and the possibility of war seemed extremely serious.

The death of the North Vietnamese leader, Ho Chi-minh, however, went some way towards bringing the two sides together again. In his last testament Ho addressed an emotional appeal to both parties to forget their differences and to join forces to support the Vietnamese people. After preliminary contacts – which were probably made during sympathy visits to Hanoi – Kosygin interrupted his journey back to Russia in mid-September to make an agreement in Peking with his opposite number Chou En-lai about a date for discussions. On 20 October negotiations started in the Chinese capital between two Vice-

Ministers for Foreign Affairs, Kuznetzov and Chiao Kuan-hua. By January 1970, it had become apparent that the discussions were achieving very little and rumours of the serious possibility of war began to circulate again, but this time the threat seemed even more explicit. Air-raid drill was held in a number of towns, and the training of the militia was intensified. At the end of 1969 the area surrounding Peking was again declared forbidden territory for foreigners, probably because of the installation of anti-aircraft artillery and other defence machinery. The tunnels for a future underground system, which had been dug for some time, were arranged to serve as eventual shelters for the civil population. Plans for evacuation were drawn up. *The Times* reported on 1 December that further underground shelters were being dug out, and similar reports came from other towns besides Peking. An ideological campaign had to be mounted to prepare the population for a renewed outbreak of armed violence. An effort was made to point out to the Soviet Union the possible domestic repercussions of a fresh invasion of a neighbouring socialist country. But veiled references in that direction probably grossly overestimated the possibilities of opposition within the Soviet Union.[3] Mao himself was perfectly conscious of this, and over a year later, this was one of the most important factors in a radical reorientation of Chinese foreign policy.

While the official line was still summed up in Mao's saying, 'People, not weapons, decide the outcome of war,' it was becoming increasingly apparent that the people's war in itself could provide no guaranteed defence against an automated war from sea and air – let alone against nuclear war. The final phase of the Vietnamese struggle had shown once more that, as more American bases were moved from Vietnam to neighbouring countries and from there to ocean-based carriers, only opposition within the United States and her allies was still capable of preventing further escalation. And while such opposition could still produce some effect in the West, the phenomenon would be unthinkable in the Soviet Union and Eastern Europe.

20: The Resumption of the Debate on Strategy

Differences between 1965 and 1970

As a consequence of the serious threat of Soviet nuclear intervention and the negligible resources at China's disposal to counter such an attack, the 'strategic debate' was resumed among
the political and military leaderships. There was thus a return
to the preoccupations of 1965, when the American threat had
led to the formulation of certain theories about the people's
war. The situation, however, was now no longer the same as in
1965, when the extension of the Vietnam war to southern China
had been a real possibility. Firstly, the threat had come from
only one of the superpowers and, secondly, was of a more
limited character. Nuclear attack was the only kind of attack
which the Chinese would not have been able to cope with; the
highly automated sea and air warfare of 1970 had not yet been
developed, and any mass intervention by American troops in
China could only have ended in a complete débâcle. If the
Americans had not been convinced of this, the Chinese certainly
were. They were quite certain that all that was needed was
preparation for a people's war on their own territory, and their
preparations were made entirely on the basis of this thinking. It
was also thought that, with regard to a possible nuclear attack,
the Soviet Union could not allow such an extension of the war
in Vietnam, in spite of continued bad relations with China. The
situation in 1970 was completely different; the threat now came
from the neighbouring Soviet Union itself, and represented a
much more direct possibility of nuclear attack. China could
hardly expect any support from the United States; not only
were relations generally bad between the two countries, but
they were also involved in specific areas of conflict, such as
Korea, Taiwan and Vietnam. China's position of diplomatic

isolation in the world also meant that very little support could be expected from other quarters either.

Since capitulation to the Soviet Union was out of the question, as was alliance with the West, the remaining alternative was preparation for armed conflict with one of the two great super-powers – or perhaps even both, from a position of almost total isolation. If the possibility were to be dealt with in a more or less adequate manner, then a considerable extension of military potential was obviously called for. Such extension could no longer simply be in the direction of preparation for a people's war; given the nature of the threat, it had to include preparation for a 'modern' war. This meant that the Chinese nuclear weapon programme, still only in its infancy, had to be completed within the context of a wide-ranging military-industrial programme. The rapid build-up of reliable nuclear potential was certainly within reach. The programme itself dated from the sixties and had been initiated after the Soviet Union had withdrawn all its previous promises of aid in that sector. The first Chinese nuclear device was detonated in 1964, a long time before any foreign observers had thought this possible. By the summer of 1967, it already appeared that the Chinese had the capacity for the manufacture of hydrogen bombs, and in April 1970 the launch-ing of China's first space satellite was enthusiastically celebra-ted. The militant song, 'The East is Red', was transmitted by the satellite and relayed by all radio stations. To the outside world, the launching indicated that the Chinese had now to be con-sidered capable of manufacturing middle-range rockets. It seems probable that China had already installed some short-range rockets on its northern borders, though unprotected launching pads could hardly have posed a serious problem for the techno-logically superior Soviet Union. Foreign observers estimated, if the present rate of development was maintained, that China would be able to build a large number of adequately protected rocket bases by the mid-eighties. China would then have become an important nuclear power. This of course presupposed that the present rate would not be increased.

But a number of prominent military leaders declared them-selves in favour of a speeding-up of the rate of development.

Most of the people in favour of this were from the air force, navy and the logistics section, while there was a marked hesitation on the part of the army command itself: Lin Piao and his chief-of-staff, Huang Yung-sheng. While it was true that they were advocates of a highly politicized army in preparation for the people's war, it did not mean that they had no eye for the strategic realities of the moment. In fact, the political aspect was finally decisive in their case: anything less than a doubling or tripling of the military development programme was considered by them to constitute capitulation to one of the two enemies.

Mao had serious objections to drastic expansion of the modern armaments industry. Firstly, a never-ending arms race would swallow up a large part of the growth margin in the gross national product. And secondly, if absolute priority were to be given to advanced sectors such as the ultra-modern electronics industry, this would introduce a factor of uneven development in China, with highly detrimental political and ideological results. Chou En-lai was in agreement with Mao, as were other military leaders from a similar background. According to them, the rise of Stalinism and revisionism in the Soviet Union had occurred because the Russians had got their priorities wrong. Chen I once had this to say about Stalin in an interview with a South American journalist: 'By encouraging industry and technology . . . without solving the agricultural problem, he contributed to the process of degeneration.'[1]

Their disagreement with the military programme eventually led Chou En-lai and Chen I to formulate an alternative course of action.

An opening towards the West?

It must have come as something of a surprise to both sides in the dispute that, with the increasing possibility of military conflict between China and the Soviet Union, public opinion in the West did not remain aloof nor even appear to take delight in the misfortunes of others, but that the leading organs of the press expressed serious concern about the matter. In their position, it appeared to the Chinese that they could not look for support to 'the people of the Soviet Union', but should rather look for help among the other 'peoples of the world', even those of the imperialist West. And what was remarkable about the situation in other countries was the way in which public opinion was mobilized in favour of Peking by established political figures, rather than by Maoist splinter-groups.

There seemed good reason for trying to discover whether the West intended to maintain the distant attitude which had placed China in her isolation. There were no important differences with the countries of western Europe; on the insistence of de Gaulle, the European Community had tried to become increasingly independent of the United States. And even with regard to the United States itself, it was not necessary to stick to a 'wait-and-see' policy. Commentaries in the newspapers of the previous few months had clearly shown that there was some sympathy for the Chinese cause. At any rate, there seemed sufficient reason for trying to establish a dialogue. Completely normal relations were still out of the question, of course, while the United States was still active in Taiwan and Indo-China, but even there certain signs of readiness to withdraw were visible. International relations, with countries in Asia, Africa and Latin America, could now be improved, since the Cultural Revolution ultras had been dismissed from their positions of power in the formulation of foreign policy. The advantage of such attempts to abandon China's position of isolation would be that military action would begin to look considerably less attractive to the Soviet Union. For these reasons, then, Chou En-lai and his supporters wanted to try their gamble in foreign policy, rather than give their support to Lin Piao and his staff in a costly arms race.

21 : Continued Dissension at Home

Army and Party

Clearly, the internal relationships of the country did not remain unaffected by what was happening on the borders. The threat of war created two opposing schools of thought on the crisis. The first wanted to limit itself for the time being to military and para-military objectives: the training of the people's militia, which had begun to fall behind just before the Cultural Revolution, and special attention for the massive drafts which had been called up for the army after the Cultural Revolution, after the virtual cessation of recruitment during that upheaval. In contrast, the second group aimed at further concentration on non-military objectives: rapid restoration of full production, replenishment of depleted reserves, and reinforcement of the administration, an area of tension at this time. There was opposition to the omnipresence of the army in civil life, especially in those sectors where they had not succeeded in adapting to their 'style of leadership'. Reproaches of 'commandism' were levelled against them: that they tried to command their subordinates, when a more comradely approach would have been appropriate; that they cut through knots instead of untying them, and were sometimes far less open to compromise than the Party itself.

During the autumn of 1969, these problems became especially pressing a number of times, since two contradictory campaigns were being effectively conducted at the same time. While a campaign for the 'four perfections', following the example of the army (excellence in military training, organization of daily work, political and ideological education and work style) was being conducted in civil life, the same work style was under bitter attack within the army. Warnings were issued against a revival of bureaucracy, formalism and subjectivism, with additional practical suggestions for combating these.

Another source of contention were the new Party organizations. Hitherto it had been the Party branches in the army which had best survived the upheavals, but new, independent Party bodies now began to come into existence again, whose primacy over all other organizations was repeatedly announced by the Peking leadership. On 23 February 1970 the national press bureau published an account of the exemplary manner in which a number of representatives of the People's Liberation Army on Party committees had carried out the orders of the Party, even if they had not agreed with them. The persistence with which this theme kept cropping up in various forms throughout 1970 suggests that it was proving difficult to get the officers to accept directives from civilian Party members. After all, had not the fact that the Cultural Revolution had been necessary shown that the Party had a tendency to degenerate, while the army had proved the strongest upholder of Maoism? Why should the old situation be allowed to repeat itself? Another argument was that many of the former Party cadres were again present in the new organizations, and that serious mistakes had in any case been committed by the newcomers. It was also argued that the threat of war was a good reason for continuing with a semi-military administration for some time. A considerable number of officers actually hesitated to give up their leading role to the representatives of the Party. Naturally, the chaos in the economy during and after the Cultural Revolution was used as a substantial argument by those who favoured a temporary semi-military administration, since it was seen to have considerable bearing on the state of the country's preparedness for war. While it is true that there was no official report of loss in production or depletion of reserves, there is little doubt that these had occurred and were probably still continuing. In industry, it had been relatively easy to get the plant working again and to make up production arrears. But the mechanisms of agriculture are more subtle: sow badly once or tend the crops badly once, and the consequences can last for years. The situation in agriculture was aggravated even further by temporary bad weather conditions. The time-honoured optimistic section on the economy was significantly missing from Lin Piao's political report to the Ninth Party Congress.

The continuing ideological fight

In the meantime, a national mass campaign to continue the revolution while increasing production was begun under the slogan, 'Make revolution, increase production'. From the beginning of 1967 there had been an alarming tendency for people to act in one of two opposite directions: either to continue the revolution at the expense of production, or to emphasize production at the expense of the revolution. Attempts were made to show that the first alternative was an 'ultra-Left' deviation, and the second a 'Right' deviation, and that to oppose revolution and production was erroneous. Any tendency towards anarchism among the younger workers was violently attacked. Many of them had become used to their relative freedom during the period of the upheavals and now tended to harm production by their lack of discipline (by arriving late or absenting themselves completely), or by their attitude of confrontation (justified by anti-authoritarian slogans from the past). The persistence of this campaign indicates that the problems in this area were also widespread.

Far-reaching decentralization of authority was another way in which the economic consequences of the Cultural Revolution were to be brought under control.[1] The financial resources at local level had increased to such an extent during the previous twenty years,[2] that the communes, districts and provinces were asked to make the initial effort to solve their own problems without turning to the central authorities to provide a solution. Large-scale programmes were drawn up with a view to making it easier for local authorities to tackle problems. Among these was a campaign for the more even distribution of trained cadres. Whereas qualified young people had tended to leave the rural areas in the past, thereby depriving the people of cadres, the process was now reversed. However, this did not prevent another bitter campaign being conducted against the younger cadres with ultra-Left tendencies, who, after 1968, had tried to skip the period of socialist transition by directly introducing communist social structures with one stroke of a pen. Right-wing tendencies were also to be held in check. Ideological study was recommended as an antidote to subjectivism and arbitrariness, simplifications of procedures against paperwork and formalism, rota systems against 'commandism' and bureaucracy. The rota system involved one-third of the Revolutionary Committee being active in a leadership capacity, one-third carrying out their customary jobs, and another studying or in residence at a May 7 cadre school at any one time.

On 5 November 1969 the *People's Daily* published a leading article under the heading, 'Pay attention to work methods', in which about a dozen lines of action were indicated to prevent a revival of bureaucracy.

1. Grasp the ideological working of the leading members well . . . revolutionization of the leading body . . .
2. Take hold of selected basic units . . . collect first-hand information . . . be clear about policy . . .
3. Grasp the work in one-third of an area . . . before dealing with the rest . . .
4. Take the whole situation in consideration . . . proceed from the strategic concept 'Be prepared against war, be prepared against natural disasters' . . .
5. Keep the masses in mind . . . listen to different views . . . obtain their approval and support . . .
6. Direct contact between the leadership and the masses . . . We must not confine ourselves to a small circle and be satisfied by reports . . .
7/8. Run Mao Tse-tung study classes well . . . Hold meetings to exchange experience in the living study and application . . .
9. Fewer but better. Meetings, documents and forms should be drastically cut down and simplified . . .
10. Provide leeway. In fighting a battle there must be reserves. If leeway for manoeuvre is not provided, one is liable to land in a passive position . . .
11. Combine exertion and rest. There must be relaxation as well as alertness. The more energetic the masses are, the greater care must be given to their well-being . . .

12. Put stress on real effect. It is imperative to work hard without fuss and do work in a down-to-earth way . . . Don't put on a show . . .[3]

It was clear that this article was intended to be studied throughout the country, thus giving the problems mentioned a national perspective. At the same time it had become clear that what had happened had been unnecessary and that the Left wing in the propaganda apparatus had failed seriously to carry out its allotted task. Harsh words were to be exchanged during the Second Plenum on precisely this subject.

The Revolutionary Committees – like the military authorities – did their best to improve their 'style of working', to make it more democratic and more effective. But there was a risk that they would be caught between two sets of problems. On the one hand, again like the military authorities (who were substantially represented on the committees anyway), they were under pressure to accept the leadership of the newly-created Party organization. On the other, they were faced with 'anarchistic' tendencies at grass-roots level and a refusal to accept their authority. One of the chief obstacles to a return to 'peace and order' was the continued existence of large numbers of ultra-Left elements among groups of young people in the provinces.

In a number of rural areas arbitrary action by the ultra-Left continued undiminished. In Taiyuan, the 2,400-year-old capital of the province of Shansi, for instance, a complete commando group was still carrying on the fight against other similar organizations and against the authorities. The situation there became so serious that the Central Committee had to intervene once again. On 23 or 24 July 1969 it issued a decree which indicated only too well the extent of the problem in Shansi and elsewhere – so well, in fact, that it is worth quoting substantially from it.

As in the rest of the country, favourable circumstances exist in Shansi. But in the town of Taiyuan and in two other places in central and southern Shansi, a handful of class enemies and evil people have infiltrated all kinds of mass organizations, and have used the techniques of bourgeois factionalism to mislead certain sections of the masses, so that they refuse to carry out the orders, directives, instructions and promulgations which have been successively issued by the leadership. This handful of class enemies and evil people have committed a whole series of extremely serious counter-revolutionary crimes. These people have:

1. Organized special groups to struggle by force and beaten, smashed, stolen, grabbed, sequestered and endangered the lives, property and security of the people and destroyed socialist revolutionary discipline . . .

2. Refused to carry out the policy decided by the centre of revolutionary great alliance and revolutionary triple unity . . .

3. Attacked the organization and units of the P.L.A., seized P.L.A. arms and equipment, beaten up, tied up, killed and wounded members of the P.L.A.

4. Destroyed railways, roads and bridges; carried out armed attacks on trains, seized means of transport; stolen the belongings of passengers and endangered their lives.

5. Forcefully occupied state banks, warehouses and shops; privately set up banks, and stolen a large amount of state property.

6. Used armed force to occupy territory; set up bases for struggle by force; carried out counter-revolutionary annexation; trampled the masses underfoot; practised fraud and extortion against the masses and handed out food and money . . .

7. Incited and threatened workers to cease work and production, incited peasants to enter the towns, struggled by force and wrecked industrial and agricultural production and the national plan.[4]

Long after the Ninth Party Congress, then, and even after the Second Plenum, there were still reports of the continuing activities of the remnants of the notorious May 16 organizations, whether in guerrilla form or not.

There was, however, a certain amount of confused thinking in this area. After the Ninth Party Congress, there was a growing trend in the People's Republic to define all Left deviationists as members of the 'conspiratorial May 16 group'; when they were not thus defined they were simply referred to as counter-revolutionaries, which would lend credence to the idea that they were nothing more than 'agents of Chiang Kai-shek' or common criminals – who would be referred to in the same terms. It is therefore frequently difficult to interpret the available information more or less reliably. But the accusation that the ultra-Left groups were often infiltrated by common criminals and nationalist agents was probably not without foundation. One indication of the possible truth of this was that the difficult situation persisted longest in those provinces in which such agents have been traditionally most active: Kwangtung, which borders on Hong Kong, Yunnan, which borders on Burma, to which some of Chiang's troops had withdrawn in the past and where they were still active.

However, as the process of stabilization progressed, the excesses became fewer and life began to return to normal, except in one aspect: political power. Only when the reconstruction and rehabilitation of the Party were complete would it be possible to talk of a return to a 'normalized' situation. And for the moment, this was not the case.

22 : Difficulties in the Reconstruction of the Party

The situation, in which the army assumed the position of responsibility while the young Leftists were discredited by their co-workers on the grounds of excess, had never been very much to the taste of Mao and his supporters. Each time he was forced by events to accept further limitations on the activities of the Red Guards and consequent extended participation of the army, he guarded against possible one-sidedness. This dislike was particularly noticeable in his thinking about the renewal of the Party. Although it was suggested outside China that Mao had wanted to use the Cultural Revolution to eliminate the Party completely, this was in fact incorrect. And while Lin Piao and his colleagues did not see the problem as being particularly pressing (they had of course carefully prepared the army for its political role), Chou En-lai and other members of the leadership thought it very urgent indeed. When Mao spoke about the necessity of the reconstruction of the Party in September 1967, Chou En-lai was already worried about the 'monistic leadership' which had been exercised by the army since January over the army itself, Government and Party. Philip Bridgham,[1] who quotes the relevant statement, adds, however, that it was clearly not the intention that the new Party organs should play a leading role until it could be reasonably certain that control over them was in the hands of loyal Maoists. At the time, this was still far from being generally true, and time after time it appeared that the new revolutionary bodies were in danger of falling into the hands of 'Right-wing' forces. For this reason, the reconstruction of the Party took place with a considerable amount of caution, and its primacy over other organizations was only established very gradually.

After the Twelfth Plenum of October 1968, new Party cells

began to come into existence hesitantly in a number of places. The movement was given new encouragement after the Ninth Party Congress in April 1969. And while it is true that Lin Piao's political report to the Congress contained much about the Party but very little about its reconstruction, this relationship was reversed at the First Plenum.

On the Forty-eighth Anniversary of the Party a number of new lines of policy were laid down which had probably been worked out at the First Plenum; on the same occasion, a joint leading article was published by the three main newspapers which dealt more directly than usual with the ways in which the new Party committees were to be formed. It is at that moment that the reconstruction of the Party really starts. The first stage was the recruitment of new members.[2] The membership on the eve of the Cultural Revolution probably stood at about twenty million, or almost three per cent of the population. There is every reason to think that a high percentage of Party members had decided during the Cultural Revolution to retire from politics and not to renew their membership after the movement was over. This was one reason why an attempt was now made to reach out to other sectors of the population. An extensive recruitment campaign was organized among the older peasants and workers who had not been involved in politics in the past, and among pupils from schools and students – army personnel and Red Guards, women and national minorities. The rigid rules for admission were not applied very strictly. The new Party statutes defined the conditions for membership as follows:

Article 1 Any Chinese worker, poor peasant, lower-middle peasant, revolutionary army man or any other revolutionary element who has reached the age of eighteen and who accepts the Constitution of the Party, joins a Party organization and works actively for it, carries out the Party's decisions, observes Party discipline and pays membership dues may become a member of the Communist Party of China.

Article 2 Applicants for Party membership must go through the procedure for admission individually. An applicant must be recommended by two Party members, fill out an application form for Party

membership and be examined by a Party branch, which must seek
the opinions of the broad masses inside and outside the Party. Application is subject to acceptance by the general membership meeting of
the Party branch and approval by the next higher Party committee.
Article 3 Members of the Communist Party of China must:
(1) Study and apply Marxism-Leninism-Mao Tse-tung Thought in a
living way;
(2) Work for the interests of the vast majority of people of China
and the world;
(3) Be able at uniting with the great majority, including those who
have wrongly opposed them but are sincerely correcting their mistakes; however, special vigilance must be maintained against career-
ists, conspirators and double-dealers so as to prevent such bad
elements from usurping the leadership of the Party and the state at
any level and guarantee that the leadership of the Party and the state
always remains in the hands of Marxist revolutionaries;
(4) Consult with the masses when matters arise;
(5) Be bold in making criticism and self-criticism.[3]

The first 'nuclei' to be formed in many places consisted of
old cadre members who had escaped criticism, new members
who had come up through the Revolutionary Committees, and
a large number of people from the General Political Department of the army. These 'nuclei' were responsible for the recruitment of new members. When Party membership had come
up to strength, then the reconstructed branch was allowed to
make proposals for the formation of a Party committee which
would lead and represent the base unit in question (production
or habitation unit, educational establishment, or army division).
Consultations were then to be held with the central powers
about the proposal, and when agreement had been reached, the
Committee formally took office. The Party was thus to be reconstructed from the base. Base committees were created in an
ever-increasing number of places and soon the first reports of
the creation of committees at the next level above the base
began to reach the outside world. It was about six months before
the next level was reached; by that time it had become clear that
the movement was progressing very slowly and encountering a
great number of serious difficulties. These sprang chiefly from

differences between the army and the Revolutionary Committees and from the problems connected with the restoration of a
sense of unity between old and young and Left and Right. And
while a large number of people did the best they could within
the situation, there were a number of Leftist elements who opposed everything and everyone with which they did not agree.

As it became more and more apparent that there were various insuperable contradictions in the way of further reconstruction of the Party, an effort was made to find the causes of this
situation so that a solution could be attempted. Around the
middle of 1970, increasing mention was made of study meetings
which were being held to prepare the formation of a new Party
committee. In the first place, the meetings gave various groups
the opportunity of airing their views again, which could then be
clarified in further discussion. In the second place, they func-
tioned as a kind of group-training in which all sentiments could
be expressed in the presence of an expert advisor (often a
special army officer from the General Political Department). In
the third place, they made it possible for differences of opinion
to be related to 'objective', outside criteria: the new Party
statutes, the political report of Lin Piao, the directives of the
Central Committee, and the statements of Mao Tse-tung. It
soon became clear, however, that, in spite of all efforts, the
political insight of the people remained very slight. The propaganda campaigns which took place before and during the Cultural Revolution may have tried to spread the Thoughts of
Mao Tse-tung among the greatest possible number, but this had
resulted in a distinct loss of quality. The extent of the problem
indicated that something was very wrong somewhere. In fact,
Chen Po-ta's propaganda apparatus for the formulation of
ideology had obviously failed in its attempt to raise the political
struggle to a higher level after the Cultural Revolution. It was
now unavoidable that Chen Po-ta's theoretical Party magazine,
Red Flag – for long a champion of ultra-Left dogma – would
be again forced to drop a bombshell on the ranks of ideological
factionalism. On 2 July 1970 it published an article on the matter in question with the title, 'Fight for ideological strength in

the building of the Party', which was taken from the 'Thoughts of the Mao Tse-tung propaganda team of soldiers and workers at the Pei-ta University'.

One revealing passage ran thus:

Some comrades have failed to achieve the objective of clarity in ideology and unity among comrades in a correct manner. One of the reasons for this is that they have an inadequate understanding and awareness of the dialectics of the contradictions within the Party. They hold that the thought of Party organizations and Party members should be 'pure' – that is 'pure' of conflicting ideas. This is a metaphysical, muddle-headed point of view ...

The fact that, in the course of Party consolidation, a minority violated Chairman Mao's principle of achieving clarity in ideology and unity among comrades is directly linked to their stand that the individual comes first. We have come across some people who are seriously affected by bourgeois factionalism and who, in dealing with Party members who disagree with them, resort to the wrong practice of 'criticizing, struggling against and discrediting' them in the hope of developing the self-interest of a faction or an individual in the course of Party consolidation. Such people have put the relationship between the individual and the Party on a wrong plane: they are strongly imbued with the cult of 'I am the only authority in the world'. Since their starting point is wrong, their policy is also wrong. Paying lip-service to 'weeding out the old to let the new emerge', they in fact think of 'weeding out those who are estranged from them and taking in their close or trusted friends', and thinking of 'weeding out one group and taking in a new group' in accordance with the criteria set by an individual or a small group ...[4]

Part Eight
The Second Plenum

Opposition and struggle between ideas of different kinds
constantly occur within the Party; this is a reflection within
the Party of contradictions between classes and between
the new and the old in society. If there were no
contradictions in the Party and no ideological struggles to
resolve them, the Party's life would come to an end.

Mao Tse-tung, *On Contradiction*, 1937

23: The Final Communiqué

On 10 September 1970 the *People's Daily* published the final communiqué[1] of the Second Plenary Session of the Ninth Central Committee, which had been sitting in conditions of great secrecy during the previous two weeks. It mentioned achievements and progress and put forward far-reaching plans for the immediate future, without referring to the very deep differences of opinion which undoubtedly still existed; the imposed unity of the Central Committee, which had itself been formed somewhat artificially, was still under heavy pressure because of continued discord throughout society. One of the remarkable aspects of a political system like the Chinese is that in such circumstances the regular Plenary Session of the Central Committee can be of considerable importance. As soon as deeply-rooted differences of opinion emerge, then there are two possibilities. The first is that the leadership will divide into two groups of similar size holding different opinions, which will be supported to a similar extent by the corresponding Party organs. The political centre of gravity thus shifts increasingly towards the necessity for finding practical policies to solve everyday problems of government.[2] Another possibility is that relations will continue to be confused and unclear, in which case a Plenary Session becomes especially important and, instead of simply sanctioning decisions which have been taken at a higher level, determines which policies are to be followed.

Such a situation must have arisen at the Second Plenum, in spite of the misleading impression created by the routine and cliché-ridden formulae of the final communiqué. However, some details contained in this declaration did fall into perspective in the light of subsequent events, as, for instance, the actual duration of the Plenary Session and the timing of the final communiqué. This session was a particularly lengthy one, and we have to go back more than ten years to find a longer one. And the final communiqué was only issued on the evening of 9 September, while the actual session, according to the communiqué, had lasted from 23 August to 6 September.

Another remarkable aspect of this communiqué was the absence of any mention of the allocation of jobs during the session. All that was said was that 155 (out of 177) permanent members, and 100 (out of 109) deputy members were present; it added that Mao had been the chairman of the session and that Lin Piao had delivered a speech.

The agenda of the session was not mentioned, though from the points made in the communiqué, some attempt can be made to deduce what was actually presented for discussion. Mention was made in the introduction to the communiqué of the progress made in a number of campaigns.

The remarks on the *international situation* began thus,

In response to Chairman Mao's solemn call 'Heighten our vigilance; defend the motherland', the great Chinese People's Liberation Army, the people's militia and the people of the whole country, in order to guard against imperialist and social-imperialist aggression on our country, have further enhanced their preparedness against war ideologically, materially and organizationally.

The following were named as militarily hostile forces, in order of importance: American imperialism, Japanese militarism, Soviet revisionism and reactionaries in other countries. The order in which these forces were named is particularly significant, since it reflects Lin Piao's own order of priority. On the other hand, the communiqué also expressed the opinion that Chou En-lai's diplomatic offensive should also be allowed every freedom,

On the basis of adhering to the five principles, we strive for peaceful coexistence with countries having different social systems and oppose the imperialist policies of aggression and war, and have continuously won new victories.

With reference to the *domestic situation*, the communiqué had this to say about the economy:

Rich harvests have been gathered in our socialist agriculture for eight years running, and another one is in sight this year. Industrial production and capital construction are developing rapidly. The mass movement for technical innovations is vigorously forging ahead. The launching of China's first man-made earth satellite signifies that our science and technology have reached a new level. Throughout the country prices are stable and the market is thriving. The situation is very good on the entire economic front.

This account of the facts is clearly very rosy indeed. Great progress certainly had been made, but not without a great deal of difficulty during the Cultural Revolution. This was not, however, a point of discussion among the members of the Central Committee; what was a subject for discussion were the related consequences. In the light of later published information, there seems a distinct possibility that two main tendencies had expressed themselves at the session. One group was composed of the radicals, with Chen Po-ta as the most likely chief spokesman. As chief formative influence on the ideological aspects of agricultural reform, he was an advocate of not slowing down the pace of change whenever difficulties occurred; on the contrary, he tended to favour increasing the rate of change, in the shape of more comprehensive collectivization of the land and the means of production, a further equalizing of incomes, and even greater decentralization – in short, new intensification of the struggle between the 'two lines' in the country.[3] This group of opinions was expressed as follows in the communiqué:

It is imperative to continue to implement the policy of 'grasp revolution, promote production and other work and preparedness against war' in an all-round way and, with the struggle between the two classes, the two roads and the two lines as the key, work arduously, rely on our own efforts, go all out, aim high and achieve greater, faster, better and more economical results in building socialism, and strive to fulfil or overfulfil the National Economic Plan for 1970. ... The Plenary Session approved the State Council's report on the

National Planning Conference and the National Economic Plan for 1970.

In this last passage, however, the emphasis has shifted imperceptibly to the second, more moderate approach to the problems, i.e., the approach of Chou En-lai's Government colleagues, who claim that the situation will right itself without the need for extreme remedial measures, and that central planning should be reintroduced. Here again, Chen Po-ta's opponent was probably Li Hsien-nien, the Minister of Finance, as he had been in 1958.

In addition to the economy, there was another important aspect of the domestic situation to be approached in a different way – that of political relations. These mainly concerned the restoration of democratic centralism, the relations within the new power organs (the Revolutionary Committees) between the leaders and the led, and between the mass organizations, the army and the Party. There were indeed certain areas of friction between these last two groups, which were expressed in different ways at the level of the leadership by their two principal exponents: Lin Piao and Chou En-lai. The great influence of the army at all levels had led to the development of a parallel hierarchy of command which had partly freed itself from political control. This was the reason why a more rapid reconstruction of the Party was necessary, to confirm once again the principle that 'the Party must control the gun, the gun must never be allowed to control the Party'.

Another obstacle in the way of Party reconstruction sprang from the failure of Chen Po-ta's propaganda organizations: the continuing phenomenon of Leftist apriorism and dogma still stood in the way of the restoration of unity to the country. On this subject, the communiqué had the following to add:

The whole Party must conscientiously study Chairman Mao's philosophic works, uphold dialectical materialism and historical materialism and oppose idealism and metaphysics ... The great leader Chairman Mao teaches us: 'The unification of our country, the unity of our people and the unity of our various nationalities – these are the basic guarantees of the sure triumph of our cause.'

24 : Project for a Change in the Constitution

In addition, the following passages from the final communiqué are also of considerable interest:

The Plenary Session calls on the working class, the poor and lower-middle peasants, the commanders and fighters of the People's Liberation Army, the revolutionary cadres, the revolutionary intellectuals as well as all patriotic personages throughout the country to greet the convocation of the Fourth National People's Congress with new victories! . . . The Plenary Session holds that in the excellent situation now prevailing at home and abroad, it is the fervent desire of the people of the whole country to convene the Fourth National People's Congress. The Plenary Session proposes to the Standing Committee of the National People's Congress that necessary preparations be made so that the Fourth National People's Congress will be convened at an appropriate time.

There is every reason to believe that the wording of the last part of the paragraph was a last-minute replacement of a much more precise declaration of intent. Only now do we know that there were not only very concrete propositions put forward for the convocation of a National People's Congress, but also a project for a new Constitution which would have been adopted by this Congress. This project must have led to fierce discussion on a number of subjects, though finally growing worse over the problem of the Presidency. It is very probable that it was this question which caused first Chou and then Mao to launch a bitter personal attack on Chen Po-ta, while fresh evidence of distrust of Lin Piao was beginning to take shape at the same time.

The National People's Congress is the representative body of the Chinese people, and is normally constituted after indirect general elections. While the Communist Party prepares all important political decisions, they are actually taken by general representative bodies (such as the People's Congress at national level) and carried out by administrative Government bodies. While the Party consists of the most ideologically advanced elements of the proletariat, the People's Congress represents all sectors of the population who are not considered to be counter-revolutionary. In any case, the People's Congress has great formal importance. And because of its importance, it was expected throughout China that it would be convened soon after the end of the Cultural Revolution or, more precisely, shortly after the Ninth Party Congress and after the necessary arrangements had been made by the new Central Committee. During the Cultural Revolution, several decisions had been taken which would have had repercussions on a People's Congress. The most important was the expulsion of Liu Shao-chi from the Party. This also meant in fact that he had been stripped of his Presidential function, but that decision had to be taken formally by a People's Congress; 'President of the Republic' is not a Party function.

Nothing happened, however, and there remained only the short, vaguely-worded sentence in the communiqué. Clearly, a last-minute hitch in the plans had occurred somewhere. But where? It is possible, of course, that the Second Plenum was not in a hurry to deal with the question, and preferred to deal with the reconstruction of the Party first. But a more real possibility seems to be that there were serious differences of opinion on the two most important decisions which had to be taken: on the question of the Constitution, and the question of the succession to the Presidency.

The present Constitution had been adopted in 1954 by the National People's Congress. It was principally based on a number of concepts and ideas taken from either western European parliamentary democracies (civil liberties, etc.) or from eastern European people's democracies (the forms of communist administration, etc.). The Cultural Revolution had, however, undermined a large part of the presuppositions embodied in the Constitution: either by rejecting the political content, or by simply transgressing certain clauses. The necessity for a new Constitution was obvious. For some time before the Second

Plenum there had been rumours that a project for a new Constitution had been circulating in Party circles. The information services of Chiang Kai-shek also put out reports on such a project probably intercepted in Kwangtung and Yunnan. At the end of 1970 a text (to be accepted with some caution) was produced to bear out these rumours; it was also claimed that the version embodied in the text had already been adopted by the Second Plenum.[1] There are factors which support the authenticity of this claim, the most striking being that several of the formulae in it were later used in documents published in the provinces during the following months. After all, Taiwan had already succeeded in making public the new Party statutes before the Party Congress. Edgar Snow, still one of the most reliable non-Chinese sources, has claimed that several versions were in circulation. And it is generally accepted that the Second Plenum was indeed involved in a project for a Constitution.

Like the Constitution of 1954, the project included a preamble and four sections. The preamble summed up past events, laying emphasis on the advances of the Cultural Revolution and the role of Mao Tse-tung. Further on in the preamble occurs a passage devoted to international relations. In the Constitution of 1954, the corresponding paragraph ran as follows:

Our country has already built an indestructible friendship with the great Union of Soviet Socialist Republics and the People's Democracies; and the friendship between our people and other peace-loving peoples all over the world is growing day by day. These friendships will continue to be developed and consolidated.

Now it is:

We will oppose the aggressive policies of imperialism and social-imperialism and the policy of war.[2]

The first section deals with the general principles on which the Chinese People's Republic is based. The crucial change is to be found in the first article. There is no more mention of a 'people's democratic state, led by the working class', but of a 'socialist state under the dictatorship of the proletariat, led by the working class'. The new formula was intended to indicate that a new phase of development had been entered. To avoid any misunderstanding, the words 'by means of the Communist Party of China' were added between parentheses. It is very probable that this addition was made at the Second Plenum itself, since it is the only phrase in the whole piece which is between parentheses. Some people clearly feared that there was a possibility of misunderstanding in this sector, especially by such a person as Lin Piao. Further clarification of the new situation was offered by the phrase, 'socialist society covers a relatively long historical period'. The intention was obvious: some Left-wingers, like Chen Po-ta, were under the mistaken impression that the period of communism had already started.

Another passage which had undoubtedly caused differences of opinion between the ultras and moderates was that concerning the question of ownership. In the old Constitution a number of forms of private property were designated, as well as a large number of sources of private income, which were to be respected by the State. Some Left-wingers, again probably Chen Po-ta, had continued to insist, after the Cultural Revolution, that all forms of individual exploitation be abolished in the country. There still appears to have been strong opposition to this and a feeling that such a measure would be premature. It is for this reason that the following statement was probably included: 'Under conditions which guarantee the absolute precedence and development of the collective economy of the people's communes, members of the communes are allowed to manage private areas of land on a small scale.'

The second section of the project for the constitution included, as before, a survey of the structure of the state, though somewhat less extensive than in the previous version. The passage on the Revolutionary Committees is especially striking in this context – not because of what has changed since 1954, but because of what has not changed. The Revolutionary Committees came into existence during the Cultural Revolution as temporary organs of power, at the same time replacing the Party, which was in a state of dissolution, and carrying out the administrative tasks which had been the preserve of the administrative apparatus up to that point. There was considerable interest in what would happen after the Cultural Revolution: would the Party be abolished, or reconstructed from the Revolutionary Committees, and would the combination of functions continue to exist? We have already seen that the Party was in the process of re-building, but nothing has yet been said of the fate of the Revolutionary Committees. In fact, they were given the function which had in the past been fulfilled by the local 'people's council'; in other words, they became ordinary executive and administrative bodies, controlled by the local people's congresses. The definition of their tasks was almost the same, apart from one important difference; they could, after the example of the Paris Commune, be deposed.

The third section of the project for a Constitution contained the description of the basic rights and duties of the citizen; this was considerably shorter than the previous version, in which the traditional formulation of the West had kept a place.

And finally, the fourth section concerned the flag, the national emblem and the capital of the country, and incorporated no significant changes. The whole document represented a considerable simplification and shortening of the Constitution; instead of the previous 106 articles, it now only had thirty. But there is another point which is worthy of note. The second section, on the structure of the state, was now made up of only four sub-sections, instead of five. The sub-section omitted was the one ... concerning the Presidency. Behind this omission lies the key to the drama of the Second Plenum and to subsequent events.

25 : The Intrigues of Chen Po-ta
Around the Presidential Succession

A manoeuvre by Chen Po-ta

The problem which created the present situation was striking by its very, almost unbelievable, absence. The principal reason for pressing on with the preparations for a People's Congress was the question of the Presidency. The Central Committee had certainly deliberated the matter at an earlier date. The most obvious solution was for Mao to become President and Lin Vice-President. But there were serious disadvantages in this solution. In the first place, Mao did not want the Presidency, as he had made clear several times. As far as Lin was concerned, there would undoubtedly be opposition to any further extension of his power, in the event of Mao's death. Lin was also in favour of an immediate solution which would put his own position beyond question – namely its incorporation in the constitution, just as his position in the Party was laid down in the Party statutes. But few regarded Lin as a suitable candidate. A candidate acceptable to all parties, who would heal the wounds of the Cultural Revolution, was needed, and Lin did not really stand above the different interests. In fact, on examination, there did not seem to be any solution to the problem. The Central Committee itself was obliged to examine the matter, and Lin submitted a text as the basis for a project for a Constitution. This document, however, did not include a section on the Presidency, probably by prior arrangement with Mao. This section was also missing from the version which was put into distribution later. What was present in the document, however, were a number of paragraphs in which Lin's name was explicitly mentioned, and always in connection with that of Mao.[1] The implications of this should not be misunderstood. When these particular paragraphs were later criticized by Mao, he claimed that Lin had added them of his own accord and that he had not been given the text to read prior to its being made public. At the time however, there was no hunt for hidden motives – at least not openly. All this was to change when a movement developed during the plenary session which wanted to solve the problem of the Presidency immediately, by pressing Mao to accept finally. At first sight, this looked like another expression of attachment to Mao, and in the light of the confused reports on the secret meeting considering the question, it is difficult to interpret with any certainty exactly what happened at the Second Plenum. According to one version, the main figure in the intrigue was Chen Po-ta. He is said to have asked to speak during the meeting and to have delivered a seemingly unprepared speech on the subject of the Presidency. His position made it certain that he would have an attentive audience. He then proposed 'spontaneously' to nominate Mao as President, thereby manoeuvring the Chairman into a difficult position.[2] Mao's nomination would almost certainly automatically make Lin Vice-President, and, even if there were other candidates, Lin would still be the strongest. The nomination of Mao was almost an apolitical deed which would produce few objections, but that of Lin was not at all. On the contrary, it would bring a sudden upset to the delicate balance of power which had been established among the leadership with so much difficulty after the Cultural Revolution. The President was not just a representative figure: he held the most important decision-making powers in the whole country. The Constitution of 1954, which was still valid, expressed the position of President as follows.

The Chairman of the People's Republic of China, in pursuance of decisions of the National People's Congress or its Standing Committee, promulgates laws and decrees; appoints and removes the Premier, Vice-Premiers, Ministers, Chairmen of Commissions or the Secretary-General of the State Council; appoints and removes the Vice-Chairmen and members of the Council of National Defence; confers state orders and titles of honour; proclaims amnesties and grants pardons; proclaims martial law; proclaims a state of war; and orders mobilization.[3]

Any significant possibility of opposition would thus be eradicated, since Lin would also become Party Chairman, in the event of Mao's death, while still remaining commander-in-chief of the army. And of all the qualities required to govern such an enormous and diverse country, Lin Piao only possessed a fraction. If Mao ever wavered over the acceptance of the Presidency, his mind was now made up by the question of the Vice-Presidency. After rapid consultation, the proposal was again resolutely rejected by Mao. At the same time he must have wondered what possessed Chen Po-ta to make the proposal in such an arbitrary way, against his express wishes, and in such a way as to be sure that it would be carried through by popular acclaim. Did Chen want to bring about a transfer of power into the hands of the hard-liner Lin, so that the position of his own radicals would be strengthened, and that of moderates, like Chou, weakened? Was he acting in good faith, or was this simply a case of straightforward court intrigue? Whatever the explanation, he had clearly placed himself in a difficult position, reminiscent of the man who was uncertain about his position and therefore wanted to declare his loyalty '110 per cent'. Or was he simply a petit-bourgeois hiding behind revolutionary rhetoric? The result, in any case, was that Chen Po-ta had to face a full-scale attack. His whole political career was closely examined, bringing reproaches of ultra-Left deviationism, dating from the time of the Great Leap Forward, as well as during the Cultural Revolution. As chief of propaganda, he was accused of being the chief culprit responsible for the shortcomings in the ideological education of the masses, and thus responsible for the difficulties experienced in the restoration of unity and the reconstruction of the Party. He was finally deposed during the Second Plenum, or at least not more than a week after its end, from his position as a member of the Standing Committee and, obviously, from the position of propaganda chief. And when an intensive campaign for ideological education to correct faulty ideas was initiated shortly afterwards, he was not responsible for its organization, but became its object. His name was linked with that of the man he is said to have fought against as against no other: he was described as a 'Liu-type pseudo-Marxist and political swindler'.

Was Lin Piao forming a faction?

Lin Piao still remained out of range, although some people probably suspected him of having consciously inspired Chen's ambiguous proposition; for the moment, he was beyond reproach. What is striking, however, is that it was he who resisted Chen's dismissal longest, and it took several months before he seemed to have accepted it. His attitude during the Plenum did not fail to anger a number of the moderates. Worse still, Mao had again begun to doubt his capacities and intentions. It had not gone unnoticed that Lin always acted at the Plenum in a closed group with his nearest colleagues. Whether the problem being debated was one of strategic relationships, the defence industry, foreign policy, the economic situation, or the distribution of power, it was always certain that, before the discussion and vote, Lin's sextet would take the same line. They were reported to have been responsible for having the original agenda of the session amended in such a way that Chen Po-ta could place the question of the Presidency on the new agenda. This kind of behaviour was to be mentioned later when the accusations of faction-forming were made. It would even be claimed that Lin and his supporters had secretly read through all the issues for discussion before the Second Plenum.

Furthermore, there was the question of the reorganization of the Ministry of Defence. There were rumours abroad that Lin had proposed reorganizing his own department completely, as many other departments had been reorganized. But instead of simplifying the structure, he would probably have proposed considerable extension, using the threat of war as an excuse. The number of sub-departments would have been increased in such a way as to constitute an almost complete parallel with the rest of the Government apparatus. In the past there had only been one example of such a parallel organization: the Party. This initiative, although it was not carried through, also tended to create distrust. Did this indicate that Lin intended to hand the central role in the country over to the army on a definitive basis – the role which the army had played during the Cultural Revolution?

Faction-forming

The cracks in the foundations were now reaching to the roof. Although the Ninth Central Committee had presented itself under a banner of unity, this was far less easy to proclaim at grass-roots level. The impossibility of reconciling radicals and moderates in everyday life confronted the leadership with the question of what might be the cause of this persistent tension. The Cultural Revolution had taught the people to think in black and white, and not in different shades of grey. Now that these nuances were being applied some of the 'straightforward' cultural revolutionaries were apparently afraid of losing their prominent positions. These feelings also manifested themselves in the Standing Committee and the Political Bureau; and were indeed to determine relations between the four remaining members of the top leadership: Mao Tse-tung, Lin Piao, Chou En-lai and Kang Sheng. The position of the latter, however, was never clear. Repeated lengthy absences caused speculation about his possible demotion or fall, but there is more reason for thinking that he had been ill for some considerable time. For the time being, then, his role in affairs was only marginal.

All events revolved round Mao. His role was pre-eminently that of the visionary who maintains a position above the different parties, only to take an active role when 'non-antagonistic' contradictions have become 'antagonistic'.

Immediately under Mao came Lin. Since his swift rise to be the chosen successor and deputy of Mao, he had now begun to familiarize himself with his new position. During the Cultural Revolution he had made constant efforts to ensure the predominance of the radicals, using his central army apparatus to achieve this.

Chou En-lai, on the other hand, was a thorough-going politician and diplomat; he was enough of a radical to follow the broad lines of Mao's vision, enough of an organization man to help the realization of the plans involved, and enough of a realist to amend them if their full execution seemed impossible at the time. During the Cultural Revolution his principal task had been to keep the movement on the right path and to prevent excesses (which had often been made possible by the actions of Lin and Chen Po-ta). The remarkable position adopted by Lin and Chen clearly demonstrated that they were afraid that Chou, who had not played an important part in the First Plenum, was now becoming a more important opponent. Chen Po-ta, who occupied the weakest position and therefore felt obliged to move to the attack, had aimed too high. Lin Piao, however, was strong enough to limit himself to sealing off his 'independent kingdom', the central army apparatus.

As the ulterior motives at play within the Party leadership brought the members of each group closer together, so the groups themselves became more sharply differentiated. Members of the Standing Committee tried to strengthen their links with their supporters in the Political Bureau, and vice versa. The situation was now clearly unstable and preparations began to be made for the eventual confrontation. Not everyone, perhaps, was conscious to the same degree of the direction in which events were moving, nor of the gravity of the situation. Based on the various alliances, then, the groups began to crystallize into more definite shape, and it only needed the right situation for a group to become a faction. The search for mutual support did not, of course, always lead to the forming of a faction; this was also determined by the necessity for and the type of alliances involved. Chou, for instance, also had support from among the regional commanders, although he now no longer really needed it, since he was slowly but surely winning that of Mao. The only instance of the formation of a real faction was the one which came into being around Lin Piao.

A closer study of the kind of alliances which led to the formation of sub-groups among the political leadership in China will be helpful at this point. Roughly speaking, these alliances can be grouped into three categories: alliances based on political opinions and political style, alliances based on institutional affiliation, and alliances based on personal relations. In other words, objective, semi-objective and subjective affinities. In normal situations, this is also the order of importance of the types of alliances, but in the kind of situation which existed during and after the Second Plenum, all the types of alliance tended to be equally important.

As far as *political opinion* alliances are concerned, the difference between progressive and moderate is hardly relevant within the present context. There was in any case no official Right wing at the time, since it had been eliminated. The differences between moderate Left, radical Left and ultra Left are also hardly worth considering within the present situation. For example, those uncertain on the Right would tend to compensate this by taking a 'firm stand' on the Left. Clearly, the converse would apply. It would therefore be extremely risky to try to apply political labels to the participants in this situation; and it would seem much more sensible to confine oneself to examining the proportions of opinions for and against in any particular issue. Differences in *political style* do provide some guidance. For instance, the political behaviour of Lin Piao, Chen Po-ta and Chou En-lai can be characterized in terms of subtlety or dogma, diplomacy or tactlessness, democracy or authoritarianism. A second important category of alliances is that based on *institutional affiliation*, which involves identification of interests and a common base within the power structure. One example of this was the formation on the eve of the Cultural Revolution of an important group affiliated to the Party apparatus, the youth league and the trade unions. The same kind of influence was exerted by the government apparatus, although here divisions occurred along the lines of the different sectors: agriculture, industry, finance and defence. And during the Cultural Revolution numbers of institutions were created, such as the Revolutionary Committees, on which people based their interests and position. Another form of institutional affiliation was formed by the degree to which one was linked either to the central powers or to the provinces. Some clearly represent the interests of one particular region – an important Chinese tradition and one which tended to be accentuated during the chaos of the Cultural Revolution – and this was especially crucial in delimiting the spheres of interest of the military group.

The third important group of alliances was that based on *per-*

sonal relationships. And here it is not so much a question of similarities in character, or of personal sympathy, but rather of whether people have worked satisfactorily together in the past for a certain length of time. Family relationships can be important, but those of marriage, rather than birth. Some of the Chinese leaders became acquainted as young revolutionaries and married later, and others introduced their marriage partner into politics. There were also affiliations based on a common place of study (for instance, at the Whampoa Military Academy at which Chou En-lai was political commissioner in the twenties). Periods spent abroad could also cement personal alliances (Chou and Chen I, for instance, had both worked in France), as could a common home region. There were also the differences between those who had worked 'underground' in the 'white regions' which had been under the control of Chiang Kai-shek, and those who had worked in the 'red regions', and the common interest of those who had fought in the same army corps.

These and similar alliances often continue for a long time, and the study of them is a favourite occupation among China-watchers and Pekinologists, who sometimes overestimate their value. On the other hand, it would be foolish to underestimate their significance in the situation surrounding the Second Plenum.

Part Nine
Maoists Against Mao –
Mao Against Maoists

'Sometimes I wonder', I said, 'whether those who shout
"Mao" the loudest and wave the most banners are not – as
some say – waving the Red Flag in order to defeat the
Red Flag.'
Mao nodded. He said such people fell in three categories.
The first were sincere people. The second were those who
drifted with the tide – they conformed because everyone
else shouted 'Long Live!' ('Wansui!') The third category
was insincere. I must not be taken in by such stuff.

Edgar Snow, *The Long Revolution*. Conversation with
Mao, December 1970

26: The Mao Cult and Leftist Dogma

The expression 'to wave the red flag in order to defeat the red flag' acquired a more specific meaning in the campaign against Chen Po-ta: both his rise and fall as the ideologist of the radical Left of the Party were closely linked to his position as chief editor of the theoretical Party publication, *Red Flag*. Shortly after the Second Plenum, a campaign was commenced against ultra-Left dogmatism and the Mao cult which were regarded as having gone too far. Mao's own attitude in this context had been ambiguous from the beginning. In some circumstances he was prepared to consider the personality cult as a necessary evil; in others, he regarded it as the cause of a hypocritical attitude which could be highly dangerous. During the 'fifties he had already shown some reservations with regard to the Stalin cult, although he did not think the latter's 'bootlicker' Khrushchev qualified to pronounce his condemnation of the matter.[1]

During the Cultural Revolution, Mao had realized that it was only the use of his personal prestige that had made it possible for him to protect the revolutionary principles against revisionist tendencies and to mobilize the population against the all-powerful Party bureaucracy. Mao spoke in greater detail about the personality cult in his famous conversation with Edgar Snow on 10 December 1970.

We discussed my account of our last talk, in January, 1965, in which I had reported his acknowledgement that there was indeed a 'cult of personality' in China – and moreover there was reason for one. Some people had criticized me for writing about that. So, he said, what if I had written about a 'cult of personality' in China? There was such a thing. Why not write about it? It was a fact . . . At the time of our 1965 colloquy, Mao continued, a great deal of power – over propaganda work within the provincial and local party committees, and especially in the Peking Municipal Party Committee – had been out of his control. That was why he had then stated that there was need for more personality cult, in order to stimulate the masses to dismantle the anti-Mao Party bureaucracy. Of course the personality cult had been overdone. Today, things were different. It was hard, the Chairman said, for people to overcome the habits of 3,000 years of emperor-worshipping tradition. The so-called 'Four Greats' – those epithets applied to Mao himself: 'Great Teacher, Great Leader, Great Supreme Commander, Great Helmsman' – what a nuisance. They would all be eliminated sooner or later. Only the word 'teacher' would be retained – that is, simply schoolteacher. Mao had always been a schoolteacher and still was one. He was a primary schoolteacher in Changsha even before he was a Communist. All the rest of the titles would be declined.[2]

Mao's ambiguous attitude towards the problem of the personality cult leads us to the attitude of other members of the leadership, before and after the Cultural Revolution. The first is Lu Ting-i, the 'revisionist' Minister of Culture and the director of the propaganda division of the Party. He was violently opposed to the creation of a Mao cult at the very time when this was seen as necessary by the Maoists. In the autumn of 1965 he joined the opposition with Liu Shao-chi by supporting Khrushchev's criticisms of the Stalin cult.[3] Six months later, this was to play a part in his downfall. His successor Tao Chu prepared the way for an expansion of the Mao cult, while his opposite number in the military leadership, Hsiao Hua, initiated a Lin Piao cult. Tao Chu was deposed at the beginning of 1967, to be succeeded by Chen Po-ta, who left much of the practical organization of the propaganda machine to Wang Li. The expansion of the Mao cult continued. The fall of Wang Li and Hsiao Hua did not bring about any change in the situation, and the cult continued to linger on under Chen Po-ta.

One of the causes of the continued deviations of the propaganda chiefs was thought to be the influence of 'bourgeois' prejudices which caused them to evaluate situations incorrectly. Philosophical idealism and apriorism (instead of a materialist approach) were responsible as much for 'leftist' deviations as for 'rightist' ones, which therefore tended to amount to the same thing. These deviations were thought to spring from traditional Chinese habits of metaphysical speculation. In the campaign against Liu Shao-chi mention was made of his notion of 'self-cultivation', which was influenced by the Confucian tradition and to be noted in his book *How To Be a Good Communist*. In the case of Chen Po-ta, criticism was made of his work on the philosophy of Lao Tzu, and of his *On Human Nature, the Nature of the Party, and the Nature of the Individual*. Liu's opposition to the Mao cult when circumstances demanded it, and Chen Po-ta's advocacy of the cult at times when this could lead to the development of a dangerous situation, were both taken as evidence of apriorism.

The failure of Chen to adjust his policies to the situation in the later phases of the Cultural Revolution brought about a two-fold deviation. Firstly, instead of bringing about a deeper understanding of the processes of radicalization, Chen's methods went so far as to make the process meaningless, which was expressed in increasing dogmatism on the ideological level, and factionalism on the political. Secondly, the fact that the cult had been taken too far had produced all sorts of undesirable side-effects. The elevation of Mao to the position of a demi-god had caused him to become isolated from the mass of the population. It was later said that Chen and Lin had allowed this to happen to strengthen their own position. This 'deification' also tended to spread to others among the leadership, such as Lin Piao. The intrigues of the Second Plenum, however, brought further development of the Mao cult to a definite halt. The merits of Mao were restored to more realistic proportions, which can easily be seen from a quick glance at the half-yearly indexes published by the *Peking Review*. The section devoted to Mao and his thought was now reduced from six or seven paragraphs to two. The special synopsis of the quotations of Mao was removed completely, and the quotations tended to be used much less out of context. The number of images of the Chairman was drastically reduced, both in the press and on public buildings. The rituals surrounding the reading of the *Little Red Book* began to disappear slowly from public life.

New editions of the classic texts by Marx, Engels, Lenin and Stalin now began to be published on a large scale . . . a sector of publishing which had suffered considerably from the rapid growth in the publication of texts by Mao.[4]

It was hardly surprising that the new developments introduced a further element of confusion into the situation. Many Party members at the lower levels knew that something was happening but were puzzled as to exactly what it was. They observed that a conflict had taken place during the Second Plenum, that Chen Po-ta had been deposed, and that he was being accused of being 'Left in appearance but Right in essence'. This only became a commonly-held opinion at a later date, but for the moment the extent of the issue was confused.[5] It had been rare in the past for a political purge to be limited to a single individual and, even more significant, recent movements had almost always ended on a higher level than that on which they started, although this possibility could hardly be faced in this instance. The most obvious course for the present situation to take seemed to be further expansion of the campaign against other former members of the Cultural Revolution Group. This could, in the first instance, have meant Kang Sheng, although he had always been thought of as a moderate from the beginning of the Cultural Revolution. Secondly, Chiang Ching and her colleagues could have been associated with Chen Po-ta. For a certain period she had been the most prominent advocate of the 'Left current' in the Cultural Revolution. The fact that she was Mao's wife, however, made it unlikely that she would be purged, and she and her colleagues had in any case dissociated themselves at a relatively early stage from the excesses. There are some indications that she had had criticism directed against her for her connection with some of the Red Guard organizations, but this had never seriously undermined her position.

Another conceivable direction in which the campaign could be extended was towards the central army apparatus. When Chen Po-ta's closest associates had in the past tried to use over-enthusiastic ultra-Left elements to achieve a number of political aims at home and abroad, Lin's closest supporters had also used similar elements to increase the power of the central army apparatus. The personal role played by Chen Po-ta at that time had now been recognized. Where a complete reappraisal of the May 16 movement, which had contributed to his fall, would finally lead was anybody's guess for the moment.

27: Strengthening the Position of Chou En-lai

In judging the significance of the revival of the May 16 controversy, it is well to remember that Chou En-lai had played a central part in the elimination of that movement. He had acted as the catalyst in the conflict between ultras, radicals and moderates. Together with the regional commanders, he had been the target of the 'irresponsible' actions of the ultra-Left. It was around him that the coalition to block any further advance of the ultras gathered – first made up of the regional commanders, and later involving the Shanghai section of the Cultural Revolution Group. He had always claimed that the responsibility for deviations lay among the leadership, rather than among the grass-roots workers.[1] This responsibility was again mentioned on the fall of Chen Po-ta, and even afterwards continued to be a matter of concern. Mao treated the question of Leftism in 1967–8 extensively in his conversation with Edgar Snow. On the worsening of relations with foreign countries, Snow reports Mao to have said that: '... those officials who had opposed my [Snow's] return to China in 1967 and 1968 had belonged to an ultra-Leftist group which had seized the Foreign Ministry for a time, but they were all cleared out long ago.' On the violence against 'revisionist militaries' Snow writes:

Later the conflict during the Cultural Revolution developed into war between factions – first with spears, then rifles, then mortars. When foreigners reported that China was in great chaos, they had not been telling lies. It had been true. Fighting was going on. The other thing the Chairman was most unhappy about was the maltreatment of 'captives' ...[2]

The attention given to this conversation, especially in Peking itself, is remarkable. On 26 December 1970, the 77th birthday of Mao, the conversation was given pride of place in the

People's Daily. A photograph of the two men in conversation, taken when they met, was accompanied by the announcement that matters of 'the greatest importance' were being discussed. At the beginning of the same month, between Snow's interviews with Chou and Mao, the American journalist sent a letter to the new French paper *La Nouvelle Chine* containing this cryptic passage: 'The present moment is well chosen for the launching of such a publication, since the coming year promises to be exceptionally interesting.'[3]

It was only afterwards that it became clear why he was so certain that this would be so. The sudden resuscitation of the May 16 affair meant that the time-bomb which had been placed beneath the leadership was on the point of exploding. This was made even more obvious when the Australian journalist Wilfred Burchett returned from a visit to Peking. On 24 May, he published a sensational article entitled 'The plot against Mao'.[4] Burchett can be considered to be speaking for the most part from 'well-informed sources'. On the subject of 'the May 16 plot', Burchett writes that 'some of the ultra-Leftists managed to camouflage themselves so well, that several of them were elected to positions of great responsibility during the Ninth Party Congress'. This seems to point clearly to Chen Po-ta, but it is striking that he mentions 'several', but who were they? Burchett quotes his informants: 'The leaders are known, their names will undoubtedly be published when the time comes and they are no longer in a position to cause trouble.' In July more similar statements were published. The most important is that of the Franco-Polish journalist K. S. Karol, an expert in international communism: 'The investigation into the May 16 movement is by no means closed, since it has not yet been established who the high-ranking persons were who controlled it.'[5]

While the revival of the May 16 affair again disrupted relations between the radicals and moderates within the leadership, which had only been stabilized with much difficulty, a large-scale campaign was getting under way at grass-roots level of even more thorough criticism of the Left wing. This campaign was directed not only against those who were still trying to achieve their aims through violent means, but against those

who were trying to achieve these aims by different methods.
The determination of some Red Guard organizations to stick to
their traditional methods is demonstrated by a report that, as
late as March 1970, an abortive attempt was made on the life of
Premier Chou En-lai when he was driving to Peking airport to
meet Prince Sihanouk (after the C.I.A. had supported the *coup
d'état* in Cambodia).[6] Theer were also reports of attempted dis-
ruptions in other places. Thus, according to some reports, a
group of twenty-six Red Guards were tried for the political
murder of the chairman of the Revolutionary Committee of the
province of Yunnan.[7] At the same time, the events of 1967–8
were the subject of reappraisal everywhere. William Hinton
gives us a dramatic report (his source is a tape-recording) of a
mass criticism meeting at Tsinghua University in March 1971.[8]
The criticism concerns the famous rebel leader of the first hour,
Kuai Ta-fu, who had been closely connected with the May 16
movement as the inciter of the violent factional battles of 1968.

Li Wen-yuan's sixteen-year-old daughter stood in the centre of the
stage facing an audience of thousands. She showed not the slightest
trace of fear or self-consciousness.

It was you, Kuai Ta fu, who grabbed away my father's life as he
stood guard at the edge of the cornfield! It was you and the evil
May 16 Group! This blood debt must be repaid! When I look at
my father's photograph it is as if he stood before me still, telling me
the bitter history of our family before Liberation; it is as if he were
sitting there at midnight studying Mao Tse-tung's writings after a
long day's work; it is as if he were standing in Tien An-men square
on National Day waiting for Mao Tse-tung's inspection. In my ears
I hear my father's voice. Before my eyes I see his face and the tears
roll down my cheeks.'

From the back of the Meeting Hall came the shrill voice of a girl
student: 'Kuai, you owe a blood debt to the working class!'

Then from every throat in the audience came the thunderous response: 'Kuai, you owe a blood debt, a blood debt to the working
class!'

'But when I remember that my father fought for the revolution
and died for the people, I dry my tears and grow strong,' continued
Little Li in a voice that strained the ears with its intensity. 'The more
I think the more I hate the May 16 Group that took my father's
life.'

Kuai, sitting on the right side of the stage, stared straight ahead through the thick lenses of his square-framed glasses. He was the only person in the hall who did not join in the shouting. Two of his former Regiment comrades, Jen Ch'uan-chung and Ts'ui Chao-shih, sat across from him on the left. As the slogans mounted in number and excitement they stood up to take a more active part, but Kuai never moved at all.

'I will be a loyal Red Guard forever. I will carry the revolution through to the end. I will never quit the battlefield until all cow-devils and snake-gods have been wiped out!'

As Little Li finished, both her arms raised high in the air, a student rushed across the stage with the dead worker Li's bloodstained shorts in his hands and thrust them in front of Kuai's face.

'Look, take a look at these! Is this not proof of your crime?'

'Smash the May 16 Group!' shouted the crowd. 'Smash Wang-Kuang-Ch'i!'[9]

Kuai Ta-fu displayed uncharacteristic reserve in his self-criticism. It can be supposed that he never had much difficulty in appearing more innocent than he really was (this had been apparent several times); it was also possible that he was in possession of certain information which led him to believe that a new reversal could still change the situation in his favour. We know from other sources that a group of people from Lin Piao's entourage started preparing a 'Left-wing' coup at about the same time. This coup was to fail some months later.

In the meantime, the struggle against old and new 'May 16 conspirators' was also resumed in other places. In June 1971 the 'red diplomat' Yao Teng-shan (who had taken control of the Ministry of Foreign Affairs four years before) was reported to have been tried, and there were reports that in August a large-scale search was carried out in Canton to eliminate the remnants of the underground Leftist network.[10] The developments had a direct effect on relations among the members of the leadership: condemnation of Yao Teng-shan [11] contributed to the rehabilitation of the old minister of foreign affairs Chen I, and therefore to a strengthening of Chou En-lai's position. Similarly, the discrediting of Kuai Ta-fu strengthened the position of Hsieh Fu-chih, his opponent on the Revolutionary Committee of

Peking. The position of these two Vice-Premiers now became extremely important: Chen I was on the brink of an important diplomatic offensive, and Hsieh Fu-chih, as Minister of Public Security, was to play an important part in curtailing the influence exercised by the Minister of Defence, Lin Piao.

As the campaign against the ultra-Left was continued, the position of Lin Piao weakened, while many of the officers who had tended to affiliate themselves to Chou En-lai suddenly began to figure prominently again after months of absence from the political scene. On 1 May, then, three moderate members of the important Military Commission suddenly appeared in public again: Chen I, Nieh Jung-chen and Hsu Hsiang-chien. It now looked as though the discrediting of the ultra-Left was approaching its completion and that it was on the point of having consequences on the members of the leadership. At about the same time Barry Burton expressed the opinion in an article that the downfall of Chen Po-ta was certainly not the end of the matter,

The responsibility for the 'drag out' ultra-leftism of 1967 and its consequences still apparently remains a latent, fundamental political question within the C.C.P. leadership ... It is possible that the entire 'May 16' question may still again resurface in Peking, and that additional prominent party and military leaders could be removed as a result of continued fall-out from this explosive question.[12]

Burton is an analyst working for the C.I.A., which in the meantime had found a further reason for keeping itself informed of relationships within the Chinese leadership: Edgar Snow, at the request of Chou En-lai and Mao Tse-tung, appears to have initiated a dialogue with Nixon and his advisor Kissinger. This contact was to create a sensation not only in the context of international relations, but also within the context of internal relations in China.

28: Reorganization in the Army Command

The intrigue surrounding the question of the Presidency at the Second Plenum, criticism of the personality cult, and the revival of the May 16 affair – all this pointed towards Lin Piao. He himself was undoubtedly aware of this, and later tried to make up for his opposition to the dismissal of Chen Po-ta. On 21 July 1971 the *People's Daily* quoted Lin Piao's appeal for criticism of the 'extraordinarily ambitious "little, little, ordinary person".' The use of such sarcasm by Lin was rather misplaced: he himself, like Chen Po-ta and other radical Left-wingers, had also made a ritual of openly expressing humility.[1]

Furthermore, it was clear that Lin Piao had slowly fallen down in the hierarchical order to the level of Chou En-lai.[2] At this point the leadership was also reminded of Lin's opinions on 'human nature' and on 'genius' in general and that of Mao in particular, as they were expressed in his speech of 18 May 1966. Mao later expressed reservations about Lin's remarks in his letter to Chiang Ching and pointed out to Lin in private the anti-Marxist nature of his statements. After the events of the Second Plenum, Mao considered it necessary to return to the subject within the context of a larger but still closed circle:

I have talked with Comrade Lin Piao telling him that some of his statements were not appropriate. For example, he said there has only been one genius in the world in the last several hundred years and only one in China during the last several thousand years, which does not comply with fact. Marx and Engels were contemporaries and there were less than one hundred years between them and Lenin and Stalin. Thus, how can we say only one has appeared in the last several hundred years? There were Ch'en Sheng, Wu Kuang, Hung Hsiu-ch'üan and Sun Yat-sen in China; thus, how can we say that there has only been one in several thousand years? You overdid it when you talked about 'apex' and 'one sentence worth ten thousand sentences'. One sentence is one sentence. How can it be worth ten thousand sentences? No provision shall be made for state chairmanship and I will not serve as state chairman. I have said so six times. If each time I had made one sentence, there should have been sixty thousand sentences. But, they have never listened to me. Therefore, my words are not even worth half a sentence; they equal zero. Only when Chen Po-ta talked to them, was each sentence worth ten thousand sentences. On the surface they were talking about enhancing my prestige, but who knows what was really in their minds. To make it clear, it was actually an attempt to enhance one's own reputation. It is also said that I am the founder and leader of the People's Liberation Army but Lin is the personal commander. Why can't the founder be the commander? I am not the only founder either.[3]

But although Lin Piao might have been reprimanded in private after the Second Plenum, nothing of this was known in public. On 1 October 1970, the Twenty-first Anniversary of the People's Republic, he made a speech on Tien An-men Square in Peking, following tradition.

His appearance there, however, did not mean that there had been no developments in the meantime which had a direct bearing on his position. To begin with, immediately after the end of the Second Plenum, a new director of the Party organization within the army seems to have been appointed. What was especially striking about the new appointment was that the new director was not a typical Lin-man; he was Li Te-sheng, the former commander of the military district of Anhwei and chairman of the Revolutionary Committee of that province. An independent figure, he was more a representative of the moderate regional commanders than of the central army apparatus. It was true that he had become commander and chairman of the Revolutionary Committee after he had started to give support to the Left wing in the province, but he never hesitated to criticize thoroughly that same Left wing whenever he found it necessary. Immediately after the Ninth Party Congress he had warned a 'Unity Congress' of cadres in his province against extremist tendencies: 'Some of our comrades cherish the idea they would rather be "Left" than Right, rather refuse to let people join our ranks than expand our ranks and rather put people under surveillance than "liberate" them. They are afraid of upholding principles simply for fear that they may be branded as Rightists.'[4]

Such statements show that the appointment of Li Te-sheng was a success as far as the regional commanders were concerned, in their attempts to reduce the political influence of Lin Piao in the army to more reasonable proportions.

At this point Mao himself took the initiative for the introduction of further measures. He later had this to say about it:

I have always made a point to grasp the question of line and principle. I will not make concessions on major questions of principle. After the Lushan meeting I adopted three measures: one was to cast stones, one to blend with sand and one to dig up the corner stone. After criticizing and repudiating plenty of materials gathered by Chen Po-ta, which had deceived lots of people, I approved for distribution the report by the 38th Army and report by the Tsinan Military Region opposing arrogance and conceit. I also gave instruction on one document concerning a long discussion meeting which had done nothing to criticize Chen. My method is to get hold of these stones and write down instructions for the public to discuss. This is what I call the method of casting the stone. When clay is too concrete, no air will pass through; however, blending it with a little sand will allow air to pass. The Military Commission needs to be blended with a few more people. Reorganization of the Peking Military Region is digging up the corner stone.

What do you think about the Lushan meeting? For example, what on earth was the No.6 briefing of the North China Section? Was it revolutionary, semi-revolutionary or counter-revolutionary? Personally, I think it was a counter-revolutionary briefing.[5]

It is not known what his 'No.6 briefiing' contained. It is possible that it referred to the Committee meeting held before the Second Plenum, during which Li Hsueh-feng again mentioned Lin Piao's ideas on 'the genius' of Mao, preparatory to Chen Po-ta's proposition that Mao should be made President. It is known, however, that it led to the thorough reorganization of the garrison of Peking and the Military Region of North China. The commanders Cheng Wei-shan and Li Hsueh-feng were subjected to serious criticism. The meeting at which the decision to do this was taken (December 1970–January 1971) was considered as much a test case by the moderate wing of Chou En-lai as by the radical wing of Lin Piao. Shortly before that meeting Chou told Edgar Snow that the army did not stand for everything in China. He also said that he would 'soon' be able to establish that personally. From statements made by Mao to Snow at the end of December, it was clear that Mao too was preoccupied with the problem. From information which became available later, it appears that Lin and his supporters took the reorganization as a serious defeat.

Measures were also taken in other sectors to moderate the dominant influence of Lin's central army apparatus. Probably as a result of the hidden struggle for the control of the army among the central leadership, Hsieh Fu-chih's public security apparatus was gradually detached from the army again, to which it had been subordinated at the end of January 1967 when the army started actively intervening in the Cultural Revolution. At the same time that the military potential in the regions was being strengthened, the training of the people's militia was started again; this had been suspended by Lin Piao during the Cultural Revolution.

Further discrediting of Chen Po-ta slowly began to affect Lin's position in public too. Not only did the criticism directed at Chen rub off on him (concerning the personality cult and the furthering of the activities of the May 16 movement), but the deepening implications of the intrigue around the question of the Presidency could not possibly leave him untouched either. How, then, were those intrigues evaluated by Mao?

At the Lushan meeting of 1970 they engaged in surprise attacks and underground activities. Why were they afraid of coming out in the open? Apparently, they were plotting against someone. They first engaged in deception and then in surprise attacks. Three of the five standing members were not informed, neither were the majority of the comrades in the Political Bureau, except those several big fighters, including Huang Yung-sheng, Wu Fa-hsien, Yeh Chun, Li Tso-peng and Chiu Hui-tso as well as Li Hsueh-feng and Cheng Wei-shan. They did not allow one word to leak out and then launched a surprise attack. Their action did not last only half a day or so, but continued for two and one-half days from 23 and 24 August to noon on the 25. Their action must have had a purpose. When P'eng was organizing the military club, he delivered a challenge. However, they were even worse than P'eng's. How contemptible was their way of doing things!

In my opinion their surprise attack and underground activities were organized and had a programme. Their programme was nothing but a creation of a state chairmanship, the advocating of the theory of 'talent', opposition to the line of the 'Ninth Congress' and the overthrow of the three-point agenda of the Second Plenary Session of the Ninth Central Committee. A certain person was anxious to become state chairman, to split the Party and to seize power. The question of genius was a theoretical question; they advocated idealist empiricism, contending that whoever opposed the theory of genius opposed me.

I have never been a genius. I have read Confucius for six years and capitalist literature for seven years. I began studying Marxism-Leninism only in 1918. How can I be a genius? Those adverbs ['Chairman Mao has ingeniously, comprehensively and creatively developed Marxism-Leninism' etc.] have been deleted several times by me. The Party Constitution had been finalized by the Ninth Congress; why didn't they open it for a look? 'Some Opinions of Mine' was written after I talked with a few people and made some investigation and study; it was intended to criticize the theory of genius. I do not mean we should drop the term genius; a genius is merely a person who is a little smarter than others. A genius cannot succeed by himself, but only with the help of several persons. A genius must rely on the Party, which is the vanguard of the proletariat. A genius must rely on the mass line and collective wisdom.

The talk by Comrade Lin Piao was made without consulting me, nor was it checked by me. They did not disclose their opinions in advance, presumably because they were sure about their views. It seemed that they would succeed. However, when they realized it wouldn't work, they were upset and did not know what to do. Their courage in the beginning seemed to be able to level Lushan [or Lu Mountain] to the ground and have the momentum of stopping the movement of the earth. However, several days later, the record [of Yeh Chun's speech about Mao's genius] was quickly recalled. If it was justified, why should it be recalled? It indicated that they were afraid and panicky.[6]

These campaigns and their attendant criticism were drawing

closer and closer to Lin Piao. In April 1971, a special meeting was held in connection with the events which had taken place at the Second Plenum, to discredit Chen Po-ta even further. The actions of Cheng Wei-shan (of the Peking garrison) and Li Hsueh-feng (North China region) were also censured again. A new element was that self-criticism was now demanded from the whole group surrounding Lin Piao: his wife and secretary Yeh Chun, his chief-of-staff Huang Yung-sheng, and his deputies, Wu Fa-hsien (air force), Li Tso-peng (navy) and Chiu Hui-tso (logistics). Significantly, the meeting was chaired by Chou En-lai and attended by a select company of ninety-nine high-ranking Party members and army personnel, including two divisional directors from the general staff. Lin Piao is said to have objected violently against the presence of such a large gathering. Although Mao Tse-tung expressed satisfaction with the self-criticism, and the matter now seemed closed, it was still quite clear that this meeting for the purpose of criticism and self-criticism signified humiliation for a large number of people in Lin's immediate entourage, and could be considered as marking a very definite change in the direction of the tide. Only immediate intervention could reverse the trend.

29: Breaking out of Diplomatic Isolation

The world table-tennis championship was held in Tokyo around the middle of March 1970. There were teams from all over the world, including Western Europe, Canada and the United States. There was an exchange of reciprocal invitations, and the Chinese representative invited his opposite numbers from several Western countries with whom Peking maintained diplomatic relations to a friendship tour through the People's Republic, after the championship arrangements. For the first time, too, the United States was approached. It had now become theoretically possible for Americans to travel to China, since Washington had lifted the ban on travel to China on the day that the table-tennis players left for Tokyo. A series of nocturnal telephone calls between Tokyo and Washington produced the decision to allow fifteen American players, together with a number of Western Europeans and Canadians, to cross into China.

A common aim was achieved: the barrier of silence was broken. The American visitors returned impressed with the Chinese way of life, and the phantom image of the 'red dragon' and the 'yellow peril', which had existed for several decades in the mass media and the public mind, began to disappear. The United States government gradually began to relax the economic blockade of China, in the hope of a new (and immeasurable) market.

As the capitalist press began to employ the term 'ping-pong diplomacy' to indicate the resumption of a Chinese foreign policy, no one could have guessed how quickly this opening would lead to a complete upset in the political balance of China itself, of Asia and of the whole world. Peking and Washington were both feeling the need to resume contact, although there could be no question of normal relations for the moment. Too much had happened for this to be immediately possible: the Cold War, the American and subsequent Chinese interventions in Korea, American intervention in the Chinese civil war by supporting Chiang Kai-shek and protecting him in Taiwan, and American intervention in Vietnam, Laos and Cambodia. China was still surrounded by a circle of American military bases. The absence of relations between the two countries, then, was not so much the result of a lack of understanding and acquaintance-ship, but rather of a continuing and deeply-rooted animosity and aggression.

At some point in time, however, the United States was rele-gated to second place as an enemy of China. And in 1968 there was some hope for a rapid end to the war in Vietnam. A second relevant development was the increasing tension with the Soviet Union. China had to choose between two enemies, of whom the Chinese had now decided that the United States was the less dangerous. China was separated from the United States by a large ocean, whereas it had a long common border with the Soviet Union. There were also other factors: the threat of mili-tary conflict with the United States seemed to be diminishing, while the threat of the Soviet Union was increasing. The course of the Vietnam war had demonstrated that there was influential opposition to it within the imperialist camp, which could be used. There was no such possibility in the Soviet Union. Finally, although China was closer to the Soviet Union ideologically, this also involved greater risk of a 'fifth column'; in the event of war with the Soviet Union, was it not possible that many of those who had been defeated in the Cultural Revolution (and even before) would aim at establishing a kind of 'Vichy government'? If Peking wanted to expand its relationship with the United States, the need remained to bring diplomatic considerations into line with strategic ones; in fact, official relations with the United States do not exist to this day, while there are still all kinds of larger and smaller links with the Soviet Union.

On the American side, Nixon had also changed his approach to Asian affairs during 1969. The United States declared that she was going to withdraw all ground forces from Asia in due course. In the event of conflict allies would be able to count 'only' on logistical support and on 'limited' support from the air. The traditional and only diplomatic contacts between China and the United States (between their ambassadors in Warsaw) were resumed in January 1970 at the request of the Americans, after they had been broken off in 1968. There was a project for more extensive contact, but nothing came of this after C.I.A. support for the *coup d'état* in Cambodia, in the hope of averting defeat in Vietnam by capturing hide-outs and supply bases which the Vietnamese Liberation Army had established in neutral territory. The hoped-for result, however, did not materialize. Sihanouk received the support of Peking and the discussions in Warsaw were countermanded. In China, the biggest anti-American demonstrations for years were held. On 20 May 1970 one of Mao's rare statements on foreign policy was published, which emphasized the Chinese standpoint:

Unable to win in Vietnam and Laos, the U.S. aggressors treacherously engineered the reactionary *coup d'état* by the Lon Nol–Sirik Matak clique, brazenly dispatched their troops to invade Cambodia and resumed the bombing of North Vietnam, and this has aroused the furious resistance of the three Indo-Chinese peoples. I warmly support the fighting spirit of Samdech Norodom Sihanouk, Head of State of Cambodia, in opposing U.S. imperialism and its lackeys. I warmly support the Joint Declaration of the Summit Conference of the Indo-Chinese Peoples. I warmly support the establishment of the Royal Government of National Union under the Leadership of the National United Front of Kampuchea. Strengthening their unity, supporting each other and persevering in a protracted people's war, the three Indo-Chinese peoples will certainly overcome all difficulties and win complete victory.

While massacring the people in other countries, U.S. imperialism is slaughtering the white and black people in its own country. Nixon's fascist atrocities have kindled the raging flames of the revolutionary mass movement in the United States. The Chinese people firmly support the revolutionary struggle of the American people. I am convinced that the American people who are fighting valiantly will ultimately win victory and that the fascist rule in the United States will inevitably be defeated.[1]

The main point of Chinese foreign policy can be summed up in this quotation from Mao's declaration: 'The danger of a new world war still exists and the people of the world should be prepared for it. But the main trend in the world today is revolution.'

At the same time, it remained apparent that Mao Tse-tung was still very conscious of the numerous internal contradictions of American imperialism and the necessity of at least breaking the deadlock. In this he was supported by Chou En-lai, though Lin Piao remained opposed to it. He saw considerable advantages in the exploitation of these contradictions, on both the strategic and diplomatic levels. It was for that reason that a certain ambiguity became apparent at the beginning of 1971 in the Chinese attitude towards the United States. While violent opposition to American intervention in Asia continued to be voiced, Edgar Snow and several other Western mediators were sounding out Washington's readiness to establish a dialogue. As fresh invasions were taking place at the beginning of 1971 in Laos and Cambodia, the *People's Daily* carried the following warning headline over several columns on its front page: 'Nixon, don't lose your head!'

The aid of Indo-Chinese revolutionaries was perceptively increased, and there were declarations of readiness for 'the greatest national sacrifice'.

This was the situation when the American table-tennis players arrived in Peking. The group received V.I.P. treatment, not only by the Western press but also at the hands of the Chinese Government. They were received personally by Chou En-lai who seized the opportunity of making the meaning of this sporting encounter clear:

Contacts between the people of China and the United States have been frequent in the past, but later they were broken off for a long time. Your visit to China on invitation has opened the door to friendly contacts between the people of the two countries. We believe that such friendly contacts will be favoured and supported by the majority of the two peoples.

The table-tennis players were followed by other American groups who came to visit China. The positive attention of the American press and public was enormous, while opinion on the

People's Republic was completely reversed. Firstly, a majority of the American people declared itself in favour of admitting China to the United Nations. Mao and Chou had done very well out of their gamble. Within a few months, China's diplomatic position in the world had changed considerably for the better; and America itself was obliged to abandon its policy of holding China at a distance.

Part Ten
Conflict

Some people may create trouble, and some people are
creating trouble. There are many ambitious conspirators.
They are representatives of the capitalist class eager to
overthrow the political power of our proletarian class. We
shall never let them succeed. A group of sons-of-bitches
wants to take chances, and is waiting for opportunities.
They want to kill us and we have to suppress them. They
are pseudo-revolutionaries, pseudo-Marxists, and
pseudo-believers in Mao Tse-tung's thought; they are
traitors. They rebel even when Chairman Mao lives. They
obey perfunctorily and rebel in reality. They are
ambitious conspirators, create trouble, and want to kill
by various means. He said he did not know about his
wife's affairs, but how could he not know?

Lin Piao on Lu Ting-i, 18 May 1966

30 : Differences of Opinion on Foreign Policy

Kissinger's attack of 'flu

In the summer of 1971 world attention shifted from China to the Indian sub-continent, where Pakistan and India seemed once more about to go to war. Elections in Pakistan had caused relations between the eastern and western parts to deteriorate completely. The western part of Pakistan made up the larger part of the country's total area, had the smaller population, the greater rate of consumption, and the lower rate of production; it did, however, dominate the eastern part, where the demand for greater autonomy produced a huge victory in the elections for the Awami League of Mujibur Rahman. The military government of Pakistan refused to recognize the results of the elections and rejected the demands for greater autonomy. Uprisings were followed by bloody repression by the army, and masses of refugees began to stream into India, bringing considerable difficulties in their wake, which India then used as an excuse to interfere in the conflict. The Americans remained undecided as to which side they should support in the conflict: they were rivals with the Soviet Union in India, and with China in Pakistan. This was the background to President Nixon's decision to send his advisor Kissinger on a fact-finding mission. During a journey into the interior, shortly after his arrival in Islamabad, Kissinger suffered a mild attack of influenza. Accompanying journalists were informed by official spokesmen that the attack was not serious, but the Presidential advisor would have to stay in bed for a few days. By 12 July Kissinger had recovered. He finished off his discussions and flew back to Washington. Three days later Nixon made a sensational announcement: his advisor had not remained out of sight for a few days because of influenza, but because he was carrying out an important mission. In fact, from 9 to 11 July he was not in Pakistan at all, but ... in China, where he had had conversations with Chou En-lai and other top Chinese officials. In so doing, he had already cleared the way for a visit to China by Nixon.

At the same time, Peking also released the news to the world, though in somewhat more sober tones. The *People's Daily* wrote: 'Knowing of President Nixon's expressed desire to visit the People's Republic of China, Premier Chou En-lai, on behalf of the Government of the People's Republic of China, has extended an invitation to President Nixon to visit China at an appropriate date before May 1972.'[1]

The announcement caused enormous world-wide sensation. In the United States reactions were mixed, but a majority of people were in favour of the initiative. Most of the allies of the United States were somewhat less than enthusiastic, since they had not been informed in advance. The Nationalists in Taiwan, and the government of Saigon, were afraid of losing American support, which was the only thing which made it possible for them to maintain their present positions. Japan and a number of other countries felt they had been betrayed after many years of solidarity with the Americans in their confrontation with China. The outcome was a flurry of travelling on the part of American diplomats to offer their explanations. The Chinese leaders were also obliged to offer some explanation to their own allies. Here, the propaganda division of the Central Committee spared no pains in explaining the initiative to the population throughout the country. The initiative was also the point of fervent discussion among the leadership, to say the least; but differences of opinion were widened not so much by the actual step itself, as by the consequences on the broader context of Chinese international strategy.

Contradictory conclusions among the Chinese leadership

The Chinese leadership had always maintained its attacks on the superpower-hegemony, claiming repeatedly that China herself did not want to be a superpower and wished to continue to show solidarity with the countries of the Third World. The claim in itself was certainly no guarantee of the country's intentions. All countries in the process of becoming superpowers invoke altruistic motives as they go about establishing their position. Colonization by the Western European powers was justified by 'a duty to civilize the rest of the world'; Japanese expansion took place 'in order to liberate the Asiatic brother countries from colonial yoke', and 'to create a Greater Asiatic Sphere of Welfare'; American imperia.st acts were directed towards 'the defence of the free world against totalitarianism, fascism and communism'; and Soviet Russian 'social imperialism' was excused on the grounds that it was 'in order to defend the integrity of the socialist bloc against subversion'. China's anti-superpower ideology could therefore theoretically be an ideal stance for achieving precisely that position.

Chou En-lai, it is true, had always expressed support for the countries of the Third World; this does not, however, alter the fact that it was 'his' diplomatic offensive which had now placed China in an essentially different position from other countries in that sphere. Before the Cultural Revolution Lin Piao had set himself up as the strategist of the Third World countries, by proclaiming the invincibility of the people's war. His enthusiasm for China's *avant-garde* role in the world had, however, caused him to be regarded very much as a Chinese chauvinist. A great number of people, both in China and abroad, felt that the invitation to Nixon did herald the beginning of a move by China towards a superpower policy, in spite of all the reassuring noises made to the contrary. There is no doubt that this point was raised at the session of the Standing Committee and the Political Bureau, who were dealing with the matter. It is clear, too, that different groups held varying opinions on the existing superpowers, on the degree to which they each separately presented a threat, and on the most suitable policy for facing them. Lin Piao and his supporters were undoubtedly much more orthodox in their view of Western imperialism (if only because 'they had never been there') than Chou En-lai and his colleagues, who were more closely acquainted with the contradictory aspects of Western political reality. In addition, attitudes to the Soviet Union also have to be taken into account. This was a country about which almost everyone knew the positive and negative aspects at close quarters; its revisionism was universally condemned but, in the last analysis, not everyone held the same views of Chinese–Soviet relationships. Everyone wanted to continue the ideological fight with the Soviet Union – if need be, according to Lin Piao, together with the fight against the United States. But if priority had to be given to one of the confrontations, then it must be to the struggle against imperialism: better a bad socialist than a good capitalist, so reasoned Lin and his colleagues. Chou and other officials, on the other hand, believed that Soviet revisionism was dangerous in a much more real way, and that it was, in any case, much easier to take advantage of the contradictions in Western imperialism.

Once again it was Mao's opinion which proved decisive. He chose the line recommended by Chou En-lai and rejected that of Lin Piao, turning to a close study of foreign policy. ('Now I act like a student by reading two volumes of reference materials each day. Therefore, I am familiar with some international affairs.'[2])

From 23 July on, Lin Piao made an inspection tour of various army divisions. According to him, this was to examine the readiness of the troops, but according to later accusations, it was in fact to make sure of the loyalty of his subordinates. As far as possible, he now avoided all contact with Mao and Chou. And although one particular policy had been decided upon, disagreement on the subject still remained.

31 : Differences of Opinion on Domestic Policy

The reconstruction of the Party

In the middle of August 1971 the last provincial Party committee was constituted. While the delegates at the Ninth Party Congress and the members of the new Central Committee were largely co-opted from above, later elections were very much grass-roots affairs. First came the reconstruction of the Party cells at the lowest levels (agricultural work-teams, workshops in industry, villages and districts), then the purging of the rank and file and the recruitment of new members, the formation of election committees, the elections of higher Party organs in the communes, the districts, and finally in the provinces. A similar process took place within civil and military institutions, and within both old and new people's organizations. This process was already fairly advanced by the time of the Second Plenum. One reason for proceeding as swiftly as possible with the reconstruction was that deep differences of opinion had shown themselves to exist during the process. It was hoped that the period of reconstruction would be over in time for the Fiftieth Anniversary of the Party (1 July 1971), so that a number of important decisions could be taken, such as those connected with the People's Congress, the constitution and the Presidency. In fact, the process was only finished six weeks after the anniversary date, and the various differences of opinion had deepened in the meantime, making the composition of the new Party committees a matter of the greatest importance.

At first sight, it looked as though recent trends had simply been strengthened in the composition of the new committees. Of the twenty-nine secretaries of the provincial Party committees, twenty-two were from the armed services, as against four before the Cultural Revolution. Not all of these, however, were genuine military personnel; at least eight out of the twenty-two had joined the army as political commissioners before or during the Cultural Revolution. And, in this instance, the significance of the high representation of olive-green uniforms was quite different from that in the case of the Revolutionary Committees and the Central Committee. The military representation on the new Party committees was not a sign in favour of Lin Piao and the central army apparatus, but rather of the regional commanders who now formed the largest group in the new bodies. Of the ten regional commanders known to have been members of the new bodies, not less than seven were first secretaries of provincial Party committees. Another three were deputy secretaries. Of twenty-seven district commanders, five were first secretaries and twenty-two were deputy secretaries. And while Lin had managed to establish some kind of control over a large number of regional and district commanders in 1967–8, a moderate group of 'strong' regional commanders had now begun to form in support of Chou. This was to have decisive significance in the renewed confrontation.

The Constitution and Presidency once again

According to unconfirmed reports a meeting of the Party leadership was held somewhere in the provinces on 18 August, presumably to prepare for the Third Plenary Session of the Central Committee. The principal task of the meeting was to advance the preparations for the People's Congress which could now be held in the autumn of 1971, while the principal document under consideration was the definitive version of the project for the Constitution; the task which was likely to cause most discussion, however, was still if and how the Presidency was to be filled. The meeting was thus faced with the problem of carrying on where the Second Plenum had left off, although the situation was naturally very different now. As far as Lin Piao, Huang Yungsheng and the other central army leaders were concerned, it had become a matter of sink or swim. Understandably, they saw it as not so much a question of their own personal fate, but rather for what they considered to be the Maoist achievements of the Cultural Revolution, which they believed to be threatened by a return to former methods. On the other hand, Chou En-lai, the central Government apparatus and the regional army leaders were all equally convinced that the time had come for it to be made clear once and for all to Lin and his supporters that they could not control virtually all sectors of political life. The discussion on this point was again embittered by the question of the Presidency. While it was true that Mao's nomination for the Presidency (and his automatic succession by Lin) had been shelved, not everyone may have grasped the fact that a direct nomination of Lin had also been made impossible. Furthermore there was just a possibility that another candidate from Lin's entourage could be proposed for the position, such as his chief-of-staff Huang Yung-sheng, since he might also be presented as the ideal compromise figure to satisfy the regional commanders. Anyone believing in this possibility was soon disillusioned. During the meeting, a movement to have the individual-style Presidency abolished altogether began to make itself felt; the supporters of this movement wanted to see it replaced by a form of collective leadership. And if this was not sufficient setback for the central army leadership, strong opposition began to develop at the same time against the inclusion of Lin's name next to that of Mao in the constitution. As Chou remarked, 'The inclusion of Lin's name as Mao's successor in the Party statutes of 1969 had drawn the ridicule of the nations and fraternal parties of the world.' He went on to say, 'The party regulations of the Ninth Congress had a pervasive feudalistic coloration; and if the successor is also written into the Constitution it will supply anti-Chinese and anti-communistic elements with even more pretexts.'[1]

The discussions were again very intense, as they had been the year before. Once again, Mao took sides with Chou. No final decision was reached, however, and the meeting broke up in a very tense atmosphere. The only outcome of the meeting, as far as outside observers could see, was that the convocation of the People's Congress was again being delayed. Feelings among the leadership were far from cordial as the meeting was adjourned.

Mao's visions

The ruling Chinese triumvirate now genuinely seemed on the verge of a split. Chou returned to Peking to devote himself to Government matters. He made public appearances virtually every few days – at receptions, for instance – and appeared to act as if nothing had happened. The two other members of the leadership trio disappeared completely from sight. Mao behaved as he had always done in political crises: he retired into his favourite, heavily-guarded residence in Shanghai, to which he invited both supporters and opponents for consultations. During these audiences, he gave a detailed exposition of the nature of the present crisis. These conversations were summarized and distributed among Party members six months later.[2]

Mao first referred again to 'the struggle between the two lines', the right and the wrong, which everyone had studied for the Fiftieth Anniversary of the Party on 1 July. He summed up the nine most important crises in the Party's past: from that concerning Chen Tu-hsiu in 1927, to that concerning Chu Chiu-pai, Li Li-san, Lo Chang-lung, Wang Ming, Chang Kuo-tao, Kao Kang (and Jao Shu-shih) and Peng Te-huai, to that involving Liu Shao-chi at the time of the Cultural Revolution. Then Mao reached the tenth crisis which had begun with the dismissal of Chen Po-ta and had continued with the criticism of the faction formed by Yeh Chun, Huang Yung-sheng, Wu Fa-hsien, Li Tso-peng in April 1971, and ended with the doubts surrounding the role of Lin Piao. In the past it had been customary for the behaviour of the central figure in a political crisis to be later subjected to critical investigation. This time, however, Mao said, 'No personal summing-up has been made this time for the sake of protecting Vice-Chairman Lin.'

In the light of the events of August 1971, this state of affairs no longer seemed tenable:

Of course, he [Lin] must share part of the responsibility. What should be done to those people? It is necessary to adopt the policy of education, namely 'learning from past mistakes to avoid future ones and curing the sickness to save the patient'. It is still necessary to protect Lin. No matter who committed the mistake, not to talk about unity and line is no good. After returning to Peking I will again send for them for talks. They do not want to see me, but I want to see them . . . Some of them may be saved but some may not . . . All depends on their practice. There are two possibilities: one is that they rectify their mistakes and the other is that they may not. Those who have committed mistakes in principle and in line and orientation and are the leading culprits will find rectifying difficult. In history, did Chen Tu-hsiu rectify his mistakes? Did Chu Chiu-pai, Li Li-san, Lo Chang-lung, Wang Ming, Chang Kuo-tao, Kao Kang (+ Jao Shu-shih), Peng Teh-huai and Liu Shao-chi rectify theirs? No, they did not. I have talked with Comrade Lin Piao telling him that some of his statements were not appropriate . . .

Mao also commented on the misguided behaviour of Lin's wife, Yeh Chun:

I have always objected to having one's wife serve as director of one's office. In Lin Piao's office, it is Yeh Chun who serves as office director. The 'four persons' [Huang Yung-sheng, Wu Fa-hsien, Li Tso-peng and Chiu Hui-tso] must first see her in order to ask for instructions from Lin. [But] all work must be done personally, read personally and replied to personally. We should not rely on secretaries and give them too much power. My secretary handles only reception work; all papers are selected and checked by me. We must do our own work lest some mistakes should occur.

It is clear that Mao was taking this opportunity to allude to the criticism which had been earlier expressed of his own wife, Chiang Ching. Unlike Yeh Chun, however, she had been almost entirely responsible for her own actions, nor had she acted as the only contact between her husband and the outside world. It is also fairly clear that Mao must have had a pretty good idea that Yeh Chun was instrumental in creating and organizing the faction around Lin and his four generals. Mao also went to great lengths to inform the authorities in Shanghai and Nanking, who bore equal responsibility for his security, about the risk of conflict which had arisen. 'These opinions of mine are made only as personal views, they are only casual remarks. Don't draw any conclusions now; let the Central Committee do it', he said modestly. But he also added, 'We must be careful. First of all the army must be careful [the regional army command in Nanking], and secondly, local authorities must be careful' [the Revolutionary Committee of Shanghai]. 'Don't be conceited. If conceited, one will commit mistakes. The army must be united and streamlined. I don't think ours will rebel,' he said confidently. At the same time he addressed himself to his chief-of-staff (although it is not clear whether he was present when Mao was expressing these opinions) with a barely concealed warning:

Nor do I believe that you (Huang Yung-sheng) can command the Liberation Army to rebel either. There are divisions and regiments under the army. There are also commanding headquarters, the political and logistics departments. Will they all listen to you?

These allusions were clearly to Huang himself (the headquarters command), his eventual allies (the logistics department), and his opponents (the reformed political branch) in the central army apparatus. Until a year before, the last-named department had been Lin's most important weapon in the domination of his independent kingdom, but it had been placed under the control of an obvious moderate, the regional commander Li Te-sheng, at about the time of the Second Plenum. Although this paragraph looks innocent enough in the published text, it was in fact a warning shot intended for the Lin faction. It also contained a considerable amount of bluff, since Mao was fully aware that the political and military power of the Lin–Huang group was still great enough to cause disruption. His attention was particularly aroused at the 18 August meeting by a proposition put forward by the central army command and approved by the Central Committee, and published two days later.[3] It contained some recommendations made by the command of the military region of Canton (the power base of the chief-of-staff Huang Yung-sheng) for the continuation of the army's participation in non-military fields, which it had originally taken on itself before and during the Cultural revolution. Mao told his audience in Nanking and Shanghai: 'In the space for official reply by central authorities I added the words "study conscientiously" so as to arouse the attention.'

If at that time his doubts amounted only to reservations, they were soon to grow into suspicions. Some of the matters mentioned in this document were:

(a) The slogan 'Learn from Taching [a model oil-refinery] in industry, from Tachai [a model agricultural commune] in agriculture, and the whole country must learn from the People's Liberation Army.' This slogan had been current during the Cultural Revolution, but before the Liberation the following words had also been added: '. . . the People's Liberation Army must learn from the people in the whole country'. Mao was in favour of reintroducing this original addition.

(b) The task of the army to 'support the Left' and 'exercise military control', which had been formulated in 1967, was retained in the document in the same wording, but Mao recommended an amendment here:

Now that local Party committees have been established, they should be allowed to practise unified leadership. If decisions have already been made by local Party committees on certain matters, is it not justified to ask military units for further discussion?

(c) The most important matter raised was perhaps that of the formation in certain army divisions of special groups of political activists which (again going back to the procedures of the Cultural Revolution) were holding training sessions in the form of 'cultural congresses'. Mao also expressed his doubts about the formation of such cells and wanted to know under whose leadership these groups were placed:

How about the effect of those conferences of activists? It, too, deserves study. Some of the conferences are good but some are not. The major problem is that of line. If the line is not correct, the conference will not proceed well.

He was obviously worried that, like the General Political Branch in the past, these groups would form an army within the army.

Mao's fears seemed to be increasingly well-founded. In Peking, Chou En-lai received reports from the information services of Hsieh Fu-chih that the leadership of the special groups of political activists set up by Huang Yung-sheng within some army units was untrustworthy. In addition, the whole Lin Piao faction was reported to have gone to Canton after the meeting of the middle of August, officially to ratify the decision of the Central Committee, but in fact to deliberate on the situation and to discuss possible measures. Mao summoned Liu Hsing-yuan, who had for years been one of Huang's closest colleagues, to see him in Shanghai. According to popular gossip in Canton, the conversation[4] went as follows: 'What is your impression about Huang Yung-sheng?'

Liu Hsing-yuan, knowing nothing about the truth, answered: 'I have followed Comrade Huang Yung-sheng for more than 10 years. He has a strong will, is a good boss.' Mao Tse-tung immediately said seriously: 'Huang Yung-sheng is a swindler of the Liu Shao-chi type.'

Liu Hsing-yuan felt cold sweat flowing down his spine, secretly cursing himself for the mistake. But he was quick to change his course and immediately added: 'The Party and Chairman Mao are wise and correct. I will follow Chairman Mao closely all the rest of my life to make revolution.' Mao Tse-tung was greatly pleased, as if he had taken some tranquillizing pills, and gave Liu his confidential instructions.

Although a story which came via Canton and Hong Kong cannot be taken as being reliable in all its details, it was clear that something dramatic was brewing.

Part Eleven
The Background to the Plot

On this tiny globe
A few flies dash themselves against the wall,
Humming without cease,
Sometimes shrilling,
Sometimes moaning.
Ants on the locust tree assume a great nation swagger
And mayflies lightly plot to topple the giant tree.
The west wind scatters leaves over Changan,
And the arrows are flying, twanging.

First stanza of Mao Tse-tung's poem 'Reply to Comrade
Kuo Mo-jo', 9 January 1963

32: Discovery of a Plan for a Putsch; the Flight of Lin Piao

Lin Tou-tou and Lin Li-kuo

Like his sister, Lin Li-kuo was the child of Lin's first marriage, which had taken place in the autumn of 1937 in Yenan. Their real mother was Liu Hsi-ming, and Lin's second wife, Yeh Chun, was thus only their stepmother. At the beginning of the Cultural Revolution they were both probably receiving educations which prepared them for service in the air force. Unfortunately, we know nothing about Li-kuo's career during the Cultural Revolution, but we do know a great deal about the activities of Tou-tou. She had belonged to the 'Red Flag' Red Guards of the Aeronautical Institute in Peking, a group which moved rapidly during the first few months from 'Right-wing loyalism' to 'ultra-Leftism'. Originally it was closely connected with those groups which formed the so-called First and Second Headquarters, in which the children of Party bosses played such an important part, and which, in spite of their small size, disposed of a wide range of facilities in Peking for their commandos, including hiding places, cars, stencil machines and loudspeakers. Close links were later established with the Third Headquarters, and the newly-formed Fourth, the 'May 16' group. The 'line' of this Red Flag group was an almost classic demonstration of 'waving the Red Flag to defeat the Red Flag', of 'petit-bourgeois' wavering – which over-compensated by being ultra-revolutionary. After being closely connected with the supporters of Liu Shao-chi, they were later in the vanguard of those who condemned him. The same kind of behaviour could be illustrated with regard to Tao Chu and many others. The group was also indirectly involved in the 'civil war' at Tsinghua University.[1]

Although it is not known to which groups Lin Li-kuo belonged, it was almost certainly to similar kinds of organizations as his sister. He was, however, rather older than his sister, and was probably nearing the end of his education so that, thanks to the influence of his father, he was able to join the radical Leftist air force leadership during the Cultural Revolution; he was in this position when the removal of people of similar persuasion to himself – like Yu Li-chin in 1968 – from influential positions began to take place. For the time being, however, he was a leading young officer, deputy director of the strike command of the air force, and acting commander of an air force based on the crucial border with the People's Republic of Mongolia.

During the previous few months, Lin Li-kuo had travelled a great deal more than seems to have been necessary for the simple fulfilment of his official function. He had gone to some trouble to cement old friendships and establish a number of fresh ones. He had also formed around himself a group of young radical and ambitious air force officers – a course of action which almost looks too much like the classic preparations for a *coup d'état* to be true. The officers belonged to two groups: those within the central air force command, and those belonging to various branches of the air force which were stationed in Eastern China. These were made up chiefly of men from Nanking (Kiangsu Province) and Hangchow (Chekiang Province). These provinces were also close to Shanghai which, as an industrial centre, was under the central administration; it was also the centre of Maoist power, as well as being the town of Mao's favourite residence. It was there, according to unconfirmed reports, that a number of unidentified aircraft and/or commando units carried out attacks on 8 and 10 September with the obvious intention of abducting or killing Mao.

Lin Li-kuo's innermost circle of friends consisted of seven people. Apart from himself there were: Yu Hsin-yeh, deputy director of the political bureau of the central Party committee of the air force (within the headquarters office in Peking); Chou Yu-chih, also deputy director of the bureau; Chen Li-yun, political commissioner of the air force command in Nanking; Wang Wei-kuo, political commissioner of the fourth army of the air force, and deputy member of the Central Committee; Li Wei-hsin, deputy director of the secretariat of the political branch of the fourth army of the air force.

The last-named was the first to talk.

The '571' plan

'I have not seen the "571" plan, but Yu Hsin-yeh said boastfully on 11 September that Lin Li-kuo had left the plan and an actual example of an armed uprising (recently summarized by Yu Hsin-yeh) to the attention of the Minister, Lin Piao, and the director, Yeh Chun, at Peitaiho.'[2] The suspicion that it was the group around Lin Li-kuo which carried out the attacks around Shanghai seems fairly well-founded. This suspicion is further confirmed if we look at the descriptions of the preparations, the plan itself, and Li Wei-hsin's confession. The idea for the plan was first put forward after the Second Plenum and was further elaborated after what took place around the beginning of the year: the turbulent meeting of the North China bureau in December 1970 and the complete reorganization of the military command for the area around Peking in January 1971. At the end of February Lin Li-kuo saw his father and stepmother in Suchow. They were pessimistic about the future and presumably took no care to hide it, although it is not certain whether they encouraged their son to carry on with his plans for a coup. Lin Li-kuo travelled to Shanghai and Hangchow to hold discussions with friends for the first time about possible action:

We must use violent revolution to stop a gradual counter-revolutionary change in the form of a peaceful transformation. On the contrary, if we do not use the '571' *kung ch'eng* [armed uprising] to stop peaceful transformation, then, once they succeed, no one knows how many heads will fall to the ground and no one knows how many years the Chinese revolution will be behind schedule. A new round of power struggle will be inevitable. If we do not control the leadership of the revolution, the leadership will fall on others.

At the end of March he returned from Hangchow with Yu Hsin-yeh and Li Wei-hsin to Shanghai, where they were joined two days later by Chou Yu-chih from Peking. Between 22 and

24 March they worked together in the utmost secrecy on a project for a possible armed uprising:

This project is classified as top secret, which will not be revealed to anyone without approval. It is absolutely necessary that all actions be taken in accordance with order. Develop the spirit of Eda Gima. [the Japanese marine establishment during the Second World War] We must be determined to die with our cause if we fail. All those who leak out the secret, neglect their duties, waver in their determination and betray our cause, shall be severely punished.

The conspirators gave the code name of '571' to their project (which may refer to May 1971, just as the May 16 conspirators were called '516'). The pronunciation of the codeword is almost the same as that of the words meaning 'armed uprising', and also (in Pekingese only) 'Wu Han uprising', referring perhaps to the previous conflict between radical and conservative elements in the army. The text of the plan began with the intriguing words: 'After *several years of preparation*, the ideological, organizational and military levels have been raised considerably. We possess a certain ideological and material foundation. In the whole country, only our force is in high spirits. . .'

From these words, it could be assumed that the conspiracy was in fact the resumption of the activities of one of the underground political clubs which had flourished during the Cultural Revolution. But whereas the seven leading conspirators had still been undergoing training or were still junior officers four or five years before, they now held key positions in one of the most important army branches, the air force.

As we can see from the plan, their inspiration was that their nucleus was small, but: 'Compared with the foreign "571" *kung ch'eng*, our force is much stronger and therefore we stand a much greater chance of success. Even compared with the October Revolution, our force should not be any smaller than that of the Soviet Union.'

The air force would, as in all such coups, play an important part. The plan had this to say on this aspect:

The geographical space for manoeuvring is big, [but] the mobility of the air force is excellent. Comparatively speaking, it is easier for the air force to control the political power of the whole country though a '571' armed uprising [because] military regions will aim at local independence. [There are] two possibilities: control of national political power and creation of 'independent kingdoms' ... The broad territory provides a big space for manoeuvring, which – plus the mobility of the air force – will be advantageous to surprise attack, co-ordination, detour and even retreat ...

The first aim of the plan was to set up groups of 'political activists' within various air force units. This was justified by the people concerned by reference to the procedures current during the Cultural Revolution. But the education was less on a cultural than on an ideological plane, and the training involved more 'special duties' than straightforward military training. It is not clear whether the creation of these commandos was exclusively the responsibility of the officers concerned, or whether their creation had been made possible by the chief of the air force, Wu Fa-hsien, just as their spread throughout the whole army was to be later made possible by the general staff of Huang Yung-sheng (through the propagation of the report on Canton). What is clear is that the formation of the special groups must have advanced considerably during this period in a number of places, such as Peking, Shanghai and the surrounding towns. The text of the plan goes:

Training group: A training group will be formed ostensibly for the purpose of cultivating cadres. It is necessary that recruits be well qualified and secrecy maintained. About one hundred persons will be quartered in Hsin-hua No. 1 Village. Cadres of the training group are very important and therefore must be well chosen. It is not enough to rely solely on the cadres of the training group; the Shanghai Group must try to win over other people. The group would be headed by Ch'iu Cho-hsian and Chiang Kuo-chang and every single member or two members of the group must control one unit of the Fourth Army of the Air Force. Each individual assigned to control a certain unit must assume a post in that unit. In addition, the Training Group must be equipped with more automobiles and guns in order to acquire mobility. Wang Wei-kuo may be called upon to 'manufacture guns'. It is necessary to master a few more skills in military science and to cultivate good feelings towards the 'Minister' (Lin Piao) and the 'Vice Minister' (Lin Li-kuo) politically.

The initial aim of the conspiracy is said to have been the isolation of Mao Tse-tung, his wife Chiang Ching and their closest
colleagues, Chang Chun-chiao and Yao Wen-yuan, so that they
could be later faced with a *fait accompli* and persuaded to join
the rebel side. Li Wei-hsin said:

When Lin Li-kuo asked me whether Chang's house is in the jurisdiction of your Garrison Department, I replied I did not know. Lin
Li-kuo then asked me to find out. I remembered I could ask Li Sung-
t'ing, director of the Garrison Department, who said Chang's house
was in our jurisdiction, since we sent guards and daily necessities. I
reported the situation to Lin Li-kuo; I was engaged in counter-
revolutionary activities for their counter-revolutionary plan. After
getting rid of Chang and Yao, Lin Li-kuo said, 'Let Wang Wei-kuo
and Chen Li-yun transfer part of the Air Force units in Nanking, if
necessary, to control Shanghai. Then, unite forces of the country to
issue statements of support to force the central authorities to express approval. Should Hsu Shih-yu lead troops to intervene, then
Wang Wei-kuo would be assigned to protect Shanghai to press for
peace talks in this situation of confrontation. If worst comes to the
worst, carry on guerrilla warfare in the mountains. In this case,
Chekiang would be our first destination.' Lin Li-kuo also mentioned
that this problem was discussed with Chen Li-yun during his trip
to Hangchow. He said the plan would be written by Yu Hsin-yeh on
the basis of the idea concluded in Hangchow.

When Mao and his supporters had been neutralized in Shanghai, Chou En-lai and his allies in the Government, army and
Party would be arrested in Peking and elsewhere. Another possibility was that eventual advantage could be taken of a meeting
of the Party leadership and everyone arrested at the same time.
This could be particularly important in the case of the regional
commanders who had stood up against Lin and for Chou in
1967–8. The conspirators hoped to be able to eliminate the
most important strong men, such as Hsu Shih-yu of the Nanking region. Chen Hsi-lien of the Shenyang region, and members of the Political Bureau. As far as the other districts and
regional commanders were concerned, some of them would
probably temporarily not involve themselves, while others could
be neutralized by local Left-wing civilians or army personnel.

In any case, the air force would have control over the larger part of the country. The central positions would then inevitably be taken over by Lin Piao and his faction in the central army command.

The draft plan, as it had been worked out in March, looked as if it had every chance of succeeding, provided that everything had been thoroughly prepared and that nothing was unduly hurried. But, in fact, the relevant events followed each other with increasing speed. In April, the criticism of Chen Po-ta was extended to other members of the Lin faction, and further extended in May and June; in July and August an insoluble conflict arose over domestic and foreign policy. Li Wei-hsin had this to say:

Yu Hsin-yeh said to me in July and August in Hangchow that at the joint meeting which criticized Ch'en and rectified the working style, Lin Li-kuo was nervous and sized up three possible developments of the meeting (1) general discussion, (2) rectification extended to the General Affairs Section of the Military Commission, and (3) purge involving the 'Minister' (Lin Piao). Later they estimated that the first two were most probable.

The group now began to become more nervous, especially after the crisis had come out into the open in mid-August. This possibility had already been foreseen in the original draft of the plan:

Both we and the enemy are riding the tiger and finding it difficult to get down.

The present, superficial balance cannot last long; the balance in contradictions is only temporary and relative while imbalance is absolute.

This is a life and death struggle! Once they secure power, we will be ousted and sent to jail. Either we swallow them up or they will swallow us.

[Therefore]

Two timings in strategy:

One, we are prepared and can get rid of them; and

Two, when we realize that the enemy is opening its mouth to swallow us, and feel the seriousness of the situation, we have to make up our minds to do something whether we are ready or not.

It now looked as though this last-named situation was developing and that the various parties to the plot would be forced into rapid action. There could thus be no question of carefully co-ordinated action by commando groups throughout the whole country, but only of one single coup: the attempts on Mao had to bring about a transfer of total power over the Party and the army into Lin Piao's hands. And if that did not succeed, then Mao would have to be eliminated in some other way. This was the sudden move to action which had led to the events catalogued by General Wang Tung-hsing in the People's Palace, on 11 September 1971.

Was Lin Piao involved in his son's plans?

To what extent and at what point in time did Lin Piao become involved in Lin Li-kuo's plan and in the air force putsch-group? It is certain that Lin Piao was already in political decline before the Second Plenum. It seems certain, too, that he was being reproached with having formed a faction when attempting to oppose the reduction of his influence at the Second Plenum. After the setbacks of January, April and August 1971, he was determined to try to maintain his position. But it is much less certain whether he knew of his son's plans long in advance. The fact that he attempted escape after the crisis had broken need not in itself mean that he had explicit foreknowledge of the plans. It is unlikely, however, that anyone in Peking would be interested in this subtle difference: the accusations against Lin were sufficient to relegate him to 'the rubbish bin of history'. As far as foreign observers are concerned, it seems worth-while to consider whether Lin Piao had not been placed before a *fait accompli*, first by his son, and eventually also by his wife.

The two versions of the '571' plan

The main problem in finding an answer to this question is in the information available to us. The information is defective,[3] and contradictory. This is especially true of the most important set of documents on the so-called '571' plan – 'Document no. 4'

– which consists of four sections, and from which passages have been quoted above. The dossier is said to have been compiled by an *ad hoc* investigating committee of the Central Committee and distributed among the more important Party members. In April 1972 an incomplete version was intercepted and published by Taipei. This was followed in August by the publication of what Taipei claimed to be the complete version of the dossier.[4] They were later confirmed as authentic by Peking. Both the earlier and the so-called 'complete' versions contained a number of very strange entries; this is especially so in the case of the latter. If the versions are compared closely, however, it becomes apparent that they did not come from the same original text.

The original version mentions the existence of a small nucleus of people who counted on being able to defeat a possible military counter-attack with the help of the air force; the group also thought that the central army command would be sympathetic towards their initiative and that the Soviet Union, if not offering overt approval, would not interfere.

The more complete version, however, mentions the possible use of bacteriological and other secret weapons, which would seem to have very little relevance to the situation in question, and of the complete and immediate complicity of the central army command, the air force, and also the Soviet Union.

From the examples given it would seem that the second version is not only fuller than the first, but of completely different origin: the two descriptions of plans suggest different original texts, contexts and ideas.

We shall, then, mainly use the first version as the basis for our reconstruction of the events of September 1971 in the People's Republic, since the second could very well be an *ex post facto* completion of the original incomplete notes.

Remarks on the terminology of the '571' plan

The choice of the various code names gives parts of the document a peculiar appearance: Mao Tse-tung is called 'B52', the plotters' group and their opponents are designated by the words 'our fleet' and 'their fleet', and the units of which they dispose are referred to as 'vessels'. If 'fleets' is taken to mean 'air fleets' and 'vessel' 'aircraft', and it is remembered that 'B52' is the name of the most notorious American plane (America being China's greatest enemy in the eyes of the Lin Piao group), then these code names point to the young air force officers, who here and elsewhere display an extraordinarily naïve approach to their plans.

This established, we can now answer the central question of our investigation: would Lin Piao, though not considered an advanced theoretician, have drawn up such a text? The answer to this must be negative. And although there are several suggestions in the first version of the '571' plan that Lin Piao, Yeh Chun and Huang Yung-sheng had incited the Lin Li-kuo group to draw up the plan, and to have been involved in the preparations of September – there is nowhere any concrete evidence to substantiate this suggestion.

The role of Yeh Chun

While there are no directly incriminating references to Lin Piao himself in 'Document no. 4' on the '571' plan, this is not the case with the description of the preparations preceding the plan, and the subsequent confession of Li Wei-hsin. But although references were made, they are not in themselves decisive: the meeting of Lin Piao and his family in February 1971 need not have been anything more than a normal family occasion, and all further indications of Lin Piao's involvement are based on suggestions made to this effect by Lin Li-kuo so that his friends would be persuaded to join the conspiracy.

There is, however, another aspect which deserves our attention: this is the evidence which points to the involvement of Lin Piao's wife, Yeh Chun.

Very little is in fact known about her. She was about twenty-two years younger than Lin and had been his secretary in the General Political Department after his nomination as Minister of Defence in 1959. Their marriage probably took place around 1960. Yeh Chun only started to come to the political foreground when she was about 40 years old, but soon after her marriage she began to show remarkable ambition. A few years before the publication of Lin Piao's article on the invincibility of the people's war, an article by Yeh Chun – unnoticed at the time – appeared in 1962 in the *People's Daily*; occupying a whole page, it concerned itself with a number of wars which had taken place in China in the past and . . . with Mao's opinions on the people's war. The coincidence is remarkable; the same historical examples were given in Lin's speech of 18 May 1966, which also related to earlier publications by Yeh Chun.[5] This leads one to wonder whether in fact Yeh Chun was not Lin Piao's source of inspiration. And it is not only on the theoretical level that this seems to have been the case; on the practical level, it was she who had acted as Lin's liaison officer with the General Political Department, which had continually increased in importance from 1962 onwards. After Lin, the person with whom Yeh Chun identified most easily was Chiang Ching. During the Cultural Revolution she had admired the latter's leading role as the champion of the young revolutionary Red Guards. A foreign journalist reported that Yeh Chun had adopted the position of cheer-leader at mass meetings at which Chiang Ching was delivering a speech.[6] It is far from certain, however, that the admiration was mutual, and in any case they went their separate ways after the Cultural Revolution.

In 1968 Yeh Chun was nominated to a key position in the secretariat of the important Military Commission; the following year she made her debut on the Central Committee and, together with a couple of Lin's generals, in the Political Bureau. From then on, she acted as the director of Lin's personal staff – a state of affairs which many people found difficult to accept. Lin, though, was a relatively retiring person and preferred all his contacts with the outside world to take place through her.

In April 1971, when Lin's four generals were forced to express self-criticism for faction-forming at the Second Plenum, Yeh Chun was also forced to express her apologies.

What she also did, according to Li, was to sound out the opinions of Huang Yung-sheng, Lin's chief-of-staff.

Although foreknowledge of the plan by Yeh Chun is suggested by Lin Li-kuo to his friends (with even greater emphasis than the supposed foreknowledge of Lin Piao), this is the first and only time in the chronological reconstruction of events that one of either parent is mentioned by another source, and it is Yeh Chun, and not Lin Piao. Given what we know about the nature of the plan for a coup by Lin Li-kuo, Lin Piao's ideas, the position of Yeh Chun, and the relationship between them, it seems possible that Yeh Chun may have been the missing link between the Lin Li-kuo group and the Lin Piao group. Those implicated can be grouped into four categories according to time and perhaps to degree of involvement:

1. Lin Li-kuo and his air force offcers who, in March, started to draw up the plans for a coup of their own accord;
2. Yeh Chun, who originally had only vague knowledge of their plans, but later became increasingly interested in them;
3. Lin Piao, who hardly knew what was happening for a long time, and was perhaps finally presented with it as the last means of escaping the crisis;
4. The four generals and other high-ranking military personnel who were only involved indirectly as a group.

This explanation is not unattractive, since a large part of the inconsistencies in the story of the 'Lin Piao plot' thereby become understandable.

Part Twelve
Stabilization

I remain alone in the cold autumn . . .
Line from a poem by Mao Tse-tung, 1925

33 : The Information Campaign

Now that the military danger seemed to have passed, and the political crisis among the leadership was being resolved, a widespread information and propaganda campaign was initiated to inform the population about what had happened. At the same time it would pass on the ideological lessons which had been learned from the events. It took at least a month for the whole Party to be informed in a more or less discreet fashion, and at least six months before every important item of information had been released internally. Between 11 and 13 September, probably only the Political Bureau and part of the Central Committee knew what had happened. After the events of 30 September, 1 and 3 October (the day on which the fact of the plane crash was confirmed in Peking) the whole Central Committee was probably informed, and then the provincial Party and Revolutionary Committees, the commanders of the military regions and districts, and the heads of the main government departments. On 3 October, the radio station at Hupei was still mentioning the 'shining example of Lin Piao' – but after this his name disappeared.[1]

The announcements made at this stage, however, were still shrouded in the greatest secrecy, and delivered personally to the relevant authorities by armed courier. There was obviously still a fear that forces either at home or abroad would try to take advantage of the situation.[2] During the second half of October the first reports on what had really happened began to leak through to the outside world; but the sensational stories which were carried in the newspapers of Hong Kong, Taipei or Tokyo were generally not taken seriously by more cautious Western observers – wrongly, as it happens. At the end of October the first restrained references to the matter began to appear in the

Chinese press, but even these were still only intelligible to insiders.[3]

As usual, the propaganda attacks were still seemingly aimed at persons or groups which had already been discredited (Liu Shao-chi and Chen Po-ta) but, reading between the lines, more and more indications pointing towards Lin Piao and his group appeared. It is usual practice in China for a fresh line of attack to be based, as it were, on a previous campaign which had already been assimilated by the majority of the Party and the population. The campaign against Chen Po-ta (partly intended as a warning shot) was gradually extended towards Lin. The attacks launched in the autumn of 1971 against Liu Shao-chi and Chen Po-ta contained a number of indirect references to Lin. Let us look, then, at two examples of this campaign, the first of which appeared at the end of October and contained a new and fierce attack on Liu.

The attack emphasized Liu's 'landowner-relations'. He had in fact come from a family of rich farmers, though his own father had been a teacher. It immediately became obvious that the key to the present purges lay in this attack. A number of observers thought it might even have referred to Chou En-lai who had been brought up by his grandfather in an educated mandarin family. But it is much more probable that it was a reference to Lin Piao, whose father had owned a textile work-shop. Liu's exaggerated 'devotion to his family' was also under-lined: as a high Party official, his wife had played an important part in the actions of the work-group at Tsinghua University, and their children had been the leaders of dubious Red Guard organizations. Here, too, it was probable that these reproaches were intended for Lin Piao, whose wife and children had also occupied key positions.[4]

The attacks were as effective as they were complicated. They were effective because an attack on Lin Piao delivered in this way did not have to be postponed until everybody had been fully acquainted with the facts. It was also based on a campaign with which the readers of the relevant articles were already familiar. Both the form and content of such attacks finally led to the discrediting of the person for whom they were really intended by the simple fact of associating him with someone already discredited. Although the use of the term 'Liu-type', applied to people who had been the bitterest opponents of the man, may appear to most foreigners (and probably to a number of Chinese) as conscious deception, there is a perfectly solid justification for this approach: as far as the Party is concerned, it shows that the Chinese revolution can be turned from its true course both by slowing it down or by urging it on in too radical a way.

To illustrate the intricacy of this method of attack let us look at another example. At the end of 1971 a fierce attack appeared in *Red Flag* on a certain Hu Feng. This presumably attracted attention in China because everyone had forgotten who Hu Feng was.[5] In the attack, however, he is introduced to the readers as the stereotype of the two-faced, ultra-Left, Marxist intellectual, and a prototype of Chen Po-ta. It is worth noting at this point, though, that Chen Po-ta's name and surname were still not mentioned in the press, even though he had already been deposed for a year. (By comparison, it was several years before this was done in the case of Liu Shao-chi.) The article contained, among others, the following passage:

All counter-revolutionary double-dealers – however deep they may lie hidden, however much artifice they may use to camouflage themselves, and however many ruses they may try – do not ultimately escape from the far-sighted penetrating investigation of Chairman Mao, and the all-comprehending network of hundreds of millions of revolutionary people armed with the Thoughts of Mao Tse-tung. Strict though their counter-revolutionary inner discipline may be, fast though they may hold to their alliance ... the strength of proletarian dictatorship and the proper method used by the Party always succeeds in splitting their unity. They have not many unswerving followers and in the end they find themselves isolated; opposed by the masses and deserted by their followers, they fall into a detestable, shameful state ... Naturally the unmasking of the counter-revolutionary double-dealers takes time; a certain process also is needed to enable the revolutionary people to recognize the falseness and the inner nature of the hidden counter-revolutionaries.

Before their total revelation they may disguise themselves and deceive some people; but once their true faces have been revealed, people see how little substance is to be found behind their imposing false front.

This is a very important document. Attention has shifted almost imperceptibly from Hu Feng to Chen Po-ta, and equally imperceptibly towards Lin Piao. A barely-concealed and complete summary of the whole crisis of 1970 and 1971 is given – including the intriguing allusion to the 'thorough investigation of Chairman Mao'.

But the revival of the criticism of Hu Feng at that particular moment involved even more historical parallels, which were clearly meant to be taken as such:

(a) Hu Feng had been the chosen pupil of Mao's favourite modern author Lu Hsun but, shortly before the latter's death in 1936, they had quarrelled over 'Trotskyist tendencies' in the Left-wing Writers' League. In the same way, Lin Piao had later been Mao's most devoted pupil until – because of a dispute on the subject of Chen Po-ta's deviationism – there had been a break between them.[6]

(b) Hu Feng had been purged at the time of the Kao Kang affair in 1954, because he had insisted on greater liberalism in the cultural sector, just as like-minded intellectuals were to allow the campaign 'Let a hundred flowers bloom together and a hundred schools of thought contend', to deviate in the same way; similarly, the ultra-Left had allowed the Cultural Revolution to depart from its original objectives. On his fall, Hu Feng was personally attacked by Mao as a 'hypocrite, his smile covering insults'.[7]

(c) The 'Left-wing current' had already been condemned during 1967 as a 'counter-revolutionary conspiracy-clique of the Hu Feng type', thereby giving the label its later significance.[8]

Behind the conjuring up of the figure of Hu Feng at that particular moment lies a whole complex of historical allusion which points towards the Chen/Lin affair. It is significant in this context that Mao presented the readers of the *People's Daily* with a quotation from Lu Hsun at the end of October: 'The enemy does not cause me undue worry. What is most fearful and disheartening is an arrow in the back from an ally and the satisfied smirk of those in my own camp.'

The information campaign had probably got through to all Party committees by the beginning of November, including those in the remotest provinces; events had thus entered a new stage. On 7 November the first 'personal' attacks on Lin appeared. While it is true that he was not yet mentioned by name, the attacks were no longer in the disguised form of attacks on other figures. On 7 November, the *People's Daily* (in an article taken from *Red Flag*) spoke of 'a few emperors, princes, generals, ministers, sages and prophets . . . who tried to reverse the wheel of history'. On the same day, an article was read out over the radio of the province of Chekiang which had been written by a local soldier who was supposed to have played an important part in preventing Lin Li-kuo's coup. (The capital of the province, Hangchow, was the scene of the planning of the coup, the local air force base had probably been the starting-point for a raid on Shanghai, and had perhaps also been the place where things first began to go wrong. The radio station broadcast included the following:

The Liu Shao-chi-type political swindler said that struggle within the Party causes a multitude of sufferings in the Party. This is nonsense. The happiness of the proletarian class consists in annihilating exploitation by the exploiting class. What Liu Shao-chi called suffering, is the suffering of renegades, secret agents, plotters and ambitious men, and suchlike counter-revolutionaries hidden in the Party. When these men are dug out they turn into heaps of dog's dung of humanity. They say they suffer: it is good for them . . . In the course of fifty years of ferocious struggle within the Party, Chen Tu-hsiu, Chu Chiu-pai, Li Li-san, Lo Chang-lung, Wang Ming, Chang Kuo-tao, Kao Kang (+Jao Shu-shih), Peng Te-huai and Liu Shao-chi have been smashed under the guidance of Chairman Mao, and our Party has become purer and stronger. Struggle within the Party is a good thing. It would be deplorable if Liu Shao-chi etc. – political swindlers did not get punishment for their crimes. When they have been caught these scoundrels make a show of misery and say that there is too much suffering in the struggle within the Party. They vainly try to avoid total extinction. This effort is futile.

34: Purges

Meanwhile, the proceedings against the Lin Piao group, the Lin Li-kuo group, and all those who had been shown to be connected with their actions, had started. Lin Piao, his wife and his son were dead, while a number of members of Lin Li-kuo's sextet had presumably been arrested already. The turn of all others involved came later. Lin Piao's 'four generals' had been arrested immediately. Dozens of other high-ranking officers were also arrested; these were mainly from the air force, the navy, the logistics department and other 'technological' army units (including the railway department). A total of about forty high-ranking officers were removed in this first round. Apart from those from the headquarters units in Peking, they came chiefly from the eastern region: Nanking, Canton, Fuchow and Wuhan. Politically speaking, the political leadership of the post-Cultural Revolution period had received a serious blow: in the course of one year two of the five members of the Standing Committee had disappeared (Chen and Lin), six of the twenty-one permanent members of the Political Bureau, and sixteen of the 279 permanent and deputy members of provincial Party committees and Revolutionary Committees.[1] An interesting detail is that part of the leadership in the province of Szuchuan, which was known to be very Left-wing, had also been removed. It was clear, however, that the elimination process was not going to end at the first forty. On 26 December the *Hunan Daily* demanded: 'These men must be criticized until they stink and the poison must be totally cleansed. This is not the work of one or two days. The struggle of the lines must never be relaxed.'[2]

During the following months the investigation spread like an oil slick. The number of arrests began to run into hundreds, while the number of suspects now totalled several thousand.

According to foreign estimates, tens of thousands of people were criticized during 1971-2 for their behaviour towards the Left-wing current of 1970-71. Apart from the Cultural Revolution, this was undoubtedly the greatest purge in the history of the Party.[3]

The first phase of the information and denunciation campaign began to near its end at the end of 1971 and the beginning of 1972; in the meantime, everyone had been informed of the official version of the struggle, although it was several months before all the background details were finally revealed. The next phase was to get everyone to participate in criticism of the group which had been eliminated. This varied from the revival of long-forgotten or suppressed scores to the writing of papers ideologically examining the denounced statements and writings. The uncertainty and confusion at the beginning of the denunciation campaign was greater than ever before. The only comparable situation was that which existed at the beginning of the Cultural Revolution. But the campaigns against Peng Chen and Liu Shao-chi had been mainly directed against their Right-wing deviationism, which was more easily accepted than a campaign against the Left-wing deviationism of Chen Po-ta and Lin Piao. And neither Peng nor Liu had been continually praised for over five years in the mass media as the closest comrade-in-arms of Mao Tse-tung. It was understandably very difficult for many people to comprehend the change. The following account was given of the denunciation campaign held in February in Kunming, capital of Yunnan, under the chairmanship of the military commander Wang Pi-cheng:

Wang observed that a few cadres had shown some fear in criticizing Lin's counter-revolutionary programme. They are afraid that some cadres 'have a low cultural level', thus 'are unable to clearly explain the questions, and engage in criticism', and that the masses 'have low consciousness', thus 'are unable to clearly differentiate one thing from another and even could produce a side effect'. Some other cadres, Wang pointed out, failed to adequately realize difficulties on how to thoroughly criticize Lin's counter-revolutionary programme, thus showing a certain 'simple emotion'. As a result, they did not make sufficient efforts to criticize. They think that nothing at all is worth discussing, and thus are quite satisfied with superficial arguments and run-of-the-mill criticism.[4]

Similar reports came in from other provinces. Greater reluctance on the part of the party cadres from the province of Heilungkiang was mentioned: 'Many of them agree in words with what was done, but only in words. In fact, "they do not throw themselves into the class struggle and the struggle of lines; they behave as if they were all above this." They hesitate and moan and pull back their tails in fear.'

In the province of Kwangtung the question was asked: 'How is it possible that, after the victories of the class struggle and struggle for the correct line and above all, of the great Cultural Revolution, a renewal of acuteness in the struggle gives us the feeling that this has come too suddenly, so that we find it difficult to understand?'

The doubts went even further in the 'Left-wing' province of Szuchuan:

Some said: 'Why is it that this vermin was not dug out earlier?' This question, the Party-secretary said, ignores Marxist laws. 'Contradictions within the Party between correct and incorrect ways of thinking are not necessarily antagonistic. This happens only if the man who is wrong adheres to errors that have attained a certain magnitude. There is a definite process in counter-revolutionary activities that are aimed at seizing power for the bourgeois class enemy within the Party, and there is a certain gradualness in the way in which they reveal themselves.'

This happened with the Liu-type men. 'They raised the standard of revolution, but secretly they were plotting counter-revolution. To protect themselves and to cover their future actions they did not reveal themselves until an unmistakable climax had been reached. Investigation itself requires a definite process and a certain gradualness until the counter-revolutionary face [of the evil men] has thrust itself into notice. Naturally the class enemy wait for a suitable occasion, though they cannot hide for long. Then the time-bombs laid within the Party are found, one after another, and the hidden dangers are disposed of.'[5]

The accusations

What had been happening, was a lengthy process whereby – to put it in Maoist terms – non-antagonistic opposition within the Party was developing into antagonistic opposition, and whereby – to put it in more general Marxist terms – quantitative or gradual differences in opinion were developing into qualitative or essential differences. Only after lengthy 'education' on these lines by the Party leadership is a response from the Party base produced and the information from above thus supplemented by denunciation from below.

The various pejorative terms which had been employed during the past few months, such as 'relic of factionalism, opportunist, counter-revolutionary hypocrite, bourgeois-individualist conspirator, secret agent of the landowners, reactionary, imperialist, revisionist, traitor, renegade, career-minded', were slowly being put to good use. Various accusations were now being assembled, as they had been in the past. This meant that:

(a) the full responsibility of Lin's 'actual' faults (such as faction-forming, militarism, and career-mindedness) were ascribed to him as well as to his generals;

(b) he was said to be equally responsible for the aprioristic propaganda policy of Chen Po-ta (encouraging the personality cult, underestimating the role of the masses, ideological dogmatism);

(c) he was accused of being involved in the Left-wing current during the Cultural Revolution.

This last point was to become especially important, although it had played only a subordinate part in the crisis of the summer of 1971: the correction of the course of the Cultural Revolution was thus no longer limited to a condemnation of the marginal excesses of a small group of ultras, but was now extended to a discussion of important elements of the mainstream of that movement. The taboo which had prevented the moderates from opposing the radicals had now been broken. But this was the only way in which a basis could be established for rectifying the course of the Revolution and restoring unity.

It was for these reasons that the renunciation campaign only began to take shape around the turn of the year, and ended up with a much wider range of accusations than the 'ten crimes' which had already been summarized by the Central Committee:[6]

1. Plotting to usurp the Party leadership, putting the individual above the Party Central and instructing that his name be inserted in the Party Constitution as heir-apparent. (April 1969)
2. Implementing the line of opportunism to counter the 'correct' line of Mao. (1966–71)
3. Undermining the 'democratic centralism' of the Party and advocating that the gun should lead the Party. (1969–70)
4. Making several attempts on Mao's life since the launching of the Cultural Revolution (1966–71)
5. Taking advantage of criticizing the 'Peng-Huang anti-Party group' before and after the 'Lushan Conference' to usurp military leadership. (1958–9)
6. Ignoring Party discipline, organizing factions and mountain strongholds, trusting only his confidants, recruiting deserters, and traitors, and forming factions in pursuit of his own selfish interests. (August 1970)
7. Raising high the red flag of studying Mao's writings to oppose the red flag, furthering his personal ambitions, and playing the biggest political trick. (Since 1969)
8. Making wanton attacks on Party members during the Cultural Revolution, thus purging a number of leading cadres and 'our comrades' who ought not to be purged. (1967–8)
9. Opposing Mao's 'correct' foreign policy. (1970–71)
10. Maintaining illicit relations with foreign countries. (1971)

The expansion of these already considerable accusations against Lin took place in every direction. Not only was he seen to be implicated in mistakes made by others, but more mistakes in his past were now brought to light. In this context, the *Peking Review* of 25 February contained a study taken from the last number of *Red Flag* in 1971 on Mao's paper 'A single spark can start a prairie fire', written in 1930, with the sub-title, 'criticism of certain pessimistic ideas in the Party'. The conclusions of the article were clearly intended to be taken as referring to present circumstances:

Pessimism is the world outlook of the declining landlord and capitalist classes. Those who cling to such an outlook always overestimate the strength of the enemy and underestimate the strength of the people; they never have faith in the masses and do not rely on them, and they do not have faith in or rely on the Party. When they meet temporary difficulties or when the revolution is at a low ebb, they waver, run away, become traitors or resort to adventurism and putschism. When the revolution advances smoothly or is at a high tide, they often take an ultra-'Left' stand, regard all successes as their own and push a reactionary line that is ultra-'Left' or 'Left' in form but Right in essence. Persons clinging to this reactionary world outlook will inevitably set themselves against the masses, keep back the tide of history and become reactionaries vainly trying to stop the earth from rotating.[7]

But what most of the readers of the *Peking Review* did not know, and what most of the older readers of *Red Flag* would know, was that Mao's article was originally aimed at the 'pessimists' of the old Fourth Army, and that its original title was 'Letter to . . . Comrade Lin Piao'.[8] Only later, when Lin had risen from being a young Army commander to being an important Party leader, was the title changed and the reference to Lin forgotten. Another episode in the past was to show that the part which Lin was supposed to have played in the Civil War in the resistance to Japan had not been so successful after all. His critics now announced that the successful offensive which had just preceded the Liberation in the North-east should no longer be ascribed to Lin, but to Mao himself.

Chou En-lai, strikingly enough, remained very moderate during this phase of the campaign to discredit Lin. While others were exhausting themselves in trying to 'widen and deepen' the criticism of Lin, he was still telling foreign observers that Lin had contributed many worthwhile aspects to the Chinese revolution, in spite of the false moves he had made.

The nature of the crisis was slowly becoming clearer to observers outside China. By the middle of 1972 it had reached the point where Mao Tse-tung could confirm the fall of Lin Piao to two foreign visitors, Prime Minister Bandaranaike of Sri Lanka (Ceylon) and the French Foreign Minister, Schumann.

On 28 July Peking finally decided to make a public statement on the affair, which meant in effect confirming what had already been learnt through the foreign press.

On 22 September 1972, over a year after the plane crash, the *People's Daily* made the first overt allusion to the circumstances of Lin Piao's death. A new line of criticism was opened on 13 October in the same newspaper, which linked Lin with all the ultra-Left crimes of the recent past, including 'anarchism' during the Cultural Revolution.

35: A Definite Break-through in Foreign Policy

Let us return for the moment to 25 October 1971. About three weeks after the dust had begun to settle over the Lin Piao affair, Chou En-lai was able to reap the first harvest from his foreign policy. This time the scene of the action was New York: the General Assembly of the United Nations.

When the United Nations had been formed in 1947, a seat had been reserved for the world's most populous country, China, which had been occupied by a representative of Chiang Kai-shek. After 1949, the Western powers had insisted that the Taiwan Nationalists be considered the only representatives of the Chinese people. It should be remembered that the Nationalists had only held out in Taiwan thanks to the intervention of the United States in the Chinese Civil War by the sending of the American fleet to the Straits of Taiwan.

The following decade saw, alternately, increasing isolation of the People's Republic, followed by a distinct *rapprochement* with the rest of the world. This had little effect at first at the United Nations, but the growth of the Afro-Asian bloc there began to provide Peking with an increasing number of allies in the General Assembly. In 1970 a numerical majority for the admission of the People's Republic to the United Nations was achieved for the first time, but the United States managed to raise the required majority to two-thirds by having the matter changed to the status of 'important question'. The Secretary-General U Thant, however, forecast that there would be a solution to the problem before long. This was the situation before 25 October 1971.

The collapse of the anti-Chinese front proved to be more complete than had been expected. The United States again tried to use a point of procedure at the last moment to try and protect her allies in Taiwan. This time, however, the matter was not designated an 'important question': only fifty-four members were prepared to go along with the Americans, fifteen others abstained, while fifty-nine neutral and socialist countries pronounced themselves against the procedure. This meant that the decision had in fact already been taken; the soundings of those last few days had shown that there was a small but sufficient majority in favour of allotting the Chinese seat to Peking. A resolution for this was put forward by China's ally Albania and some twenty-two non-aligned developing countries. But once it became clear that the resolution was going to be passed anyway, the majority became a landslide victory. Only thirty-five pro-Western countries declared themselves against the motion, seventeen abstained, and seventy-six countries voted in favour. The Chinese press agency Hsinhua mentioned the event on 26 and 27 October, and on the 28th the *People's Daily* gave more extended treatment to this 'irreversible historical development', and spoke of the complete failure of the American imperialists and the Japanese reactionaries to create 'two Chinas' (an attempt had been made to allow Peking in and retain Taiwan at the same time). The next day an official Government declaration offered further explanation of this 'victory for Chairman Mao's proletarian revolutionary line in foreign affairs'. The Chinese delegation to the U.N. arrived under the leadership of Vice-Minister Chiao Kuan-hua and Huang Hua, both very close colleagues of Chou En-lai and Chen I. Chen Chu was to be the permanent Chinese representative on the Security Council. On 11 November the Chinese delegation arrived in New York. And while the bitter polemics against the United States were continued in all the official publications in the People's Republic, Chiao Kuan-hua made his official speech of acceptance on 15 November. He concluded by repeating the principles of Chinese foreign policy:

We have constantly maintained that all countries, big or small, should be equal and that the Five Principles of Peaceful Co-existence should be taken as the principles guiding the relations between countries. The people of each country have the right to choose the social system of their own country according to their own will and to protect the independence, sovereignty and territorial integrity of their own country. No country has the right to subject another country to its aggression, subversion, control, interference or bullying. We are opposed to the imperialist and colonialist theory that big nations are superior to the small nations and small nations are subordinate to the big nations. We are opposed to the power politics and hegemony of big nations bullying small ones or strong nations bullying weak ones. We hold that the affairs of a given country must be handled by its own people, that the affairs of the world must be handled by all the countries of the world, and that the affairs of the United Nations must be handled jointly by all its member states, and the superpowers should not be allowed to manipulate and monopolize them. The superpowers want to be superior to others and lord it over others. At no time, neither today nor ever in the future, will China be a superpower subjecting others to its aggression, subversion, control, interference or bullying . . . [But]

We have always held that the just struggles of the people of all countries support each other. China has always had the sympathy and support of the people of various countries in her socialist revolution and socialist construction. It is our bounden duty to support the just struggles of the people of various countries. For this purpose, we have provided aid to some friendly countries to help them develop their national economy independently. In providing aid, we always strictly respect the sovereignty of the recipient countries, and never attach any conditions or ask for any privileges. We provide free military aid to countries and peoples who are fighting against aggression. We will never become munition merchants. We firmly oppose certain countries trying to control and plunder the recipient countries by means of 'aid'. However, as China's economy is still comparatively backward, the material aid we have provided is very limited, and what we provide is mainly political and moral support. With a population of 700 million, China ought to make a greater contribution to human progress. And we hope that this situation of our ability falling short of this wish of ours will be gradually changed.[1]

This statement of policy was greeted with approval in some quarters, with scepticism in others. Whether China saw herself as a superpower or not, the fact that she was seen by other nations as a superpower would increasingly influence the position she occupied in the framework of international relations.

Already during the following month, China was forced to

take up a position regarding the events on the Indian sub-continent. Together with the United States, she found herself in the position of providing political support for the reactionary government of Pakistan, which had just violently crushed an uprising in the eastern part of the country aiming at greater autonomy, and which was now confronted with military intervention by the equally reactionary government of India, supported by the Soviet Union, since this was an opportunity of getting even with an old enemy. Indian hegemony of the whole sub-continent was assured with establishment of an independent Bangla Desh. China found herself forced to express her first veto in the United Nations – against the admission of Bangla Desh, because a resolution demanding the release of all prisoners of war had been rejected by India and Bangla Desh. Although the Chinese were very cautious in their handling of the matter, and followed expressed Chinese policy in every respect,[2] many observers in the West saw this, with horror or approval, as the first step taken by Peking on the road to a superpower policy. This opinion was strengthened as the preparations for Nixon's visit to Peking advanced.

36: The Visit of Nixon; Towards New Relations

On 21 February 1972, 'The Spirit of 76', the aeroplane of the American President, landed at Peking airport; on board were Nixon, his wife, advisor Kissinger, Secretary of State Rogers, his East Asia assistant Marshall Green, some ten other officials and about twenty members of Nixon's personal staff. In addition, about ninety journalists were present. On the Chinese side, the welcoming party was made up of: Premier Chou En-lai, Vice-Premier Li Hsien-nien, Minister for Foreign Affairs Chi Peng-fei (successor to Chen I, who had died in the meantime), the acting Minister of Defence Yeh Chien-ying (Lin Piao's successor) and many others. The great surprise, however, was that Nixon was received by Party Chairman Mao Tse-tung that same afternoon. It was obvious that Mao wished to demonstrate to his own followers that he was personally responsible for the 'revolutionary line in foreign affairs'.

At dinner Chou En-lai made his speech of welcome 'in the name of Chairman Mao and the Chinese Government'.[1] After making a number of friendly remarks, he confined himself mainly to explaining the reasons for the absence of relations between the two countries. He referred to the formulation of the Five Principles for Peaceful Co-existence which had been made at the time of the Bandung conference: 'As early as 1955 the Chinese Government publicly stated that the Chinese people do not want to have war with the United States and that the Chinese Government is willing to sit down and enter into negotiations with the United States Government. This is a policy we have pursued consistently.'

President Nixon changed the subject of the conversation and struck a more dramatic note:

The world watches. The world listens. The world waits to see what we will do. What is the world? In a personal sense, I think of my eldest daughter whose birthday is today. As I think of her, I think of children in the world, in Asia, in Africa, in Europe, in the Americas, most of whom were born since the date of the foundation of the People's Republic of China. What legacy shall we leave our children?

In the heat of his oratory he forgot the children of Vietnam, where the bombing was being increased, and the daily paper of Hanoi, *Nhan Dan*, did not fail to take note of this cynicism. Nixon became completely lost in his own demagogy and after the appeal 'Let us start a Long March together', he went on to quote a saying by Mao Tse-tung on the continuation of the revolution: 'So many deeds cry out to be done and always urgently; the world rolls on. Time passes. Seize the day. Seize the hour.' He continued pathetically: 'This is the hour. This is the day for our peoples to rise to the heights of greatness, which can build a new and better world!'

If the Chinese were bewildered, they certainly didn't show it.

During the four following days, however, the atmosphere became considerably cooler when it became apparent that the Chinese did not wish to make policy concessions, while the United States was not prepared to abandon its position on Indo-China and Taiwan.

There are essential differences between China and the United States in their social systems and foreign policies. However, the two sides agreed that countries – regardless of their social systems – should conduct their relations on the basis of . . .

and then follows China's Five Principles for Co-existence, a paragraph which is almost word for word identical to Chou En-lai's toast of 21 February.

With these principles of international relations in mind, the two sides stated that:
– progress towards a normalization of relations between China and the United States is in the interest of all countries;
– both wish to reduce the danger of international military conflict;

– neither should seek hegemony in the Asia–Pacific region and each is opposed to efforts by any other country or group of countries to establish such hegemony; and

– neither is prepared to negotiate on behalf of any third party or to enter into agreements or understandings with the other directed at other states.

Both of the first points had clearly been put forward by the United States; the first refers to a passage in the final paragraph, and the second to a passage in the paragraph summarized above, 'peace, freedom and progress' ('lessen the risks of confrontation through accident, miscalculation, or misunderstanding'). The last point had been clearly put forward by China, and referred to Indo-China. Then the declaration broached the subject of Taiwan which was treated – probably on the insistence of the Chinese – as a 'domestic question' and not as a part of foreign policy. The ways again parted here: 'The Chinese side re-affirmed its position', the U.S. side declared:

The United States acknowledges that all Chinese on either side of the Taiwan Strait maintain there is but one China, and that Taiwan is part of China. The U.S. Government does not challenge that position. It reaffirms its interest in a peaceful settlement of the Tai-wan question by the Chinese themselves. With this prospect in mind, it affirms the ultimate objective of the withdrawal of all U.S. forces and military installations from Taiwan. In the meantime, it will progressively reduce its forces and military installations on Taiwan as the tension in the area diminishes.

With regard to this last problem, later interpretations were to differ. Chou En-lai was reported to have promised 'off the record' that no violence would be used, even though the matter was essentially a domestic one. At the same time, he is said to have drawn Nixon's attention to the fact that he could not very well expect tension in the area to diminish as long as there were Americans in Vietnam. The withdrawal from Indo-China was a condition for the normalization of relations. For this reason, the final paragraph was a considerable disappointment for Nixon who had hoped to bring about an exchange of permanent missions, preparatory to the resumption of diplomatic relations. 'The two sides agreed that they will stay in contact through various channels', so runs the rather vague wording, 'including the sending of a senior U.S. representative to Peking from time to time for concrete consultations to further the normalization of relations between the two countries and continue to exchange views on issues of common interest.'

And the declaration then ends with the generalities which somehow seem unavoidable on such occasions.

While Nixon, Kissinger and Rogers flew back to Washington, Rogers' assistant, Marshall Green, parted from the rest of the party to undertake a tour of Asian capitals to reassure America's allies. Chou En-lai later travelled to Hanoi for a similar purpose. Although agreement had been reached on virtually none of the points raised, the opening of the dialogue with the United States had laid the foundations for a rapidly growing hope of peace in Asia and the world. As far as Asia was concerned, the results of this could be seen on all fronts within a year:

(a) in Korea, discussions were started between North and South about possible reunification in the future;

(b) after the United States, Japan also reopened the dialogue with China and diplomatic relations were resumed soon afterwards;

(c) the clear admission by the international community that the Taiwan problem was a Chinese domestic affair first exacerbated the bitter feelings of Taiwan; later, however, it seems to have created the conditions for a possible peaceful political solution in the future;

(d) the Americans now felt themselves forced to withdraw their troops from Vietnam and to sign the Paris agreement, after a long delay, even though they still left for the time being enough men and material in South-east Asia to continue the armed struggle;

(e) after the coming to power of a reformist government led by Bhutto in Pakistan, which accepted the independence of Bangla Desh as a *fait accompli*, China and India also began a cautious dialogue.

Whichever way one looks at it, the break-through of an intelligent Chinese foreign policy, encouraged by Chou En-lai, had forced other Asian nations to reopen communications which had been moribund for ten or twenty years. This in itself was a remarkable development in a part of the world which contains half the population of the world, but which had hitherto acted as though the largest country – China – did not exist.

Epilogue

Practise Marxism, and not revisionism; unite, and don't
split; be open and above-board, and don't intrigue and
conspire, and unite to win still greater victories!

Declaration of policy at the Tenth Party Congress

After coming to terms with the 'Left current', the great question
which was exercising everybody was: is there not a danger that
Chinese policy will move Right again over the long term, and
will there ever be another Cultural Revolution, as had been
constantly predicted?

Foreign policy, too, began to cause the Left wing, both at
home and abroad, to have doubts. The Chinese position on the
conflict over Bangla Desh was still understandable in every
respect. Nor had Nixon's visit led to any compromise on fundamental questions like Indo-China, Korea or Taiwan. However,
the accent in international relations had shifted increasingly
away from giving support to the progressive elements among
other peoples towards the normalization of relations with other
governments – irrespective of their political complexion. The
Chinese stance that these were two completely different types of
relationship, which need not be at variance with each other, was
met with increasing scepticism among 'sympathizers' overseas.
It was feared that China would find herself placed increasingly
before the dilemma which the Soviet Union had had to face
decades before: whether to lend support unconditionally to
foreign revolutionaries, thus risking the weakening of the diplomatic position, or whether to strengthen the diplomatic position
as much as possible in the hope of being in a better position to
give support to progressive forces elsewhere. The Western Left
wing, in particular – partly because of authentic doubt and

partly because of petit-bourgeois arrogance – appeared increasingly divided. The recognition of the Greek Fascist government was accepted as a logical diplomatic step which did no harm to the opposition. When it came to the normalization of relations with Spain, however, it struck many people as signicant that there was no reference to the Civil War and its background in an article on the history of Spain in the *People's Daily*. A similar phenomenon occurred with regard to the French parliamentary elections: the prominent role of the (pro-Soviet) Communist party within the Left-wing popular front was systematically passed over in silence. Not only did Peking become increasingly alienated from the progressive forces in Western Europe which had relations with the Soviet Union, such as the orthodox Communists, but it also took up a much more distant stance in relation to those progressive groups (Leftist social democrats and similar) which were aiming at a détente between East and West. On the other hand, the Chinese went out of their way to establish contacts with those conservative groups (such as the Christian Democrats in West Germany) who were opposed to multilateral disarmament and the reduction of troops. Thus it was, during my second visit to China, that Chou En-lai gained the approval of the conservatives and embarrassed the progressive elements in a group of Dutch members of parliament with whom I was travelling, by insisting that the nations of Western Europe should increase their defence budgets 'even if this was not a popular election slogan'. Similar statements were made during the following months to Pompidou and other European visitors. It is clear why the Soviet Union should appear as the enemy to be most feared from a Chinese point of view, and it is also understandable why the Chinese should believe that Russian aggression must increase in the East, while there continues to be a thaw in the West. This does not mean, however, that progressive forces elsewhere will understand Chinese attempts to interfere with the movement aimed at détente in the West. And a number of statements by the leadership in Peking must tend to lead to the 'misunderstanding' that we are witnessing the beginnings of what will become a superpower policy in the distant future.

The Tenth Party Congress

The Tenth Party Congress ratified all the important domestic and foreign developments in policy which had taken place over the last few years. It lasted a remarkably short time and its conclusions were only made public when it had ended. It had obviously been decided that no further risks could be taken and everything had been prepared well in advance. It had twice happened in the past that a People's Congress had been announced prematurely, thus giving time for tension to develop at the Central Committee plenary sessions and work sessions which were needed for its preparation and which finally only hindered its being called. This time it was to be different and, to be quite certain, the long-awaited Fourth National People's Congress was first preceded by a new Party Congress, so that the purging and reorganization of the Maoist ranks could be terminated. The Communist Party, which had barely 20 million members on the eve of the Cultural Revolution and had lost many of them during the movement itself, had now increased to 28 million members. While the situation at the time had meant that the Ninth Party Congress had to be formed largely by co-option, the 1,249 delegates to the Tenth Party Congress were chosen by the Party base – although 'consultation with the masses' still allowed a strong element of control by the leadership in the elections. It was striking that those population groups which remained seriously under-represented during the Cultural Revolution were now present in much greater strength than at previous congresses: two-thirds of the delegates were peasants, workers and soldiers; also the numbers of military personnel had diminished considerably; women made up another fifth, and the representation of young people had also considerably increased. The national minorities remained strongly represented, while a delegation from 'the province of Taiwan' took part for the first time – as would be the case at all meetings at national level from now on. After the great moral victory at the United Nations over Taiwan, Peking was now aiming at the peaceful integration of the island, which would retain a large measure of domestic autonomy. The more widely representative nature of the Party leadership was also reflected in the election of the 148 members of the praesidium and in the nomination of the Vice-Chairman of the Congress (Chou En-lai, Wang Hung-wen, Kang Sheng, Yeh Chien-ying, Li Te-sheng), and of the Secretary-General (Chang Chun-chiao). All of them came from such different backgrounds that it would be impossible to classify any two of them together.

As on previous occasions, the agenda of the Congress consisted of the following parts: the delivery of a political report, proposals for the revision of the Party statutes, and the election of a new Central Committee. This time the political report was delivered by Chou En-lai. It dealt mainly with two sectors: the domestic situation (following the elimination of the Lin Piao–Chen Po-ta faction) and the foreign situation (complicated by the threat of war with the Soviet Union).

On the subject of the domestic situation, Chou En-lai had this to say:

First of all, we should continue to do a good job of criticizing Lin Piao and rectifying style of work ...

We should attach importance to the class struggle in the superstructure, including all spheres of culture; transform all parts of the superstructure which do not conform to the economic base. We should handle correctly the two types of contradictions of different nature. We should continue to carry out in earnest all of Chairman Mao's proletarian policies. We should continue to carry out well the revolution in literature and art, the revolution in education and the revolution in public health, and the work with regard to the educated youth who go to mountainous and other rural areas, run the May 7 cadres schools well and support all the newly emerging things of socialism.

Economically ours is still a poor and developing country. We should thoroughly carry out the general line of going all out, aiming high and achieving greater, faster, better and more economical results in building socialism, and grasp revolution and promote production. We should continue to implement the principle of 'taking agriculture as the foundation and industry as the leading factor' and the series of policies of walking on two legs, and build our country independently and with the initiative in our own hands, through self-reliance, hard struggle, diligence and thrift.

The policies lying behind the criticism campaign against the Chen–Lin faction are often open to misinterpretation. When, it is said, for instance, that they exaggerated the importance of developing production, the accusations sounded very much like their own made earlier against Chou. But this has to be interpreted in the context of the discussion in 1970 on participation in an arms race and the development of the arms industry. The same is true in the case of the accusation of revisionism, which was always used against Chou by the ultra-Left. This, too, has to be examined in the light of the policy problems of 1970. There was also a tendency in the report away from referring to Chen and especially Lin as ultra-Leftists who had played the game of the Right towards calling them straightforwardly Right-wingers. This would be quite comprehensible to the Chinese, who would know the previous history of those involved, but foreign readers are likely to be confused by the report. This is perhaps even more true of the sections on foreign policy. Why does Chou, who is known as a moderate in politics, appear so much more violently opposed to the Soviet Union than anyone else? Did he want to safeguard himself against accusations from the Left (he was in fact at that very moment proposing normalization of relations), is it because he is a great Chinese chauvinist, or is he simply pro-Western? As usual, these categories are too vague to do justice to the complexities behind these attitudes. Certain aspects of Chinese–Russian and Chinese–American relations have already been discussed in previous chapters. And this is perhaps a suitable point for a more precise appraisal of Chou's thinking on the position of Western Europe and Japan.

The present international situation is one characterized by great disorder on the earth. 'The wind sweeping through the tower heralds a rising storm in the mountains.' This aptly depicts how the basic world contradictions as analysed by Lenin show themselves today. Relaxation is a temporary and superficial phenomenon, and great disorder will continue. Such great disorder is a good thing for the people, not a bad thing . . . Lenin said that 'an essential feature of imperialism is the rivalry between several Great Powers in the striving for hegemony'. Today, it is mainly the two nuclear superpowers – the U.S. and the U.S.S.R. – that are contending for hegemony. While hawking disarmament, they are actually expanding their armaments every day. Their purpose is to contend for world hegemony. They contend as well as collude with each other. Their collusion serves the purpose of more intensified contention. Contention is absolute and protracted, whereas collusion is relative and temporary. The declaration of this year as the 'year of Europe' and the convocation of the European Security Conference indicate that strategically the key point of their contention is Europe. The West always wants to urge the Soviet revisionists eastward to divert the peril towards China, and it would be fine so long as all is quiet in the West. China is an attractive piece of meat coveted by all. But this piece of meat is very tough, and for years no one has been able to bite into it. It is even more difficult now that Lin Piao the 'superspy' has fallen. At present, the Soviet revisionists are 'making a feint to the east while attacking in the west', and stepping up their contention in Europe and their expansion in the Mediterranean, the Indian Ocean and every place their hands can reach. The U.S.–Soviet contention for hegemony is the cause of world intranquillity . . . It has met with strong resistance from the Third World and has caused resentment on the part of Japan and West European countries. Beset with troubles internally and externally, the two hegemonic powers – the U.S. and the U.S.S.R. – find the going tougher and tougher. As the verse goes, 'Flowers fall off, do what one may', they are in a sorry plight indeed. This has been further proved by the U.S.–Soviet talks last June and the subsequent course of events.

It is within this complex, but not illogical, view of the development of international relations, that one must see Chinese diplomacy in the seventies.

Wang Hung-wen presented the revised Party statutes at the Tenth Congress. They did not vary greatly from the statutes adopted at the previous congress, and were largely based on the forty-one official proposals for modification which had been put forward by the various Party committees during preceding consultations. The alterations were mainly concerned with the preamble. Certain formulae were corrected in the remainder of the statutes, but the specifications of the organizational structure remained virtually unchanged. It is interesting to note that, not only have the references to Lin Piao disappeared, but that – apparently at the express wish of the Party

Chairman himself – the repeated mention of Mao's name is also stopped. Theoretical emphasis is shifted from the 'Thoughts of Mao Tse-tung' to Marxism-Leninism, while the credit for successful revolutionary practice in the past is shifted from the person of Mao to the people and the Party. The Cultural Revolution was perhaps praised even more than before, but the accent has shifted from the 'armed conquest and consolidation of political power' to 'farther-reaching, faster, better, and more efficient construction of socialism', with 'economy and diligence'. At the same time, it was established explicitly that new Cultural Revolutions would continue to be necessary, and that it was absolutely inadmissible to stifle criticism and carry out reprisals.

The last and most important point on the agenda of the Tenth Party Congress was the election of a new Central Committee. The old one had been considerably thinned out by the purging of the Chen–Lin group. The Central Committee eventually increased its numbers by about forty and reached a membership of 319. Of the 195 permanent members, seventy-five (of whom seventeen were former deputy members) were new. Of the 124 deputy members, sixty-four were new. Here, too, the trend which had been discernible in the composition of the Party Congress was continued; groups which had had little say before the Cultural Revolution were finally much better represented. This was first of all true for young people, although it is difficult to give exact statistics, since little is known of either the old or new members, and the date of birth of only eighty-four of them (and almost all of these belonging to the older generation). It is hardly surprising, then, that the average age of these is hardly lower than before. Other information, however, seems to confirm the impression that the rejuvenation of the Party membership after the Cultural Revolution was now also reflected in the composition of the Central Committee. The fact that the old demand for the formation of 'three-in-one' combinations was now made in a large number of public documents in the context of the generations (young, middle-aged and old representation on all public bodies) seems very significant in this respect. Another group whose participation in the Central

Committee was constantly increasing was that of the women. While it is true that the percentage (thirteen per cent) was somewhat lower than that of the Congress, it was still quite a lot higher than that of the Party membership. For the rest it should be added that the proportion of pre-Liberation 'heroes' (mainly soldiers) had diminished, while that of the groups who had come to the fore later – especially model peasants and workers – had increased. Participation by the central government apparatus (ministers etc.) was less, while that of the provincial and national minorities had increased. The emancipation brought on by the Cultural Revolution was being clearly felt everywhere.

Even more important, of course, than the composition of the Central Committee was that of the Political Bureau which was in fact responsible for most policy decisions. The number was fixed at twenty-one members and four deputies. With regard to its composition by age, it was clear that the elimination of the ultra-Left and the Right had made it necessary to recall some very old, and pretty well inactive, members. Thus, along with Mao, Chou and Kang, appeared other 'nineteenth-century' men in prominent positions: Yeh Chien-ying (who now assumed the military functions of Lin Piao), Chu Teh (who became chairman of the National People's Congress), Tung Pi-wu (who temporarily assumed the Presidential functions of Liu Shao-chi), and Liu Po-cheng (who became vice-chairman of the National Defence Council). In contrast to the 70- and 80-year-olds, there were now for the first time a number of 30- and 40-year-olds, among whom the best known are Wang Hung-wen and Yao Wen-yuan. With regard to the women, a model textile worker, Wu Kuei-hsien, was given a seat beside Mao's wife, Chiang Ching. In addition, several other model peasants and workers now had seats in the Political Bureau: such as, for instance, Chen Yung-kuei (from the famous agricultural brigade of Tachai), and Ni Chih-fu (a model worker from a peasant family). The elimination of the seven-man military faction of Lin Piao had considerably reduced the participation of the army, although the ranks of the two remaining 'strong' moderate regional commanders, Hsu Shih-yu (Nanking) and Chen

Hsi-lien (Shenyang) had been reinforced. Li Te-sheng (General Political Branch) and Wang Tung-hsing (special security services), who had both played a part in the elimination of Lin Piao and his group, were promoted from deputy to full members. Of the central government apparatus, only Chou's deputy, Li Hsien-nien, retained his seat. On the other hand, several hitherto marginal figures moved closer to the foreground: Hua Kuo-feng from the province of Hunan, Chi Teng-kuei from Kwangsi, and Saifudin from the autonomous minority of Sinkiang. The deceased Mayor of Peking, Hsieh Fu-chih, was replaced by his successor Wu Te. The Cultural Revolution trio from Shanghai – Chiang Ching, Chang Chun-chiao and Yao Wen-yuan – remained intact. The new Political Bureau was thus more heterogeneous and at the same time more representative than the previous one. And the same was true for the Standing Committee, whose membership now rose from five to nine.

After the Tenth Party Congress there was a clear revival of political activity. In the autumn of 1973 a new campaign of cultural criticism seemed to be rising – both in education and the arts. Around the beginning of 1974 there was a reshuffle of all important regional military commanders. In the spring of 1974 wall-posters recurred, in which some local Party leaders were attacked. Many expected a new Cultural Revolution. But in the summer some of these elements disappeared again. Apparently the movement was led in another direction. There was a sudden emphasis on the formation of mass contingents for Marxist theory by workers, peasants and soldiers. The argument was, that if Liu, Chen and Lin could get away with pseudo-Marxist ideas, this is because pre-Maoist (that is, Confucian) ideas had not entirely been rooted out. Therefore, there was sudden propaganda for 'spare time study groups' to read and discuss the classical works of Marx, Engels, Lenin, Stalin and Mao. In mid-1974 the media presented a model of such a group, formed by eight young women in the daily necessities department of Peking's Friendship store. They started their investigation into the origins of the Lin Piao deviations, but it took them eighteen months to get to the heart of the matter. Finally, they were able to distinguish between bourgeois apriorism and genuine dialectical materialism (and launch an offensive against male chauvinism in their shop on International Working Women's Day, and against the misleading of young people on Youth Day). After some initial resistance, the value of their philosophical analysis has now been recognized. One of them was admitted into the Communist Party, another one into the Youth League; three others have been cited as advanced workers in the store. In the second half of 1974, their example was followed by millions of others. The formation of these mass contingents of Marxist theoretical workers becomes a very important feature of the political scene, and may have considerable consequences for future campaigns.

The Fourth People's Congress

In 1975 I made two more trips to China. From 13 to 17 January 1975, the long-awaited Fourth National People's Congress took place. As for the Congress itself, of its 2,885 deputies, seventy-two per cent were workers, peasants and soldiers, twenty-two per cent were women. Among them are twelve 'compatriots of Taiwan Province' origin. It was preceded from 8 to 10 January by the Second Plenary Session of the Tenth Central Committee, and ended with the appointment of the new Government. Foreign observers attached great importance to the predominance of Chou En-lai, and the rehabilitation of Teng Hsiao-ping: he was appointed Vice-Chairman of the Party, first Vice-Premier, and later even chief-of-staff. Observers tended to overlook the fact that such a radical Leftist as Chang Chun-chiao was appointed as Teng's deputy in all three positions: he became a member of the Party's Political Bureau, was second Vice-Premier and head of the General Political Department of the People's Liberation Army. Finally, the other members of the so-called Shanghai group also continued to play a fairly prominent part in Party life: Wang Hung-wen as a Vice-Chairman, Yao Wen-yuan as a leading ideologist, Chiang Ching as a cultural reformer. Therefore, there was no reason to look upon the appointment of Teng in itself as 'a swing to the Right'. Also, the new Government featured quite a few new faces, some of them representatives of the Cultural Revolution generation.

To underline both the pre-eminence of the radicals and their support for the decisions taken, Chang Chun-chiao was chosen to present the report on the revision of the state constitution. On the whole, the document is congruent with that discussed at the Second Plenary Session of the Ninth Central Committee (at which Chen Po-ta tried to have Lin Piao appointed as President). Important revisions are: the abolition of the post of President, the appointment of the Chairman of the Central Committee of the C.C.P. to command the armed forces, and the administration of protocol functions by the Standing Committee of the National People's Congress.

Finally, Premier Chou En-lai reported on the work of the Government, and discussed the last year of the fourth Five-Year Plan, i.e., 1975. He summed up the political developments, mentioning a number of 'socialist new things' and the economic developments, giving data on growth. Furthermore he implicitly commented on the period 1976–80 when the building of 'an independent and relatively comprehensive industrial and economic system' must be completed, and even on the year 2000 when 'our national economy will be advancing in the front ranks of the world'.

From the emphasis on production many foreign observers concluded that new revolutionary upsurges are not to be expected any more. However, immediately after the Congress Mao and the radical-Left started an offensive to draw the final conclusions from the Lin Piao affair. If the recurrent deviations from 'the correct line' are a consequence of persistent 'bourgeois apriorism', then the question arose what its social basis is. The answer was given in two articles from Yao and Chang: inequality in general, and the rise of a 'new bourgeoisie' of Party and state officials more specifically. There are still a number of inequalities of different natures: those between individuals (as apparent in the eight-grade wage system and the unequal distribution of commodities), and those between collectivities (mental and manual labour, industry and agriculture, cities and countryside – but also between richer and poorer communes, etc.). The tendency of some of these inequalities to grow supports the rise of

a new class of well-educated cadres from urban and industrial
centres. Through the three alienations these in turn promote
Rightist (even if often apparently ultra-Leftist) policies, that
lead to Soviet-type revisionism in the end. Therefore, it is
necessary to restrict bourgeois rights, and reinforce the dictatorship of the proletariat. This ultimate stage in the *Pi Lin, Pi Kung*
campaign was prepared by the publication of a number of
quotes from Marx, Engels, Lenin and Stalin on the dictatorship
of the proletariat, and from Mao on inequality under socialism.
It was then introduced in *Red Flag No. 3* with an article by Yao
Wen-yuan 'On the Social Basis of the Lin Piao Anti-Party
Clique'. In *Red Flag No. 4* there was an even more important
article by Chang Chun-chiao 'On Exercising All-round Dictatorship over the Bourgeoisie'.

Just after New Year 1976, however, the death of Premier
Chou En-lai upset the delicate balance again. Vice-Premier
Teng Hsiao-ping had clearly been intended as his successor.
But the radical-Left, who felt that he had fallen back into his
old mistakes, launched a vehement campaign to prevent his
appointment, and this led to his renewed downfall. Hua Kuo-
feng was once again the ideal compromise, and was made the
new premier. But at the same time it was obvious that this
would not end the hidden controversy. The after-effects of the
Cultural Revolution – most dramatic in the Lin Piao affair –
will still affect the Chinese leadership for some time.

J.v.G., April 1976

Sources

My investigation into the 'Leftist current' in China between 1966 and 1972 is very much based on other publications – both books (especially where the first part is concerned) and periodicals (especially in the case of the second part).

Books

For my account of the developments which took place in the period preceding the Cultural Revolution, I have relied on:

GUILLERMAZ, JACQUES, *Histoire du Parti Communiste Chinois 1921–1949*, Payot, Paris, 1969.

GUILLERMAZ, JACQUES, *Le Parti Communiste Chinois au Pouvoir, 1949–1972*, Payot, Paris, 1972.

For information on the Chinese Party leadership my principal source has been the standard work on the subject:

KLEIN, DONALD W., and CLARK, ANNE B., *Biographic Dictionary of Chinese Communism, 1921–1965*, Harvard University Press, Cambridge, Mass., U.S.A., 1971;

and for information on Lin Piao

EBON, MARTIN, *Lin Piao, The Life and Writings of China's New Ruler*, Stein and Day, New York ,1970.

For Chinese Communist Party documents and the speeches and writings of the Party leaders my sources have been:

CHAI, WINBERG, ed., *Essential Works of Chinese Communism*, Bantam, New York, 1969;

MAO TSE-TUNG, *Selected Works*, I–IV, Foreign Languages Press, Peking, 1967–9;

FAN, K., ed., *Mao Tse-tung and Lin Piao, Postrevolutionary Writings*, Anchor, New York, 1972;

SCHICKEL, JOACHIM, *Die grosze strategische Plan, Dokumente zur Kulturrevolution*, Edition Voltaire, Berlin, 1969.

For the Cultural Revolution itself, I have based myself largely on about five books by Western Europeans who experienced the movement wholly or partly on the spot, as diplomat, scientist, or journalist, namely:

BLUMER, GIOVANNI, *Die Chinesische Kulturrevolution 1965/67*, Europäische Verlagsanstalt, Frankfurt-am-Main, 1969;

DAUBIER, JEAN, *Histoire de la Révolution Culturelle Prolétarienne en Chine*, I and II, Maspero, Paris, 1971;

ESMEIN, JEAN, *La Révolution Culturelle*, Seuil, Paris, 1970;

FOKKEMA, D. W., *Standplaats Peking, Verslag van de Culturele Revolutie*, Arbeiderspers, Amsterdam, 1970;

ROBINSON, JOAN, *The Cultural Revolution in China*, Pelican, 1969.

Additional sources on the student movement in Peking were:

NEE, VICTOR, *The Cultural Revolution at Peking University*, Monthly Review Press, New York/London, 1969;

HINTON, WILLIAM, *Hundred Day War, The Cultural Revolution at Tsinghua University*, Monthly Review Press, New York/London, 1972;

MEHNERT, KLAUS, *Peking und die neue Linke*, Deutsche Verlagsanstalt, Stuttgart, 1969 (in English: *Peking and the New Left*, University of California Press, Berkeley, U.S.A., 1969).

Periodicals

A number of magazines are published in Peking for distribution abroad. The most important is the *Peking Review* which is published in a number of languages and contains mainly political information. Next is the monthly *China Pictorial* which contains mainly photographs. There is also the monthly *China Reconstructs* which contains photographs as well as general information. Aspects of Chinese life can sometimes be found discussed in such periodicals as *Chinese Literature*.

Regular information on events in China is issued in daily and weekly bulletins from *New China News Agency*, not to be confused with *China News Agency* in Taiwan. The principal publications within China itself are: the theoretical Party paper *Red Flag* (*Hung chi* or *Hong Qi, H.Q.*), which appears every few weeks, the Party paper *People's Daily* (*Renmin Ribao* or *Jenmin Jihpao*), and the paper of the People's Liberation Army, *Chieh-fang-chun Pao.* There are other papers in the two largest cities, such as the *Peking Daily* and the intellectual paper *Kuang-ming Jih-pao* in the capital, and in Shanghai *Wen-hui Pao* and *Chieh-fang Jihpao* (*Liberation*).

On important festivals like New Year, Labour Day, the anniversary of the Party (1 July), the anniversary of the People's Liberation Army (1 August) and the anniversary of the People's Republic (1 October), or on special occasions, they often publish a joint leading article which lays down the accepted political line. Such articles are often later published in pamphlet form by the Foreign Languages Press in Peking. In Peking no foreign edition is issued of the ordinary editions of these newspapers. For articles in the Chinese mass-media we often have to depend on translations made by agencies outside the People's Republic, chiefly in Hong Kong. Many of the more interesting articles in the metropolitan and provincial press (and in some other publications) are translated into English and collected in one of the publications of the American consulate in Hong Kong: *Survey of China Mainland Press, Selections of China Mainland Magazines* and *Current Background* (a series of articles and articles in different subjects).

During and shortly after the Cultural Revolution, a lot of wall poster material, pamphlets, etc., were translated into English. This material is particularly interesting, since the information it gives is often much more outspoken than the official press. It must, however, be approached with the greatest caution, because the authenticity of many of these writings has not been established, and because they are often one-sided or exaggerated.

In addition to written source-material, there is also spoken material. Many of the important articles in the central and provincial press are read daily on one of the dozens of radio stations, which also broadcast their own news and commentaries. These broadcasts are monitored abroad and sometimes translated. The chief agency in this field is the B.B.C. which publishes a *Summary of World Broadcasts*, of which the Chinese section is put out by the *Far East* department. There are also other agencies which monitor the Chinese radio stations. All this material is naturally too large to be consulted in its entirety. The main items, however, can be consulted, since they reflect the trend, and these can be found in the weekly *China News Analysis*, and especially in the *Quarterly Chronicle and Documentation* of the important London publication, *China Quarterly*, which also contains learned studies of developments in China.

In addition to articles which come straight from China, a wide range of information reaches the outside world by other channels. First, there are the well-known 'travellers' accounts' by refugees arriving in Hong Kong, which find their way into one of the local papers and are then often translated into English or summarized by the *Joint Publications Research Service* of the American Ministry of Trade. Needless to say, this type of information should be approached with great caution, since it is often based on rumour from an uncertain source and has then been passed on by word of mouth, often by people who do not understand its importance and who therefore seriously distort it. Nor does the active trading in such information help its reliability. A final source may be mentioned in this category, which should be treated very circumspectly. These are the reports issued by agencies in Taiwan, as 'originating on the mainland'. Many of these reports are simply part of a propaganda offensive, but it has happened in the past that important confidential documents from the Central Committee have been published earlier in Taipei than in Peking. The fact that such documents are usually issued in editions of several hundreds means that some of them may reach provinces with which Taipei still has connections and it is not inconceivable that they sometimes may come into the hands of cadres who pass them on to Taipei, either from ideological or financial considerations. Generally speaking, it is important to distinguish between information which is put out by the *China News Agency*, a press agency which puts out chiefly propaganda, and information which is circulated in specialist circles in Taiwan, and which appears in semi-propaganda, semi-factual publications like *Issues and Studies*, published by the Institute of International Relations. My primary sources of information were those which came directly from the People's Republic itself. Only when there were important gaps which made the matter incomprehensible, did I then refer to other sources. I have only used the reports from Hong Kong and text from Taipei when I have considered that they had reasonable claims to authenticity. In instances of persistent uncertainty, I must leave it to the reader to make the final judgement. The periodicals mentioned can be found in most relevant university libraries. My principal researches were carried out in the Modern China Department of the Sinological Institute at the University of Leyden (director: Professor E. Zürcher) and the China Department of the Centre d'Études et de Documentation sur l'Extrême Orient at the University of Paris VII (director: Professor J. Guillermaz). I should like to express my thanks at this point for all the help I received. I should also like to mention two other publications which have been very useful. Most reports from daily papers were taken from the French daily *Le Monde*, which may be considered the best-informed international newspaper on China and the whole non-Western world. I also found the review *La Nouvelle Chine* very helpful; the review has been published almost monthly since the beginning of 1971 by an independent group of French journalists and academics. Another useful publication is the Hong Kong weekly *Far Eastern Economic Review*.

Notes

Chapter 1

1. See the documents of the Tenth Party Congress and the articles by Wilfred Burchett shortly before in *Far Eastern Economic Review*, 33, 20 August 1973, and in the *Sunday Times*, 12 August 1973.
2. According to a semi-official version, Lin Tou-tou is said to have taken the initiative herself to telephone Chou En-lai and tell him that her father had flown to her brother's air force base in Inner Mongolia from where he intended to flee to the Soviet Union. In this context, see the report mentioned below, ascribed to the Central Committee and quoted in *Joint Publications Research Service*, no. 188.

Chapter 2

1. Five different interpretations of the accident are said to have been formulated:
   — too little fuel for such a long flight;
   — the pilot lost his way;
   — the pilot was inexperienced;
   — the pilot was opposed to the escape and wasted fuel on purpose, flying in circles;
   — a fight took place in the cockpit and the pilot was shot in the head by one of the fugitives (see also *La Nouvelle Chine*, 9, p. 12.)

   The diversity of these theories merely emphasizes that Peking itself did not know exactly what had happened for a long time. In the *Hsing-tao Jih-pao* (Hong Kong) of 3 April 1972 it was claimed that a Chinese report had mentioned that the plane had been shot down by rockets from five pursuing fighters. In that case, however, the obvious uncertainty displayed by the Chinese leadership between 13 and 30 September remains unexplained. In the documents which were published for the Tenth Party Congress, mention was made of an emergency landing which failed.

Chapter 3

1. On this subject see Alan Saunders, 'Unhappy Neighbours', *Far Eastern Economic Review*, 25 March 1972.
2. Gilles Martinet and Yan Govello, 'Les mystères de Pékin', in *Le Nouvel Observateur*, 7 August 1972.

Chapter 4

1. *Peking Review*, 6 October 1959. See also Martin Ebon, *Lin Piao, The Life and Writings of China's New Ruler*, Stein and Day, New York, 1970, p. 178 et seq.
2. *New China News Agency*, 24 January 1966; *Survey of China Mainland Press*, 3627; quoted by John Gittings, 'Army–Party Relations in the Light of the Cultural Revolution', in John Wilson Lewis, ed., *Party Leadership and Revolutionary Power in China*, Cambridge University Press, 1970, p. 373.
3. There is extensive literature on the Chinese attitude to the continuing American intervention in Indo-China during this period, and this is constantly growing. The official Chinese view, and the various individual variations on the subject, form a very complex body of opinion. It is therefore difficult to give a definitive description of it at this point. An article which well illustrates how a dogmatic approach can lead to premature conclusions is that by Michael Yahuda, 'Kremlinology and the Chinese Strategic Debate, 1965–66', *China Quarterly*, 49, with a reply in no. 50 and a rejoinder in no. 51.
4. Lin Piao's *Long Live the Victory of People's War* has been published in Peking in the form of a little red book. It is his best-known work, but far from being his only one on the role of the army. Others are : about three articles written in 1938 for the paper *Liberation* in Yenan (see Donald W. Klein and Anne B. Clark, *Biographic Dictionary of Chinese Communism, 1921–1965*, Harvard University Press, Cambridge, Mass., U.S.A. 1971, p. 562); an article on 'China's Three Years' War of Liberation', published in Moscow in 1950 by *Communist International* (see Ebon op. cit., p. 157 *et seq.*; also Esposito in *China Quarterly*, 42, pp. 136–7); a *Handbook of Tactical Instructions* in 1946 (see Ebon op. cit., p. 167 *et seq.*); an introduction in 1960 to the fourth part of the *Selected Works of Mao Tse-tung* (on the third revolutionary civil war, see K. Fan, ed., *Mao Tse-tung and Lin Piao, Postrevolutionary Writings*, Anchor, New York, 1972, p.

329 *et seq.*). *Long Live the Victory of People's War* derives its fame unjustly from the theory of 'the countryside encircles the towns'. As far as can be ascertained this theory was developed by the leader of the Indonesian Communist Party, Aidit, and quoted by Peng Chen six months before Lin Piao did. (See Jacques Guillermaz, *Le Parti Communiste Chinois au Pouvoir, 1949–1972*, Payot, Paris, 1972, p. 281.)

When Lin's essay was published Chinese foreign policy was still completely dictated by the country's role as militant leader of the Third World. After the border disputes with India had considerably weakened the anti-imperialist front in Asia, a series of events occurred in Indonesia at the end of September 1965 which were to break up the Peking–Djakarta axis as well. In Algeria, Ben Bella was replaced by Boumedienne. A number of other militant Third World leaders also disappeared during this period, while the life seemed to go out of a number of revolutions. By the time the foreign policy proposed by Lin Piao was being exalted during the Cultural Revolution in 1967, the real possibilities seemed smaller than ever. The years 1966–9 were characterized especially by clashes within the wealthy nations. The chances of a successful resumption of Chinese foreign policy in the years 1970–71 lay in a completely different approach.

Chapter 5

1. Joachim Schickel, *Die grosse strategische Plan, Dokumente zur Kulturrevolution*, Edition Voltaire, Berlin, 1969, pp. 63–4, *Peking Review*, 2 June 1967.
2. Schickel, op. cit.
3. There is an extensive discussion of this in Giovanni Blumer's *Die chinesische Kulturrevolution 1965–67*, Europäische Verlagsanstalt, Frankfurt-am-Main, 1969, p. 41 *et seq.*
4. The Department of Philosophy and Social Sciences played a very important part in providing a context for the formulation of Left and ultra-Left ideologies before, during and after the Cultural Revolution. In 1964 fierce criticism had already been expressed of a university professor of philosophy who was said to have interpreted the dialectical cycle thesis-antithesis-synthesis according to the formula 'two unite in one', instead of the formula 'one divides into two'. This was a fundamental problem in the discussion on whether the class struggle continued to appear in

different forms in socialist society, and the Maoists attached great importance to its correct interpretation. At the end of 1965 and the beginning of 1966, and probably through the influence of Chen Po-ta and his supporters within the Department, a group of radical philosophers and social scientists began to form the youthful nucleus of the Peking culture critics of the first hour. They later became an important faction within the Cultural Revolution Group.

5. *Peking Review*, 2 June 1967; see also Ebon, op. cit., p. 246.
6. See Blumer, op. cit., pp. 60–61.
7. ibid.
8. ibid., p. 165 et seq.

Chapter 6

1. When this circular was published on its first anniversary, it produced a completely different effect than had been intended at the time of writing. The text of the circular is given in Schickel, op. cit., p. 127 et seq.; Joan Robinson, *The Cultural Revolution in China*, Pelican, 1969, p. 70 et seq.
2. Despite agitation by Lin Piao's supporters to have the speech published almost immediately, it was in fact only given limited circulation within China. Objections had probably been raised against the tone and content of the speech. Attempts during subsequent years to publish pamphlets of collected articles and a little book of Lin Piao quotations always proved abortive. See also *La Nouvelle Chine*, 9, p. 6. Lin Piao only received recognition in a motley collection of documents on the Cultural Revolution which appeared at the end of 1970, when he was already in decline; thirteen of the seventeen documents included were by him.

   The version of the speech which is quoted here was put out by the Red Guards and reached the outside world in 1969. This version was also published in *Issues & Studies*, February 1970; Ebon, op. cit., chapter 24. There should be little doubt as to the authenticity of this version, considering the number and content of the references to it in various other documents published in China.

3. A photocopy of this letter, in Mao's handwriting, is supposed to have been circulated in 1972 by the Party leadership to the higher military and civil cadres. It was the large numbers of copies thus in circulation which led to its falling into the hands

of the intelligence service of Chiang Kai-shek. The text was published on 4 November 1972 in Taiwan in *Chung-yang Jih-pao*, and reprinted in the following January number of *Issues & Studies*. The authenticity of it was clearly open to doubt. However, there have been cases where the Taiwan intelligence service has employed a sufficient number of informers in some border areas for it to obtain texts which have been circulated in editions of several hundreds within the administrative apparatus on the mainland. The authenticity of such texts can often be established when certain key formulae are used later in official documents in Peking, which is what occurred in this instance. The authenticity of this particular text was once again confirmed in the beginning of 1975 when it was more widely circulated in Peking and came to the attention of foreign correspondents such as Alain Bouc of *Le Monde* (4 March 1975). The only discrepancy concerns a number of derogatory references to the Chiang Kai-shek K.M.T. movement which were removed by the Taipei sources for obvious reasons.

Chapter 7

1. Victor Nee, *The Cultural Revolution at Peking University*, Monthly Review Press, New York/London, 1968, pp. 44–5.
2. Robert Guillain, 'Chine Nouvelle, an XV', *Le Monde*, 1964. Quoted in Jean Esmein, *La Révolution Culturelle*, Seuil, Paris, 1970, p. 108.
3. Schickel, op. cit., p. 137 et seq. *Peking Review*, 9 September 1966.
4. Schickel, op. cit., pp. 143–4.
5. According to William Hinton in *Hundred Day War: Cultural Revolution at Tsinghua University*, Monthly Review Press, New York/London, 1972.
6. Schickel, op. cit., pp. 146–7.
7. Philip Bridgham, 'Mao's Cultural Revolution – The Struggle to Consolidate Power', *China Quarterly*, 31, pp. 17–18.
8. Schickel, op. cit., pp. 144–5. *Peking Review*, 11 August 1967.
9. Ebon, op. cit., p. 276.
10. Complete text also in Schickel, op. cit., p. 155 et seq.
11. See Ebon, op. cit., p. 276.
12. Quoted from an extract in a discussion by Richard Baum, *China Quarterly*, 49, p. 156; extensive extracts have also been published in *L'Express*, 1–7 November 1971.

Chapter 8

1. See Schickel, op. cit., pp. 162–3; Robinson, op. cit., p. 92.
2. *Red Flag* (*Hong Qi*), 21 August 1966, translation *Selection of China Mainland Magazines*, 543.
3. Speech by Lin Piao, 3 November 1966; Ebon, op. cit., p. 286 et seq.
4. For the Chinese view of the Paris Commune, see also: John Bryan Starr, 'Revolution in Retrospect: the Paris Commune through Chinese Eyes,' *China Quarterly*, 49, p. 106; Jean Daubier, 'La célébration de la Commune de Paris,' *La Nouvelle Chine*, 3, p. 25.

Chapter 9

1. The example of the Paris Commune was abandoned after its two main principles, as published in *Red Flag*, were abused by the ultra-Left wing to justify its actions during the following six to twelve months. The first principle, that of the necessity of arming the proletariat to enable it to defend its newly-acquired power, was current during the first half of 1967 within the radical Left wing, though with a number of variations. The second principle, that of the importance of extensive democracy, appeared continually under various forms until democratic centralism was rehabilitated. Mao dissociated himself from the unbridled application of this last principle immediately after the long hot summer of 1967. By the time of the centenary, the emphasis was clearly placed again on the dictatorship of the proletariat and not on general elections.

Chapter 10

1. Yao Wen-yuan, 'Comment on Tao Chu's Two Books', September 1967, Foreign Language Press, Peking, 1968, pp. 29–30.
2. 18 October 1966. See Esmein, op. cit., p. 93.
3. See Esmein, op. cit., pp. 96, 103.
4. Quoted by Ebon, op. cit., p. 48.
5. The role of the People's Liberation Army in the Cultural Revolution is extensively analysed in: Jürgen Domes, 'The Role of the Military in the Formation of the Revolutionary Committees, 1967–1968', *China Quarterly*, 44, p. 112 et seq.; Harvey Nelsen, 'Military Force in the Cultural Revolution', *China Quarterly*,

51, p. 444 et seq.; John Gittings, 'Army–Party Relations in the Light of the Cultural Revolution', in Lewis, ed., op. cit., p. 373 et seq.; 'L'Armée de la République Populaire de Chine', *La Documentation Française. Articles et Documents d'Actualité Mondiale, Problèmes Politiques et Sociaux*, nos. 63–64.

Chapter 11

1. Quoted by Esmein, op. cit., pp. 136, 180.
2. Quoted by Jean Daubier in *Histoire de la Révolution Culturelle Prolétarienne en Chine*, Vol. II, Maspero, Paris, 1971, p. 13.
3. The most important articles are: Chi Pen-yu, 'Patriotism or National Betrayal', 30 March/1 April 1967, *The Red Flag*, 5, *Peking Review*, 20; 'Betrayal of Proletarian Dictatorship'. *The Red Flag* and the *People's Daily*, 8 May 1967; Lin Chieh, 'Down with Slavishness', *People's Daily*, 16 June 1967; Chen Li-chia, 'Down with the Capitulationism of China's Khrushchev', *People's Daily*, 6 July 1967.
4. Hinton, op. cit., p. 122.

Chapter 12

1. General: Melvin Gurtov, 'The Foreign Ministry and Foreign Affairs during the Cultural Revolution', *China Quarterly*, 40, pp. 65–102; anecdotes; ibid., p. 75; Esmein, op. cit., pp. 136, 161, 293; D. W. Fokkema, *Standplaats Peking, Verslag van de Culturele Revolutie*, Arbeiderspers, Amsterdam, 1970, p. 104; Daubier, op. cit., pp. 63–4.
2. Quoted by Schickel, op. cit., p. 12.
3. On 5 June, Chi Pen-yu defended himself against the accusation of xenophobia. Fokkema gives the following quotations:

The imperialist and modern revisionist lords have expressed the slanderous accusation that our great proletarian revolution is guilty of 'xenophobia'. We should like to ask what we do in fact reject of what comes from abroad. We always adopt a friendly attitude towards peoples abroad . . . But if 'xenophobia' means struggle against the imperialists, revisionists and secret agents who endanger the course of the Chinese revolution, then we shall not be restrained in the struggle and we shall be rid of them, as one gets rid of rubbish. (Fokkema, op. cit., p. 116).

However, after the elimination of the ultra-Left current, it was openly admitted in Peking that the Cultural Revolution had displayed strong xenophobic tendencies in the Ministry of Foreign Affairs in 1967.

4. Jean Daubier, 'Chen I, un révolutionnaire humoriste, in memoriam', *La Nouvelle Chine*, 6, p. 9.
5. Robinson, op. cit., p. 25.
6. Report by an eye-witness to the author, August 1971.
7. Reported in Hinton, op. cit., pp. 132–4.
8. Daubier, op. cit., p. 104.

Chapter 13

1. Quoted from the detailed description by Thomas W. Robinson, 'The Wuhan Incident: Local Strife and Provincial Rebellion during the Cultural Revolution', *China Quarterly*, 47, pp. 414–38.
2. Hinton, op. cit., p. 125.
3. According to a Red Guard publication of 13 September 1967, quoted in Lewis, ed., op. cit., p. 29.
4. In a speech to the Red Guard delegates from the province of Anhwei.

Chapter 14

1. According to later attacks by other Red Guard publications, such as: the half-a-dozen articles from the pamphlet *Revolutionary Students Unite, Crush the Counter-revolutionary Organization, the Sinister May 16 Corps*, Revolutionary Rebel Commune, Peking College of Iron and Steel Industry, Red Guard Congress of the Capital, September 1967, translated *Current Background*, 844; *Issues & Studies*, December 1971, January 1972; about four articles with the titles 'Towering Crimes Committed by Counter-revolutionary Clique', 'Brief Introduction of Principal Members of the Wang-Kuan-Chi, Lin-Mu-Wu Counter-revolutionary Conspiratorial Clique', 'What is Wang Li' and 'Down with Chi Pen-yu', in *Open Warfare Bulletin* and *Cultural Revolution Storm*, Canton, March 1968, translated *Survey of China Mainland Press*, 4158.
2. 'Premier Chou is the Chief of Staff of Chairman Mao and Vice-Chairman Lin. Talks Given by Comrades Chen Po-ta, Chi Pen-yu, Hsieh Fu-chih and Yeh Chun while Receiving Members of the Nucleus Group of the Conference of Red Guard Repre-

sentatives', 'On the Incident of Bombarding Chou En-lai', *Issues
& Studies*, VIII, no. 7, April 1972.

Chapter 15

1. *Current Background*, 844.
2. Ibid.
3. Yao Wen-yuan, 'Comment . . .', op. cit.
4. *Current Background*, 844.
5. Quoted by Klaus Mehnert, *Peking and the New Left*; University
   of California Press, Berkeley, 1964, from *Facts and Figures*, 13,
   December 1967.
6. *Survey of China Mainland Press*, 4088, quoted by Barry Burton,
   'The Cultural Revolution's Ultraleft Conspiracy: the "May 16
   Group" ', *Asian Survey*, XI, no. 11, November 1971.
7. See note 3 of this chapter.
8. Both publications were mentioned by Kang Sheng in his later
   requisitory against the Union. See note 13 of this chapter on the
   first publication.
9. Yao Wen-yuan, op. cit.
10. See Mehnert, op. cit., pp. 49–50.
11. According to a publication from Canton of March 1968; trans-
    lated *Survey of China Mainland Press*, 4190, quoted as docu-
    ment 5 in Mehnert, op. cit., pp. 154–60.
12. The sources of the documents mentioned are, in order:
    (a) programme, 11 October and declaration, 17 November; a
    publication from Canton, March 1968, translated *Survey of
    China Mainland Press*, 4174, and Union Research Service (Hong
    Kong), t. 51/5–6, 19 April 1968, quoted as document I in
    Mehnert, op. cit.
    (b) resolution, 21 December: a publication from Canton, Feb-
    ruary 1968, translated U RS, t. 51/5–6, 19 April 1968, quoted as
    document 2 in Mehnert, op. cit.
    (c) analysis, 12 January: translated *Survey of China Mainland
    Press*, 4190, in U RS, 19/20, 7 June 1968, quoted as document 3
    in Mehnert, op. cit., pp. 124–51.
13. See a publication from Canton, March 1968, translated *Survey
    of China Mainland Press*, 4163, and U RS, t. 51/23, 18 June 1968,
    quoted as document 6 in Mehnert, op. cit., pp. 161–72; a publi-
    cation from Canton, February 1968, translated U RS, t. 51/5–6,
    19 April 1968, quoted as document 7 in Mehnert, op. cit., pp.

173-4, ibid., quoted as document 8 in Mehnert, pp. 175-6. Much of the material from this period can be found in Mehnert, op. cit.

Chapter 16

1. This episode is quoted in Fokkema, op. cit., 144-5.
2. Chen's activities as spokesman for Mao's radical ideas on the role of the peasants and the collectivization of agriculture already dated from the period of the war against Japan, when he was still working in the propaganda department of the Party in Yenan. In 1954, he wrote *Notes on Mao Tse-tung's 'Report of an Investigation into the Peasant Movement in Hunan'* and *Notes on Ten Years of Civil War, 1927-1936* (corresponding with Parts I and II of the later edition of Mao's *Selected Works*, with which Chen was presumably involved). In 1945-6 he wrote *A Study of Land Rent in Pre-Liberation China*, which was published a year later, and translated eleven years after that. After setting out his ideas, however, he began to involve himself practically, and his mark was made several times in the context of the problems of collectivization, from the Second Session of the Political Council up to and including the Sixth Plenum of the Seventh Central Committee in October 1955 – where he gave an explanation of Mao's 'On the Question of Agricultural Co-operation' and of the subsequent 'Draft Decisions'. In the meantime he had become deputy director of the Rural Work Branch of the Party, and was to play an important part in the formation of the agricultural communes, the campaign for the Great Leap Forward and the assembly of the over-ambitious twelve-yearly programme for agriculture. In 1951, a translation was published of his general work on Mao, *Mao Tse-tung on the Chinese Revolution*.
3. Esmein, op. cit., pp. 264-6.
4. The persistent nature of the problem is illustrated by the fact that, years after the Cultural Revolution, on 26 December 1971, a directive is said to have been issued by the Central Committee on the 'Leftist' misunderstandings which had arisen about questions of distribution in the agricultural communes (*Chung-fa*, 1971, *Issues & Studies*).
5. Thus Kang Sheng went to great lengths in a speech in Changsha (see previous paragraph) to show that Lin Piao's speech of

24 October was not at all 'the appeal to continue the revolution' which it had seemed to be to some, but was, on the contrary, a violent attack on the ultra-Left.

6. Harvey Nelsen, 'Military Force in the Cultural Revolution', *China Quarterly*, 51, pp. 454 and 457; Philip Bridgham, 'Mao's Cultural Revolution: the Struggle to seize Power', *China Quarterly*, 41, p. 5.
7. Quoted by John Gittings in Lewis, ed., op. cit., p. 379.
8. Ebon, op. cit., p. 53.
9. Nelsen, op. cit., p. 400.
10. Gittings, op. cit., p. 400.

Chapter 17

1. This whole episode is exhaustively described in a special summer number of almost 300 pages of *Monthly Review*, 24, no. 3, July/August 1972, which contains William Hinton's 'Hundred Day War. The Cultural Revolution at Tsinghua University', later published as a book.

Chapter 18

1. The documents of the Ninth Party Congress have been collected and published by the Foreign Languages Press in Peking.
2. A more detailed comparison of the old and new Party statutes can be found in the *Revue du Centre d'Études des Pays de l'Est*, no. 1, Brussels, 1969. Also: L. Kawan, 'Caractères généraux des Nouveaux Statuts du Parti', *La Documentation Français. Problèmes Politiques et Sociaux, Articles et Documents de l'Actualité Mondiale*, Paris, 1971, pp. 85–6 (abridged). The old statutes are also included by Winberg Chai in *Essential Works of Chinese Communism*, Bantam Books, New York, 1969; the new statutes can be found in *China Quarterly*, 39.
3. See also Richard K. Diao, 'The Impact of the Cultural Revolution on China's Economic Elite', *China Quarterly*, 42, pp. 65–87; Donald W. Klein, 'The State Council and the Cultural Revolution' in Lewis, ed., op. cit, pp. 351–72; Donald W. Klein and Lois B. Hager, 'The Ninth Central Committee', *China Quarterly*, 45, pp. 37–56.

Chapter 19

1. Quoted by Geoffrey Hudson, 'Paper Tigers and Nuclear Teeth', *China Quarterly*, 39, p. 64 et seq.
2. According to a later reply by Moscow, this offer only concerned Russian extra-territorial areas (the so-called concessions) and reparations (for damage suffered during the Boxer Rebellion), but not changes in the border. This was later contested by Peking.
3. In this context see Andrei Amalrik on the America–Russia–China triangle in *Will the Soviet Union Survive until 1984?*

Chapter 20

1. Quoted by W. A. C. Adie, 'China's "Second Liberation" in Perspective', in Bulletin of Atomic Scientists, *China After the Cultural Revolution*, Random House, New York, 1969, p. 29.

Chapter 21

1. For evaluations of the economic consequences of the Cultural Revolution see also: R. M. Field, 'Industrial Production in Communist China 1957–1968', *China Quarterly*, 42, especially p. 54 et seq.; R. F. Dernberger, 'The Cultural Revolution and its Impact on the Economy', *Asian Survey*, XII, no. 12, 12 December 1972, p. 1048 et seq. In a later conversation with Edgar Snow (*Epoca*, 18 April 1971) Chou En-lai made the cautious statement that production in the agricultural communes had not in any way diminished during the Cultural Revolution. And for the first time he offered data on production, which had now resumed its former growth rate. For 1970 he gave the following figures: 18 million tons of steel, 20 million tons of oil, 14 million tons of fertilizer, 8½ billion metres of cotton fabric, 240 million tons of grain. China's economic development was further highlighted by the fact that industrial production was now beginning to overtake agricultural production, and the latter sector accounted for only a quarter of the G.N.P.
2. Since the beginning of the fifties the balances held at savings banks had increased almost sevenfold in the towns, and a hundredfold in the country. A third of this increase had taken

place in the last three years. (*Far Eastern Economic Review Yearbook 1970*).
3. *People's Daily*, 5 November 1969; *China Quarterly*, 41, pp. 161–2.
4. *Hong Kong Times*, 28–9 August 1969; *China Quarterly*, 40, pp. 172–3; *Joint Publications Research Service*, 48. 492, pp. 1–4.

Chapter 22

1. Philip Bridgham, 'Mao's Cultural Revolution . . .', op. cit., pp. 1–25.
2. See also *Absorb Proletarian Fresh Blood*, Foreign Languages Press pamphlet.
3. See Documents of the Ninth Party Congress.
4. BBC, *Summary of World Broadcasts – Far East Department*, 3426; *China Quarterly*, 44, pp. 239–40.

Chapter 23

1. For the complete text of the final communiqué: *Peking Review*, no. 37, 11 September 1970.
2. In this context see Parris H. Chang, 'Research Notes on the Changing Loci of Decision in the C.C.P.', *China Quarterly*, 44, pp. 169–94.
3. This becomes apparent in later attacks on Chen Po-ta. See also 'The Purge of Chen Po-ta', *China News Agency* (Taiwan), 851, p. 5.

Chapter 24

1. See also *Issues & Studies*, December 1970, January 1971, February 1972; *China News Agency*, 823.
2. Respectively 'Preamble, Constitution of the C.P.R., 1954', in Chai, op. cit., p. 272; and 'Preamble, Revised Draft of the Constitution of the C.P.R., 1970'. *Issues & Studies*, April 1971, p. 93.

Chapter 25

1. See, for instance, *Issues & Studies*, December 1970.
2. In the version circulating in Hong Kong, the intervention was ascribed to Lin. From later information, however, it appears that

this must have been based upon misinterpretation of the data. (*Joint Publications Research Service*, 183, p. 2).

3. Chai, op. cit., pp. 282–4.

Chapter 26

1. See also *On the question of Stalin*, second pamphlet in the series published in Peking 'A propos of the open letter from the C.C.P. to the C.P.S.U.'
2. Conversation between Edgar Snow and Mao Tse-tung, *Life*, 30 April 1971, also in Snow's posthumously published book *The Long Revolution*, Hutchinson, 1973.
3. See Blumer, op. cit., pp. 37–8.
4. See also the new (!) translations of Marx/Engels, *The Communist Manifesto*; Marx, *The Civil War in France*; *A Critique of the Gotha Programme*; Engels, *Anti-Dühring*; *Feuerbach*; Lenin, *The State and Revolution*; *Materialism and Empirio-criticism*.
5. See also *China News Agency* (Taiwan), 851 : 'The Purge of Chen Po-ta'.

Chapter 27

1. See, for instance, Barry Burton, 'The Cultural Revolution's Ultra-left Conspiracy: The "May 16" Group', *Asian Survey*, XI, no. 11, November 1971, p. 1050.
2. Quoted in the conversation between Mao and Snow.
3. *La Nouvelle Chine*, 1, p. 3.
4. *Africasia*, 24 May 1971.
5. *Le Nouvel Observateur*, 19 July 1971.
6. *Joint Publications Research Service*, 188.
7. *Der Spiegel*, 1971, no. 45.
8. Hinton, op. cit., pp. 275–6.
9. Hinton, op. cit., pp. 285–6.
10. *Hsing-tao Jih-pao* (Hong Kong), 24 August 1971, p. 4; *Joint Publications Research Service*, 160, pp. 9–10.
11. *Der Spiegel*, 1971, no. 27.
12. Barry Burton, op. cit., pp. 1030–31.

Chapter 28

1. This is what Nym Wales had to say in the thirties: 'The communists consider that Lin . . . ranks with the half dozen military

geniuses of recent Chinese history . . . When I first talked with him, he was regarded as the most expert and original tactician among all the military men.' And on the subject of his proverbial modesty: 'Lin . . . told me . . . that he was a veteran of a hundred battles and had never once been defeated when he led the First Army Corps. When I asked him how he could be infallible, he smiled and raised his heavy black eyebrows. "We never engage the enemy unless we are certain of victory," he replied.' (Nym Wales, *Red Dust*, quoted by Klein and Clark, op. cit., p. 567.)

2. In the index of the *Peking Review*, the entry 'Chairman Mao and his close comrade-in-arms Vice-Chairman Lin Piao; receptions and other activities' was replaced by 'Chairman Mao meets foreign guests'.

3. 'A Summary of Chairman Mao's Talks with Responsible Comrades of Various Places During His Inspection Tour', end of August, beginning of September 1971, distributed in China as 'Top secret' document no. 12. See also *Issues & Studies*, September 1972.

4. BBC, *Summary of World Broadcasts – Far East Department*, 3074; *China Quarterly*, 39, p. 152.

5. See note 3 of this chapter and 'The Struggle of Smashing the Counter-revolutionary Coup of the Lin–Chen Anti-Party Clique', Material no. 2 of the Ad Hoc Investigation Committee of the Party Central Committee; also in *Issues & Studies*, May 1972.

6. ibid.

Chapter 29

1. 'People of the World, Unite and Defeat the U.S. Aggressors and All Their Running Dogs', *Peking Review* (Special Issue), 23 May 1970.

Chapter 30

1. *People's Daily*, 15 July 1971.
2. Schickel, op. cit., document 12.

Chapter 31

1. Report ascribed to the Central Committee, *Hsing-tao Jih-pao*

(Hong Kong), 18 January 1972, quoted in *Joint Publications Research Service*, 179.
2. According to the document no. 12 already quoted, dating from 17 March 1972, which was distributed by the Central Committee within the Party under the title 'Mao Tse-tung's Talks to Responsible Comrades in Nanking and Shanghai Areas during his Inspection of the Troops', in *Issues & Studies*, July 1972, p. 95 et seq., and *Issues & Studies*, September 1972, p. 63 et seq.
3. 'Minutes of the Symposium of the Kwangchow Military Region Concerning Ideological Work', approved for distribution by the Central Committee on 20 August 1971.
4. Tien Ya Lang Tzu, 'Trip to Canton in Early Spring', *Ming Pao* (Hong Kong), 7 March 1972, quoted in *Joint Publications Research Service*, 183.

Chapter 32

1. On Lin Tou-tou see also Ebon, op. cit., p. 19. On Lin Tou-tou and the Red Flag of the Aeronautical Institute see also Esmein, op. cit., p. 137. On the Red Flag of the Aeronautical Institute see Fokkema, op. cit., pp. 84–5. See also Hinton, op. cit.
2. On 13 January 1972 a secret document was circulated by the Central Committee, labelled no. 4. In this document the origin and nature of the '571' conspiracy were further explained to the various Party bodies. In April, Taipei published a first fragmentary version of this which it claimed to have intercepted on the mainland. The fragments and/or summaries of this were originally also published in *Issues & Studies*, May 1972, *Joint Publications Research Service*, 187, and *China News Agency* (Taiwan), 897 – although the translations vary in places. The document is in two main parts:
(a) a covering letter from the Central Committee;
(b) the 'Material no. 2' on 'The Struggle of Smashing the Counter-revolutionary Coup of the Lin–Chen Anti-Party Clique,' which was made up of three elements:
  (i) an introduction by the Central Committee,
  (ii) the original '571'-plan, or at any rate a reconstruction of it,
  (iii) parts of the confession by Li Wei-hsin.
The quotations in this paragraph are taken from it.
3. At a People's Congress banquet in the spring of 1973, for the first time Chou En-lai mentioned the names of Chen and Lin, and told foreign journalists that information on the Lin Piao

affair would be released. See also *Le Monde*, 10 March 1973.

4. The complete document has also appeared in Western Europe in *Le Monde*, 2 September 1972. Other Central Committee documents on the 'plot', mentioned by Taipei, are 'chung-fa' nos. 1971/68, 1971/77, 1972/3 (of which the texts are not available), 1972/4 (the document no. 4 which is quoted in the previous paragraph), 1972/12 (which is mentioned above), 1972/24 (26 June and 2 July, with a number of very bizarre elements) and the 'letter from Mao Tse-tung to Chiang Ching' which is quoted in the first chapter.

5. See also *China News Agency*, 829, p. 4.

6. Mark Gayn, *Chicago Daily News*, 8 July 1966, quoted by Ebon, op. cit., p. 119.

Chapter 33

1. A later issue of *China Pictorial*, destined for distribution abroad, was released, showing Lin still parading at Mao's side and containing praises of Lin. This publication caused a lot of confusion, but presumably the issue had been in production for a fairly long time, and it was preferred to let sleeping dogs lie as far as the outside world was concerned, rather than create suspicion by holding publication back at the last minute.

2. Anti-Chinese sources still spoke of dissidence in the army for weeks and months afterwards. Thus, *News Tibet*, published in New York, suggested that the military commander in Lhasa had ignored the orders of Peking in the matter.

3. A discredited Chinese Party leader is usually only expelled and criticized by name or surname when the discussion of his faults is completely finished, which sometimes may take years. During this first stage of discussion, it is not definite whether the person has left the political scene for good, or whether he can be rehabilitated.

4. According to an article in *Far Eastern Economic Review*, 20 November 1971. See also Klein and Clark, op. cit., p. 1052, Appendix 6: 'Class Origin of Biographees'.

5. *China News Agency* (Taiwan), 871, p. 4.

6. In this context, see also Michelle Loi, 'Lu Xun, le plus grand écrivain moderne', *La Nouvelle Chine*, 6, pp. 28–30, in which one of his later texts, 'Réponse aux trotskyistes', is analysed.

7. See also Guillermaz, op. cit., pp. 111–12.

8. See *Issues & Studies*, January 1972, p. 87 et seq.

Chapter 34

1. See *Issues & Studies*, June 1972, and *Joint Publications Research Service*, 190.
2. Quoted by *China News Agency* (Taiwan), 871, p. 5.
3. Taipei went as far as to claim that a total of 37,000 army personnel were placed on trial in connection with the coup. See also *Le Monde*, 7 November 1972. On 7 February 1973 *Pravda* announced large-scale purges. Since no other source mentions such large-scale purges, we may take these claims to be mainly propaganda. In the same story, 200 people were said to have been condemned to death, and 4,000 to life imprisonment.
4. According to *Issues & Studies*, July 1972, p. 10.
5. According to *China News Agency* (Taiwan), 871, p. 3.
6. According to a report from Associated Press on 2 January 1972 from Tokyo, quoted by Liu Mao-nan, 'On the Lin Piao Incident', *Issues & Studies*, March 1972, p. 41 et seq. *Pravda* of 7 February also mentioned the existence of such a document. For a summary of the accusations against Lin in the Chinese press, see also *La Nouvelle Chine*, 9, pp. 12–13.
7. *Hong Qi* (*Red Flag*), 13, 1971; *Peking Review*, 7/8, 1972.
8. See Klein and Clark, op. cit., p. 560.

Chapter 35

1. The relevant passages have all been collected in the pamphlet *Irresistible Historical Trends*, Foreign Languages Press, Peking, 1971.
2. For the Chinese version of this conflict, see also Kostas Mavrakis, 'La politique internationale de la Chine', in *Tel Quel*, 50, and additions to it in 'Peintures, Cahiers Théoriques', 4/5. See also Kostas Mavrakis, 'La politique à l'égard du Pakistan', *La Nouvelle Chine*, 3, and Biren Roy-Sakar, 'La Chine et la Bangla Desh', *La Nouvelle Chine*, 6.

Chapter 36

1. The official texts on Nixon's visit have been collected in *China Quarterly*, 50, Chronicle.

Index

of, 109, 122, 125, 138, 159; setting up of, 54; Shanghai section of, 22, 125, 138, 230
Culture Group, of Chinese Government, 22

Damansky, *see* Chenpao
'Drag out' campaign (1967): Chiang Ching and, 121, 124; 'Chingkangshan' Regiment and, 158; Chou En-lai and, 124; Lin Piao and, 123, 124, 153; Red Guards and, 123; responsibility for, 234

Eda Gima, 266
Education, proletarianization of, 163–4
Engels, Friedrich, 61, 89, 183, 228, 235, 307, 310
Esmein, Jean, 151–2
European Community, 190
European Security Conference, 304

Festival of the Peking Opera, 44
Fuchow, 124, 283
Foreign Languages Institute, *see* Institute of Foreign Languages
France, 221, 300
Fu Chung-pi, 157
Fukien province, 15

Gaulle, Charles de, 190
General Political Branch, 259
Great Leap Forward: Central Committe of, 52; difficulties encountered in, 44; Mao and economic aims of, 42; plans

for, 29, 33, 34, 55, 98; Tan Chen-lin and, 130
Greece, 300
Green, Marshall, 294, 297
Group of Five for the Cultural Revolution, 45, 46, 47, 48–9, 51, 56; dissolution, 52, 54, 74, 78, 79, 95; Outline Report, 54, 55, 56
'Group of the Peking Movement', 131
Guillain, Robert, 69

Hai Jui, 49, 55, 70
Hangchow, 49, 51, 64, 264, 265, 268, 281
Han Hsien-chu, 124
Hankow, 120,
Hanoi, 295, 297
Han River, 120
Harbin, 91
Harris, Richard, 20
Hegel, Friedrich, 61
Heilungkiang province, 181, 285; Revolutionary Committee, 91, 93, 165
Hiang Chung, 64
Hinton, William, 110, 116, 232
Ho Chi-minh, 185
Honan, 154
Hong Kong, 18, 22, 119, 197
Hopei province, 154
Hopei–Anhwei wars, 60
Hopei–Manchu wars, 60
Hsiao Hua, 38, 41, 46, 98, 99, 122, 138, 153, 226
Hsieh Fu-chih, 98, 105, 110, 119, 120, 121, 129, 132–3, 137, 143, 157, 159; as member of Political Bureau, 176, 177, 307; public security

**More about Penguins
and Pelicans**

Penguinews, which appears every month, contains details of all the new books issued by Penguins as they are published. From time to time it is supplemented by *Penguins in Print,* which is our complete list of almost 5,000 titles.

A specimen copy of *Penguinews* will be sent to you free on request. Please write to Dept EP, Penguin Books Ltd, Harmondsworth, Middlesex, for your copy.

In the U.S.A.: For a complete list of books available from Penguins in the United States write to Dept CS, Penguin Books, 625 Madison Avenue, New York, New York 10022.

In Canada: For a complete list of books available from Penguins in Canada write to Penguin Books Canada Ltd, 41 Steelcase Road West, Markham, Ontario.

Some books on China published by Penguin Books

Chinese Looking Glass   *Dennis Bloodworth*

Russia, China and the West, 1953–1966   Isaac Deutscher

The Birth of Communist China   *C. P. Fitzgerald*

China: The Revolution Continued   *Jan Myrdal and Gun Kessel*

Mao Tse-tung   *Stuart R. Schram*

Mao Tse-tung Unrehearsed: Talks and Letters, 1956–1971   *Edited by Stuart R. Schram*

Red Star Over China   *Edgar Snow*

Red China Today: The Other Side of the River   *Edgar Snow*

China's Long Revolution   *Edgar Snow*

The Chinese Literary Scene: A Writer's Visit to the People's Republic   *Kai-yu Hsu*

China: The Quality of Life   *Wilfred Burchett with Rewi Alley*

Prisoner of Mao   *Bao Ruo-wang with Rudolph Chelminski*